What People Are Saying About
A 6th Bowl of Chicken Soup for the Soul . . .

"From the beginning of time, we have passed on life's most important lessons through stories. This collection will uplift, inspire and motivate you beyond your wildest dreams."

Orvel Ray Wilson, CSP
coauthor, *Guerilla Selling*

"*Chicken Soup for the Soul* stories take the unbelievable and make it believable, because the stories really happened."

Donna Nelson
president, 3N and Associates
and international speaker

"*A 6th Bowl of Chicken Soup for the Soul* will make you laugh, cry and positively change your outlook on life. As you read this book you'll find yourself thinking better thoughts, helping others more, and appreciating how fragile yet resilient people truly are. It is a brilliant compilation of emotional sparkplugs that will improve your quality of life."

Gordon Pedersen, Ph.D.
director, Insitute of Alternative Medicine

"*Chicken Soup for the Soul* speaks the language of humanity's soul. These powerful stories remind us that all cultural, national and religious boundaries are illusions. They unite us and remind us of an emerging spirituality that is destined to sweep across the planet."

Christopher Naughton
host, PBS's *New World with Christopher Naughton* and
NPR's *New World Radio*

"The stories in this book will challenge, motivate and inspire you as they have me."

Ray Pelletier, CSP, C

"Holy guacamole! *A 6th Bowl of Chicken Soup for the Soul* is another must-read and should be mandatory for every living soul. Get your helping today!"

Tom Harken
literary activist, owner, Casa Ole
and winner of the Horatio Alger Award

"The *Chicken Soup* books have won first place in my library. There are quality family values tucked into these wonderful stories. They provide motivation and inspiration for everyone."

Bob Proctor
author, *You Were Born Rich*
and international public speaker

"*A 6th Bowl of Chicken Soup for the Soul* is a genuine pearl among the many books of inspiration that are available. When you read this book it can change your life. This is not just a read, it's a *must*-read!"

L. W. Paxson
chairman, Paxson Communications Corporation

"Sometimes the simplest of stories can describe our most complex feelings. The *Chicken Soup* series gives us laughter, tears and a sense of optimism for our tomorrows. It is literally a one-a-day multiple vitamin."

Edwin L. Griffin Jr., CAE
president/CEO, Meeting Professionals International

"The *Chicken Soup for the Soul* books are the only ones I read, my wife reads, my kids read, and that we all talk about."

Marty Coyne
director of development, Ronald McDonald House

"You make us cry so much, you'll create the next great flood."

Barbara Daugherty
Lifestyles reporter, *The Valley News Dispatch*

A 6th Bowl of

CHICKEN SOUP
FOR THE SOUL®

A 6th Bowl of Chicken Soup for the Soul
More Stories to Open the Heart and Rekindle the Spirit
Jack Canfield, Mark Victor Hansen

Published by Backlist, LLC,
a unit of Chicken Soup for the Soul Publishing, LLC. www.chickensoup.com

Front cover redesign by Andrea Perrine Brower
Originally published in 1999 by Health Communications, Inc.

Back cover and spine redesign by Pneuma Books, LLC

Distributed to the booktrade by Simon & Schuster. SAN: 200-2442

Publisher's Cataloging-in-Publication Data
(Prepared by The Donohue Group)

A 6th bowl of chicken soup for the soul : more stories to open the heart and rekindle the spirit / [compiled by] Jack Canfield [and] Mark Victor Hansen.

 p. : ill. ; cm.

 Originally published: Deerfield Beach, FL : Health Communications, c1999.
 ISBN: 978-1-62361-073-9

 1. Spiritual life--Anecdotes. 2. Anecdotes. I. Canfield, Jack, 1944- II. Hansen, Mark Victor. III. Title: Sixth bowl of chicken soup for the soul IV. Title: Chicken soup for the soul

BL624 .A155 2012
158.1/28   2012913006

PRINTED IN THE UNITED STATES OF AMERICA
on acid free paper

22 21 20 19 18 17 16 15 14 13   01 02 03 04 05 06 07 08 09 10

A 6th Bowl of
CHICKEN SOUP FOR THE SOUL®

More Stories to Open the Heart and Rekindle the Spirit

Jack Canfield
Mark Victor Hansen

Backlist, LLC, a unit of
Chicken Soup for the Soul Publishing, LLC
Cos Cob, CT
www.chickensoup.com

12-10

"Will you knock it off with the
Chicken Soup for the Soul excerpts!"

Contents

2. ON PARENTING

3. ON DEATH AND DYING

Introduction

Without the stories we are nothing.

Bryce Courtney

From our hearts to yours, we are delighted to offer you *A 6th Bowl of Chicken Soup for the Soul.* This book contains more stories that we know will inspire and motivate you to love more fully and unconditionally, live with more passion and compassion, and pursue your heartfelt dreams with greater conviction, bolder action and stronger perseverance. We believe that this book will sustain you during times of challenge, frustration and failure, and comfort you during times of confusion, pain and loss. We hope it will truly become a lifelong companion, offering continual insight and wisdom in many areas of your life.

How to Read This Book

We have been blessed with readers from all over the world who have given us feedback. Some read our books from cover to cover; others pick out a particular chapter that interests them. Some simply can't put our books down from beginning to end, going through a big box of tissues en route. We've been particularly touched by those readers who have reconnected to loved ones or old friends as a result of being inspired by one of the stories.

Many times we have been approached by readers—at a speech or public appearance—who told us how one or more stories were of inestimable value during a period of trial and testing, such as the death of a loved one or a serious illness. We are grateful for having had the opportunity to be of help to so many in this way. Some have told us they keep their *Chicken Soup* book at bedside, reading one story each night, often rereading favorites. Many use these books as a family gathering experience, reading a story aloud with parents and children gathered together in the evening.

You may choose the path of readers who have gone before you, or simply enjoy reading this book with no particular pattern in mind, letting each story guide your thoughts in new directions. Find the path that's best for you, and most of all, enjoy!

1

ON LOVE

The love we give away is the only love we keep.

Elbert Hubbard

The Healing Power of Love

We dreaded Christmas that year. It was 1944, and the war would never be over for our family.

The telegram had arrived in August. Bob's few personal possessions, the flag from his coffin, the plan of his burial site in the Philippine Islands, and a Distinguished Flying Cross had arrived one by one, adding to our agonizing grief.

Born on a Midwest prairie, my brother rode horseback to school but wanted to fly an airplane from the first day he saw one. By the time he was twenty-one, we were living in Seattle, Washington. When World War II broke out, Bob headed for the nearest Air Force recruitment office. Slightly built, skinny like his father, he was ten pounds underweight.

Undaunted, he persuaded Mother to cook every fattening food she could think of. He ate before meals, between meals and after meals. We laughed and called him "lardo."

At the Navy Cadet Office he stepped on the scale—still three pounds to go. He was desperate. His friends were leaving one after the other; his best buddy was already in the Marine Air Corps. The next morning, he ate a pound of greasy bacon, six eggs and five bananas, drank two gallons of milk, and, bloated like a pig, staggered back on their scales. He passed the weigh-in with eight ounces to spare.

When he was nominated Hot Pilot of primary training school in Pasco, Washington, and involuntarily joined the "Caterpillar Club" (engine failure causing the bailout) at St. Mary's, California, we shook our heads and worried. Mother prayed. He was born fearless, and she knew it. Before graduating from Corpus Christi, he applied for transfer to the Marine Air Corps at Pensacola, Florida. He trained in torpedo bombers before being sent overseas.

They said Bob died under enemy fire over New Guinea in the plane he wanted so desperately to fly.

I never wept for Bob. In my mind's eye, I pictured my debonair big brother wing-tapping through the clouds, doing what he loved best, his blue eyes sparkling with love of life. But I wept for the sadness that never left my parents' eyes.

Mother's faith sustained her, but my father aged before our eyes. He listened politely whenever the minister came to call, but we knew Daddy was bitter. He dragged himself to work every day but lost interest in everything else, including his beloved Masonic Club. He very much wanted a Masonic ring, and at Mother's insistence he had started saving for the ring. Of course, after Bob died, that too ceased.

I dreaded the approach of Christmas. Bob loved Christmas. His enthusiasm excited us long before reason took over. His surprises were legendary: a dollhouse made at school, a puppy hidden in mysterious places for little brother, an expensive dress for Mother bought with the very first money he ever earned. Everything had to be a surprise.

What would Christmas be without Bob? Not much. Aunts, uncles and Grandmother were coming, so we went through the motions as much for memory as anything, but our hearts weren't in it. Dad sat for longer and longer periods, staring silently out the window, and Mother's heart was heavy with worry. . . .

On December 23, another official-looking package arrived. My father watched stone-faced as Mother unpacked Bob's dress blues. *After all this time, why oh why did they—the nameless they—send his dress uniform,* I thought bitterly. Silence hung heavy. As she refolded the uniform to put it away, a mother's practicality surfaced, and she went through the pockets almost by rote, aching with grief.

In a small, inside jacket pocket was a neatly folded fifty-dollar bill with a tiny note in Bob's familiar handwriting: "For Dad's Masonic ring."

If I live to be a hundred, I will never forget the look on my father's face. Some kind of beautiful transformation took place—a touch of wonder, a hint of joy, a quiet serenity that was glorious to behold. Oh, the healing power of love! He stood transfixed, staring at the note and the trimly folded fifty-dollar bill in his hand for what seemed an eternity; then he walked to Bob's picture hanging prominently on the wall and solemnly saluted.

"Merry Christmas, Son," he murmured, and turned to welcome Christmas.

Mary Sherman Hilbert

How Much Love Can You Fit in a Shoebox?

The little things? The little moments? They aren't little.

Jon Kabat-Zinn

On a cold and rainy February morning, my mom, four brothers and I cleaned out Dad's apartment. There were a thousand places we would have rather been, but we were together and the rest of the world seemed distant. With Dad's funeral scheduled for the next day, it was all I could do to take my mind off the reality of his heart attack. Everything he owned was in his apartment. He wasn't materialistic, yet every belonging seemed priceless. His countless drawings filled every room. His notepads of sketches he drew in the hospital had a flavor of who he really was. His deteriorating car and torn furniture didn't begin to describe what made him successful in my eyes.

He took life one day at a time, never taking anything too seriously. It was his best quality . . . and his worst. I was thirty-seven years old and had grown up much like him, putting tremendous value on the little things in life.

I moped around from room to room, gathering souvenirs and throwing out the garbage he never had the chance to. As I turned the corner and entered his bedroom, I quickly spotted his prized possession. It was a letter from my eight-year-old nephew declaring his unconditional love for his grampa—how much he loved him, loved fishing with him and how he hoped he would never die. Dad's heart melted and eyes watered whenever he spoke of the letter. It touched him deeply. He proudly displayed it to anyone and everyone. I gathered the cleanup crew to read it one last time. We all seemed to realize where this letter belonged—with Dad, forever.

My mind wandered back to the time I wanted to write a similar message to Dad. It was less than a year ago when I sat down to write. My heart wanted to fill the page with the traits and values I had grown to respect. Before a single word was written, my head took over and I realized Dad could never keep such a letter to himself. Even if he promised never to show it to my brothers, I somehow knew his good intentions would eventually be overtaken by his heartfelt pride. I'd be too embarrassed expressing such feelings at this point in my life. Besides, my actions had always spoken louder than words, so I didn't write it. Knowing Dad was indestructible, I always figured there'd be time.

As the years rolled on, it bothered me that I never wrote that letter. My mom wasn't getting any younger, and thoughts of not having thanked her for all the things she had done for me started creeping in. Now, instead of feeling embarrassed, I wanted to include my brothers in this project. Christmas was only a month away, and what a great present this could be for all of us to write about something we'd never thanked her for. We all had to write something because if one of us declined I knew she'd put more weight on why one didn't write anything.

It would not be an easy task to get my brothers to write. I needed a plan.

I was committed to the point of listing my brothers' names in order from who I imagined was the easiest to convince to the hardest. I determined Bob would be the easiest. He always got along with Mom. Gary would be second. He usually mailed a Mother's Day card. Mark was next. He hadn't spoken to her for six months. Even worse, he had four kids who weren't seeing their gramma, and I knew Gramma missed the kids. Rick lived in Rochester and, except for the occasional ninety-minute obligatory trips to Buffalo to see her, he had limited contact with Mom.

We all crafted our reasons for not staying in contact with Mom. My brothers and I didn't intentionally alienate her, but we didn't seem to go out of our way to stay in touch either. She seemed the perpetual martyr, and her words and tone of voice left us upset to the point where the frustration her words created overpowered our understanding of her hurt.

I sat by the phone, frozen in my thoughts. This would either happen or it would be the most embarrassing idea I ever shared with my brothers.

So there I was . . . nervous . . . shaking . . . feeling all the insecurities that kept me from writing Dad. By now, the "what ifs" were coming faster than my hands were moving toward the phone. But this time, I was determined to succeed or be humiliated.

So I picked up the phone and called Bob. I explained what I wanted to do, why I wanted to do it and what my plan was. To me, Bob was a given, no problem, just a matter of explaining the game plan. When I got done with my two-minute speech, there was a pause at the other end. "Well, it would have been a lot easier if we had written one for Dad!" he said with deadpan reasoning.

Yikes! What kind of an answer was that? I thought. This brother was the "for sure." Under other circumstances, I may have crumbled and agreed with him, but this was not the direction I had committed to take. So I restated, "Putting that aside, can you think of something you've never thanked Mom for?"

"Sure," he said.

"Well, could you write a letter and have it ready to hand me on Christmas Eve when the family gets together at Mom's house?"

"All right, I'll do it!" he stated without further hesitation. I hung up the phone, and my first thought was, *Good, I have one in the bank.* I could use that to enroll brothers number two, three and four. It was a plan. I hadn't expected Bob to give me any resistance, so I knew the job wasn't going to get any easier.

Gary was next. He replied in the sensitive, caring fashion I had anticipated. "How long does it have to be, and what do we have to say?"

Mark was next. I was nervous before I called him. Not only hadn't he spoken to Mom in months, I knew he was mad at her. I started my conversation by explaining the idea and that Bob and Gary had already agreed. I was expecting my hardest time with Mark.

I'll never forget what happened next.

As I finished, he started right into a story. "I remember when I was in junior high school and got suspended for something I didn't do. I got sent home, and Mom asked me, 'Did you do it?' I said, *'No!'* She took me back to school to face Mr. Schaefer, the most feared disciplinary teacher any student ever encountered. We marched into his office, and before I knew it, Mom was screaming at him, saying, 'If my son said he didn't do it, he didn't do it.' When she was done with him, he was somewhere under the desk apologizing for his obvious mistake."

Mark's story rolled off his lips as if it happened yesterday. I was shocked because not only had I never heard that story, but he recalled it so vividly.

Rick was next. He had a similar story to Mark's from back in high school. Besides Bob, Gary and Mark had already agreed, and my work actually seemed to get easier. It was like my brothers' stroll down memory lane rekindled a different message and memory they had of Mom. I hopefully put them back to a time when she was always there, as if she had never left. Four in the bank, at least verbally.

Two days before Christmas Eve, I called all four brothers, and each had finished his letter. My final instructions to them were to bring the letters to Mom's, and I was going to put all five into a shoebox I had wrapped to give to her.

Christmas Eve arrived. I handed the box to Mom and said, "This present is from all of us. Do not open it until tomorrow." She looked puzzled, wondering what we were up to, but agreed and said, "Thank you."

Christmas Eve was always fun at Mom's, but this year it was special for me. I knew I pulled off something I couldn't have imagined. As my brothers and their families gathered to open presents, this year was different. Closer . . . nicer . . . warmer.

I drove home that night with the greatest feeling of accomplishment. I recalled Mom talking to the grandkids and laughing all night long. Maybe the night was special for everyone. We all seemed a lot closer to her that night, or maybe it was just me hoping it was all this way again.

Christmas morning the phone rang. It was Mom. She told me how she couldn't wait until morning to open the shoebox. She read all the letters three times and cried herself to sleep. She said, "I knew you were the one respon -

sible for doing this, and it was wonderful." I told her we were all responsible for doing this, and it was long overdue.

I never knew what my brothers wrote in their letters, not completely. As for me, I included a story of when I was ten years old and wanted to go to a sports competition. I can't remember the exact words, but it went something like this: "No one seemed to feel it was a big deal, but you saw the disappointment in my face and said, 'I'll take you.' You sat in the rain for over an hour as I tried my best to win a prize. I don't think I ever thanked you, but it meant a lot to me."

I also told her how hard it must have been for her to raise five boys with all of us being a little closer to Dad. "We knew he got the easy job of playing good guy while you were forced to be the one who disciplined us when we were bad. You were the one who taught us right from wrong, fair and unfair, and to apologize when we were wrong. You did that, and I thank you."

Mom had longed to hear such words for years. It was always in our hearts but never got translated to her. I always saw her cry after cooking Thanksgiving dinner. She would prepare all day, while Dad, my brothers and I gobbled it up and proceeded to the living room to tend to our own priorities.

I see a lot of Mom and Dad in me, and I couldn't be happier. I started out wanting to do something for Mom to show her how we felt. We got to revisit our appreciation for her and how she had always been there for us.

In hindsight, I really did it for Bob, Gary, Mark, Rick and me.

I hung up the phone that snowy Christmas morning, reclined on the couch and looked up to imagine Dad wiping a tear from his eye.

Seems everyone got something special out of this Christmas.

Jim Schneegold

Discretion Is the Better
Part of Marriage

Seventeen years ago on a cold and blustery Saturday, I stood in the arch of a sanctuary with baby's breath in my hair and a foolish grin on my face, too big of a ninny to realize that I ought to be scared to death.

As a swell of Mozart filled air that was thick with my great aunt's Chantilly, my nervous, tuxedo-clad father bent down to whisper what I thought would be words of paternal wisdom. "It's not too late," he hissed, waving a wad of bills. "If you want to weasel out of this, I'll give you five hundred bucks and a Greyhound ticket any place you want to go."

I didn't tell my soon-to-be husband, Jeff, this story for several years. It wasn't that Dad didn't like "that tall kid"—he did—but the combination of watching my sister's impulsive first marriage unravel and knowing that Jeff and I had met less than five months before was making him a little gun shy.

That problem was soon remedied. As some wit said, marriage remains the most efficient way to get acquainted. We met over Labor Day, got engaged at Thanksgiving and married in the windiest January on record. Between immediately moving out east where neither of us knew a soul and then having a child before our second anniversary, we got to know each other (as my southern Missouri relatives would say) right soon.

Though seventeen years hardly qualifies us for one of those fatuous anniversary greetings from Willard Scott, we've been married long enough to know a thing or two. Before the honeymoon was over, we were certain that the bozo who wrote "Love means never having to say you're sorry" had obviously never been married. While having the last word might be intellectually satisfying, it's mighty chilly on your own side of the bed. We've also been married long enough to know how much fun it is to have private jokes that drive our children crazy. It would take us a very long time to explain to them why the terms "garlic milk shakes" and "bluebird watching society" set us off, and besides, you had to be there.

We were relieved to discover that we don't have to enjoy the same things to enjoy each other. We both like long road trips on blue highways, old houses and junk shops. After that, we part company. I like Victor Borge; he likes Jimi Hendrix. I love exotic travel; he has never had a passport. He loves musicals where the ruddy villagers burst inexplicably into song; I like Ingmar Bergman dramas in which pale, suicidal sisters communicate in cryptic whispers. He likes to dance; I have two left feet.

Over the years, we've discovered that discretion is the better part of matrimony. He has not once pointed out that I am routinely responsible for 75 percent of the long-distance calls on the phone bill. When I see the telltale yellow of a parking ticket on his chest of drawers, I permit myself no more than a raised eyebrow. He doesn't comment when I stay up until 2 A.M. reading a mystery even though I've been whining about how much I have to do the next day; I pretend I don't know he blows a half an hour and a few bucks at the video arcade each time he takes the boys to the mall. I nod in agreement when, with ambition born of a Saturday morning, he says he's going to patch, sand and paint the bedroom after going into the office in the morning and before running errands in the afternoon (even though I know he'll be "resting his eyes" in his favorite chair before the first dribble of paint hits the dropcloth).

And perhaps most astonishingly, of all the innumerable times over the last seventeen years I have put something on and asked if it makes me look fat, he has always feigned astonished denial. Not once has he said, "What do you mean? You are fat."

We have learned that, "How can I help?" works better than "I told you so," and that "I love you" works better than "What's your problem?"

Still, if I had it to do over, I'd take the bus ticket and the money my dad offered instead of the dyed-to-match shoes, the sterling flatware and the obligatory feeding-each-other-cake shot in the deluxe portrait package. But wherever I went, I'd take Jeff with me.

Rebecca Christian

You Do It Quiet

At the time, I wasn't even sure he knew I was screaming at him, but for years afterward, he was resentful of it. He felt that I wasn't having faith in him. I don't fault myself in the slightest. I think it was a very human response. I didn't know the outcome. I was in love with this guy, and it looked like I had an awful big chance to lose him.

It was right after we got pinned—the end of my sopho-more year and Dan's junior year. Bates College had an annual clambake on Fox Island in Maine. Dan and I were sitting high on a cliff, looking down on the ocean in awe. There were tremendous waves crashing against the rocks. Then a girl we knew came running, screaming. Within seconds, we could see two people being swept away by the current. Steve, the closer one, had been smashed off a fifteen-foot rock by a wave and was floating. The other guy had tried to save Steve by tying sweatshirts into a rope and throwing them from the rocks. But as he threw, *he* fell in. He had all his clothes on, and his struggling car-ried him out farther than Steve.

When I saw Dan get out of his clothes, I started scream-ing. I knew he was a lifeguard, but this was not a normal rescue: The waves were so high that in the water you couldn't see over the crest, and after they crashed into the rocks, the undertow sucked everything out like a vacuum. I was swearing at Dan, screaming at him not to go.

But some of the other students had cut rope out of a volleyball net, and he tied it around his waist. I don't remember if I saw Dan enter the water. I know that I was watching when he reached Steve, because at that very moment I saw the other guy go down for the last time.

Dan held Steve in a carry, and they were pulled up by the rope, dragged along the barnacles. Dan's legs were all cut and bruised. The next day, they were so swollen, he could barely get his pants on. I remember the dean of students coming over and shaking Dan's hand afterward. But other than that, the college didn't acknowledge what he'd done. The student newspaper interviewed Dan, but the story was never published. It's a terrible blemish to admit that a student died on a college outing. Because it was a tragic event, people wanted to put it out of their minds. With the way it was kind of snuffed, the campus in denial, it almost made Dan feel guilty or part of a bad thing. So you learn that it's not always like it is in the fairy tales. There are going to be all kinds of reactions.

That's one of the reasons Dan rarely talks about this and about what happened later at the school and why I'm reticent to talk about it now. You have to be sensitive. There's *always* another side to the story. Think about it. When Dan got his first Carnegie Medal for heroism, one was posthumously awarded to the guy who'd fallen in throwing the sweatshirts. Even though the situation may have had a happy ending for us, it's still a tragedy for another family.

Dan's one of only four people to receive two Carnegie Medals. One of the previous winners died in the second attempt, and I think another lost a leg. Dan's lucky to have come out whole. Yes, I'm proud of him beyond words. But it's better not to dwell on it. When people ask me what it's like to be married to a hero, I tell them that when I married Dan thirty-four years ago, I was a brunette with straight hair, now my hair is curly and white. I might as well get a laugh out of it. In reality, I try not to think about it, because every day I'd be wondering if a situation is going to arise, *knowing* that Dan's likely to step forward. And not just Dan. Our daughter, Carolynn, is a water-safety instructor. Our youngest son, Michael, is a lifeguard, and our oldest, Danny, paraglides and rock climbs. Sometimes I think, *Why couldn't they all have just taken up bowling?*

Of course, I'd rather have them be who they are. What would have happened if Dan had heeded my screams and done nothing—just stood on that cliff and watched both of those guys go down? He probably would've had nightmares for the rest of his life. And I would've felt horrible.

I don't want you to get the wrong impression about Dan. You watch him mount a horse—how can I describe it? It's like he'll grab the mane and bounce up as the horse starts to gallop. When he skis, he doesn't take a lesson and learn to snowplow. He'll head to the top of a hill in a snowstorm, go down, somersault, come up with snow in his eyebrows, and do it again. But you can't stereotype him. The fact is, Dan was so scared in his first year of teaching at an inner-city school that he'd eat his breakfast, barf it up, then go in to work. Years later, when he first became principal at Winnisquam Regional High School, there were days when he'd come home and tell me that he'd wanted to hide under the coffee table.

Some people might have a hard time believing that the same guy who wanted to hide under the coffee table would voluntarily walk into a classroom where a sixteen-year-old is pointing a rifle at junior high school kids. I don't really have an answer to that. Only a revelation that

I had when Dan and I were driving to the hospital on my way to have major surgery and I thought I might have cancer. I was about in tears, and my teeth were chattering, and I said to Dan, "Look at me, I'm a wreck. I'm sorry I'm not being brave about this." And he turned to me and said, "Oh, you're being brave. Brave is not *not* being scared. Being brave is being scared and doing what you have to do."

After thirty-three years of marriage, I definitely have a clear understanding of who he is. I understand why he entered room 73. Yet to this day, it amazes me how a man who needs twenty-two pairs of glasses because he's so absentminded that he always forgets where he puts them can focus and think ahead so clearly with students being held hostage.

I learned all about it that morning, of course. But I didn't fully comprehend what had happened until a couple of years later, when I went to the room and Dan reenacted everything. A sixteen-year-old had shot a rifle in the cafeteria. Two kids were injured, and then the kid with the rifle took a bunch of students hostage. I don't want to mention the kid's name. As I said before, there's another side to every story. This might still be painful to him. We don't want to hurt him; we hope he can straighten his life out.

The questions people ask Dan about the incident are the questions that they ask themselves. They want to know how they'd react under those circumstances. But it's pointless. None of us could ever know.

Dan looked through the window in the door and saw some of his students crying while this kid was reloading his rifle with shells from a box on the teacher's desk. There were so many things to think about: posting janitors so nobody could come down the corridor; getting everybody out of the school. How much time did he have? We're in rural New Hampshire. He'd called the police on occasion and been unable to get anybody. Sometimes there's only one policeman on duty. Was he better off not doing anything? Was he putting the kids in danger by walking in? He got everybody out of the school, then held his breath and turned the doorknob.

Immediately, the gun was pointed at his head. The kid was sweating and shaking. Dan said, "If you need a hostage, you have the principal now. You can let the kids go." When the students were out the back door, Dan was so relieved. Then he began to realize, *Whoops, I'm still here.*

For forty-five minutes, the rifle was aimed at his head. He made himself keep eye contact the whole time. I can't stand to think about it—not only the reality that he might have died but what he was feeling when he was telling himself, *I hope I don't hear the trigger pulled. I hope I don't see the flash.*

The kid was saying that there was no reason to live. He demanded a boom box and to see a friend. When Dan went to the window to shout the kid's demands, the kid turned with him away from the door, where the police chief was crouching. The police chief rushed in with a gun. And then, when the kid put the barrel under his chin and threatened to commit suicide, another officer who'd crawled in seized the rifle.

There was an outpouring of appreciation from the community. I wrote my own thank-you note to the police chief. But Dan didn't even give it a thought when the Hollywood people offered a lot of money to make a movie about it. And when the superintendent asked if the second Carnegie Medal could be presented in a public way, Dan said, "No thanks." You have to realize, Monadnock Regional Junior/Senior High feeds off eight small towns that don't even have a downtown. Dan goes to Agway and gets his horse grain and turkey feed just like everybody else. We're much more comfortable keeping a low profile. Our fear is that when someone whom everybody knows in everyday life is suddenly set up as a hero—especially in our culture, where heroes are touted as larger than life—then there's something about human nature that wants to take that person down a peg.

But there are little things nobody really sees or could imagine that come out of a situation like this that make you feel good. Everyone from the family came up the weekend after the incident. Our daughter, Carolynn, cried and yelled at Dan for going into that room: "Don't you understand you're the only father I'll ever have?" Much later, when she was able to think about it, she understood. She has stepchildren. She would want the principal of their school to have the same care for their safety. But there's a difference between your emotional response and the rational response that comes later. That day, all the emotions came pouring to the surface. Dan did a wonderful job of sitting there and letting her say her piece.

Until that day, he would have told you that he resented my yelling at him at Fox Island. He didn't understand my reaction until he heard it from our daughter. When he did, he forgave me.

Cal Fussman
As told by Merry Stockwell

Blue Christmas

This is a story about Christmas, and about a box under our Christmas tree one year that wasn't big enough, by a long shot, to hold a bicycle. That box, brightly wrapped in blue tissue with a tag "Merry Christmas, Terry—love, Mom and Dad," was the object of my considerable attention, because I knew it held my main gift, and what I really wanted was a bicycle. Not any bicycle, but a particular blue bicycle from Johnston's Hardware Store on the Hill.

On the other side of the tree was another box, wrapped in red, with a tag "Merry Christmas, Steve—love, Mom and Dad." Steve, my nine-year-old brother, wanted an electric train, and he was sure that was what his package held.

It was 1958, my eleventh year, and we were living in Cedar Falls, a town I never really got to know because we moved from there to Iowa City the next fall.

We had a low, ranch-style house, pale green and brand new. It was a new street and a new neighborhood, dotted with expensive new homes.

The Hill was six blocks away and important to us, not only for its small shopping district but also because it was the site of the college my sister, Linda, seventeen, would attend next fall.

The Monday before Christmas, Steve and I headed for the Hill to do our Christmas shopping. Shivering, I plunged my hands as far into my pockets as they would go. The sky was ominously grey, and the cold wind which shook the bare branches of the trees overhead, seemed to cut right through my jacket.

"C'mon, Steve," I called impatiently to my brother. "We'll never get there if we don't hurry."

"Race ya," he cried.

We were off. I was a faster runner than he was, but sometimes with a head start he could beat me. I sprinted behind him, straining to catch up. He stopped at the corner, winded, his face red. "I won," he panted triumphantly.

Any other day I would have called him a cheater. But today was special, so I let him stay the victor. The Hill was in sight. Its lampposts were gaily strung with green cellophane chains and huge plastic candy canes that looked good enough to eat. Steve and I trudged up the hill that gave the small shopping area its name, past the soda shop where we sometimes got ice cream in the summer, past the pet store where we usually admired the parakeets and turtles. We were going to the five-and-dime to do our Christmas shopping—for the first time alone.

My brother had his savings from his piggy bank clutched in his hand, and I had four dollars, some of which I'd earned raking the neighbor's yard, in my pocket.

At the dime store we paused long enough to look in the window. There were a host of wonderful things there— chocolate Santas, dolls with long hair, miniature bright red fire trucks with a hose that sprayed water.

"You could get that for me," I announced to my brother, pointing to a round, blue sliding saucer which sat on a mound of artificial snow. "I'll share it with you."

"I only have sixty-five cents," he reminded me.

Then in we went. Steve stopped by a jar of colored combs and carefully examined one. Then he looked at me. "Don't you have shopping to do?" he demanded.

I headed for the aisle that held envelopes, notebooks and stationery. My sister would need stationery to write to us, I thought. It was a perfect gift. I debated about buying my father a notebook, since he would be going back to college in Iowa City. (At forty-five!) *Too ordinary*, I thought. I wanted to give him something special, not something silly, like the green beanie his friends were planning!

My brother came around the corner and began looking at the pencils. I picked up the stationery I'd chosen and headed for the cash register in front. I had made my mother a set of hot pads, but I wanted to give her something else as well. Suddenly I spotted the perfect gift, a pair of pale blue earrings that would just match her new dress.

I had enough money left to buy baseball cards, bubble gum and a miniature flashlight for Steve. After I paid for my presents I waited for him outside.

Soon he emerged, beaming, a small bag in one hand, a nickel in the other. "Let's go wrap them," he said.

We went home by way of the hardware store, so I could look at my bike. It wasn't my bike actually, but I was saving money to buy it. I wanted it more than anything else in the world. It was a slim blue Italian model; I'd never seen another one like it. I planned to ride it to school, to the ice cream shop, and to see my best friend Cathy, even though she only lived a half block away from me. Next fall, I'd ride it all over Iowa City.

The hardware store was busy, and Mr. Johnston was waiting on a customer. He wouldn't have time to talk today. I would take a quick look at my bike and be on my way. My brother waited by the sporting goods while I went to the back where the bicycles were. There it was, on the end, as blue as the whole sky, just waiting to be ridden. I reached over to touch the blue and white seat, and stopped cold. Hanging from the handlebar was a tag, handwritten in capital letters, SOLD, it said.

It seemed like my heart stopped and time stood still. For three months, ever since the first day I saw it, I'd been saving my money to buy that blue bike.

I ran from the store, fighting back tears. Now somebody else would ride down College Street on my bike, somebody I knew, or, worse yet, a stranger who would carelessly leave it out in the rain and snow to rust and grow old.

On the way home, Steve and I walked slowly. I didn't notice the cold. He wanted to talk, but I was thinking about the bicycle that almost was, the bicycle that wouldn't be. One thing was certain. I could break open my bank. I no longer needed the twelve dollars I'd saved. I started to think of what I would buy with it.

This, our last Christmas in Cedar Falls, would be a truly blue Christmas now, I knew. Next year, we would no longer have the ranch house with its two fireplaces. Instead, we would have a tiny tin barrack left over from World War II, so small it was barely larger than my bedroom in Cedar Falls. Instead of a fireplace it would have an oilstove; instead of a picture window looking out over a spacious green lawn, it would have windows so high you couldn't see out and no lawn at all. My mother said we had to save money, and cut back. She was going to find a job while my father went to school.

I didn't look forward to the prospect of cutting back or moving. I liked Cedar Falls, the shops on the Hill, my school, and my best friend Cathy. But I knew education was important. It had brought us to the new ranch-style with the huge sloping lawn planted with Russian olive trees and weeping willows. That house was miles and miles from the ramshackle houses my father had grown up in, dark, drafty tinderboxes bordering smelly, smoky factories. And it would take us even further—to the university town where my father hoped to get a Ph.D. degree, and then to some other university town where he would become a professor.

If I had my blue bike, I thought brightly, *I wouldn't mind moving so much.* Then, remembering how much my father had gone without as a boy, I decided to put the bicycle out of my mind. There was Christmas to think about, and presents to wrap.

By the time my brother and I got home, my spirits had picked up and we burst excitedly through the door, throwing off our jackets and hats. I heard Bing Crosby on the record player singing "White Christmas." That meant my father had gotten out his Christmas records while we were gone. He was sitting by the fireplace, where a fire was crackling, reading. Occasionally he'd sing a few bars, his off-key tenor voice echoing Crosby's.

My mother was baking, humming as she worked. She was making sugar cookies shaped like bells and reindeer, sprinkled with red and green sugar. My brother and I sat down and had two each, warm from the oven, at the picnic table we ate from in our kitchen. The tempting scent of cookies baking drifted through the warm and cozy house from room to room, as Bing Crosby sang and I wrapped my packages. When I put them under the tree I spotted several small rectangular packages that my brother had wrapped.

One was addressed to me, "Merry Christmas, Terry," the card read, "and no peeking."

A piece of tinsel had fallen off the tree and I put it back on a low branch, then stepped back to admire the tree. Decorating it was a family affair, and each year we dragged out the box of ornaments and happily examined its contents. There were little candle-shaped lights with colored water inside that bubbled when you plugged them in. There was tinsel, which we carefully removed from the tree each year and saved.

At night, when the room was dark and the Christmas tree lights were on, the living room seemed to take on a special glow, a blue glow, as if that tree were the center of the universe and all the promise of the world lay in that room. That tree represented warmth, happiness and security.

"Look," my mother said, "it's snowing."

The sky that had threatened snow all day opened up, and soft flakes fell softly to the ground, piling up around the steps, blanketing the yard, and draping the small pine trees outside. A hush came over the neighborhood and in every picture window, it seemed, the colored lights of Christmas trees twinkled. Even the snow shimmered, catching and reflecting the blue lights strung on trees across the street.

After dinner my father told about Christmas when he was a boy. He told about the time there wasn't enough money for presents, or even food. It was a faraway world that I only knew through his stories, and even though I had seen the rundown houses where he had grown up, I had trouble feeling the reality of going hungry, of going without presents on Christmas day.

Some of his Christmases were happy, and those were the ones I liked to hear about best. I liked to hear about the year he and his brother got a wooden sled, which they found leaning in the snow against their house on a bright Christmas morning. I liked to imagine my father going downhill at top speed, the snow flying in his face, momentarily blinding him, his peals of laughter.

But I would always think about going hungry. I secretly hoped I would never know a Christmas without date pinwheel cookies, and the oranges my mother always put in my stocking.

Suddenly I knew what I would give my father for Christmas—the money I saved for my bicycle. I ran to my room, and on a piece of paper I wrote, "Dear Dad, this is for your education." I carefully folded the paper and in it I put the money I had saved for my bicycle—twelve one-dollar bills. I put the paper in a shoebox. He'd never guess in a million years what a shoebox as light as a feather held. Carefully I wrapped it and put it under the tree.

And then, it was Christmas! Christmas morning, and my brother and I were up at dawn, trying to rouse my parents from their bed. We waited impatiently while my mother made her way slowly to the kitchen and started the coffee in the percolator. My brother and I poked at the presents under the tree, and emptied our stockings of their ribbon candy, oranges, apples and trinkets. Couldn't my mother hurry? Why did they have to have coffee?

Finally the great moment came, as we all assembled around the tree. The anticipation was high. I had come to terms with the fact that there would be no bicycle, but that big box held something else, some wonderful surprise. I knew that. We began to open our presents. My grandmother had sent me pajamas. She had given my sister embroidered pillow cases. My sister had given my father a moustache cup for drinking his coffee. My brother opened a football, and whooped.

Then there was the big box for me, and I shook it to see if it rattled. It didn't.

"Try to guess," my mother said. I couldn't and finally ripped the paper from it. There inside was the big blue saucer from the five-and-dime. It had snowed just in time. My father opened a red flannel shirt my sister had made, and my mother opened the comb from my brother and ran it appreciatively through her hair. "Thank you sweetheart," she said to Steve. My sister opened the stationery and laughed. "I guess this means

I'll have to write," she said, giving me a hug.

Finally, my brother picked up his big box. He started to say "A saucer for—" and then something in the box rattled. His eyes opened wide. With my mother cautioning him to save the paper, he gently opened the box. It was an electric train set with a cattle car and a yellow caboose.

"It's just like the Illinois Central," he said.

Then I saw my father holding the shoebox, a puzzled gleam in his eyes. Carefully he untied the ribbon. He reached inside and slowly withdrew the note.

For once he didn't say anything. When he finished reading what I had written, he looked at me, then my mother. His eyes seemed to fill with tears.

Had I ruined Christmas? We all watched him in uneasy silence. Then, as he handed the note to my mother, he stood up, put on his new shirt, tucked his new comb in one pocket and the money in the other. "Looks like I'm all ready for college," he said, laughing.

Then his expression changed and he looked at all of us. "This is the most wonderful Christmas I've ever had. I hope it is for you too," he said. He winked at my mother.

My mother was smoothing the hot pads I had given her with her hands. She had put on the blue earrings. The way she smiled at me showed how pleased she was.

While my father was pretending to be drinking from his moustache cup, I picked up the coal black locomotive from my brother's train. "It's beautiful," I said.

He whispered, "Maybe you'll get a bike for your birthday."

"Maybe," I acknowledged. My birthday was eleven months off, and the coasting hills would have to do without me for now.

But then a realization came over me, suddenly, as I picked up the blue pencils my brother had given me. Christmas was more than giving presents, or receiving presents.

It was my brother stretching his allowance to buy us gifts. It was the care I had put into making those hot pads. It was my sister being there, before she went to college. It was my mother bustling in the kitchen, singing "Silent Night," and my father getting out his Bing Crosby record for the umpteenth time. It was carols and cookies and colored lights, a family in a small town on a morning when the snow fell thick and fast. It was love and sharing and being together. It was intangible stuff—memories, tradition, hope—it was catching, for a moment, a glimpse of peace.

My mother interrupted my thoughts. "Terry, could you please see if the coffee is ready?"

Dutifully I hurried to the kitchen, where I could smell a cinnamon coffee cake baking. My mouth watered. "It's ready," I called, and I took out two coffee cups. Then I turned to see if the plates were on the table for breakfast.

I could not believe my eyes. There, parked next to the picnic table, was the bicycle from the hardware store, shinier, sleeker and bluer than it had ever been before, shimmering like a vision. Taking a deep breath, I ran over and touched the gleaming chrome, the leather seat, the tires.

Softly then Bing Crosby began singing "White Christmas" in the living room. I smiled. It might be a white Christmas for everyone else, with plump snow-capped evergreens on soft white lawns. It was a blue Christmas for me. Blue was the color of promise and possibility, of next year and always, of the roads I would follow, on that bike and others. Blue was the top of the hill, the wind at my back, freedom. With a flourish I kicked up the kickstand and wheeled my bike toward the front door.

Terry Andrews

Daisy's Trip

Daisy stood on Abe's lap in the front of his faded blue truck. She licked his face. His fingers were buried in her neck.

"I've never seen Pop so happy," said Peter Galan, Abe Galan's son. "Since Mom passed away, that dog has been his life."

And vice versa, evidently. Ten-year-old Daisy just completed Modesto's version of *The Incredible Journey*, a tracking so amazing even dog experts marvel.

"Daisy tracked her master four miles to a place she had never been before, over a route that her master never walked." It defied logic, but that didn't mean a dog couldn't do it."

Daisy yaps. She's half Chihuahua. She's a soprano.

The journey began last Friday, when Daisy watched Abe's children drive away with her master. They took him to Memorial Medical Center, where he was to undergo cancer surgery.

Another car came and carted Daisy to the house where Rachel, Abe's daughter, lived. Daisy was supposed to stay with Rachel while Abe was away.

No one filled Daisy in on the plan.

The first night she never slept. She paced the floor and whined.

The second night, Rachel let Daisy sleep in the yard. Daisy spent the night digging. She tunneled out before dawn.

Rachel called all of the brothers and sisters at six-thirty in the morning and said, "My God, Daisy is gone."

The extended Galan clan gathered at Rachel's home and fanned out like soldiers.

They walked every step of the neighborhood, taping posters to all the poles. They scoured the street where their dad lived. They knew it would kill him if he lost that dog.

Darkness fell, and still no sign of Daisy.

Meanwhile, Memorial staff was mesmerized by a stray dog. Daisy just sat there by the emergency entrance, and every time the doors opened she'd run in. Someone would chase her out, and she'd turn around and run back in. For hours she did this, starting before dawn.

Employees considered calling the pound, like they do with other strays. But Daisy was different. She was clearly looking for someone. She even made it into the main hallway and was sniffing at the doors.

Paramedic Nina Torres took her to dispatch, where Lou Menton and her partner LaVonda Barker soothed her with a blanket and a Wendy's hamburger. Then she just curled and slept.

Dispatch tried to page the master. "Will the owners of a light tan dog please come to security. . . ."

By six-thirty that night, another one of Abe's daughters —Chris Hackler—made the long walk down Memorial's hall to tell Dad the bad news.

He was coming home the next day. They had to let him know about Daisy. He went nuts when they told him. He tried to get out of bed to go look for her himself."

Chris went out into the hall to compose herself and (as is her fashion) began telling her tale to whoever would listen. Good thing because a woman overheard her and said, "Hey, they've been paging all day for the owner of a lost dog."

The woman went with Chris to call security, who called dispatch, who called the dog "Daisy" to see if it was a match.

Her ears shot right up.

A security guard told Chris she couldn't bring a dog into the hospital, "but if I don't see you do it, I guess there's nothing I can do about it."

Chris wrapped Daisy in a blanket and carried her infant-style into the elevator. A man in the lift tapped her on the shoulder: "Pardon me. Your baby's tail is showing."

Chris told everyone on the elevator the Daisy saga, so everyone on the elevator had to get off with her and watch the reunion. Twenty people were in the hall when Chris handed Abe the bundle: "Dad, I have something for you."

Daisy popped out like a showgirl.

Abe let out a yell, and Daisy started barking. The rest of them were crying like babies.

When Abe was well enough to return home, Daisy's new friends gathered outside to bid them adieu. "We like it when things here at the hospital end happy," Torres said as she planted a big kiss on Daisy's wet nose.

Abe turned to the crowd outside his truck and waves.

Daisy licked her chops and beams. Birds gotta fly, fish gotta swim and Daisy had done found her man.

Diane Nelson

Lilies of the Valley

On a table lay approximately fifty miniature china slippers whose colors ranged from the palest of pastels to vivid pinks and burgundies. They were trimmed with tiny ruffled lace and flowers: rosebuds, violets and lilies of the valley. The mall was hosting Antiques Week.

"This is quite a varied collection," Ellen said to the salesman standing behind the table.

"I bought them at a farmhouse auction," he replied. "A widow was selling just about everything she owned to move to the city. She said she received the first one when she was twenty years old. Slippers were popular miniatures to collect at the turn of the century. They are still well received today; one of my best sellers, in fact."

Ellen couldn't help wondering on what occasion the widow either bought, or was presented with, a special miniature. Maybe it was an anniversary, or her birthday. Perhaps her grandchildren purchased a slipper as a Christmas present.

I'll bet if these shoes could talk, they would divulge a great deal about the joys and sorrows of this woman and her family, thought Ellen. *Why didn't she give these heirlooms to her children or grandchildren?*

Ellen began to tire of the large package she carried in her arms. A rest was in order. She spied a bench directly across the aisle. With a sigh, Ellen sat down, placing her parcel between herself and a short, white-haired lady. Facing the woman, Ellen asked, "Are you interested in antique?" Tears came to her eyes and she brushed them away with her wrinkled hand.

"Why, mmnnn, yes, I was," the woman answered. "Did you notice the salesman in the booth across the way? He recently purchased my entire collection of antique slippers."

Ellen leaned down toward the woman. "Tell me what happened," she whispered.

"You've heard the expression 'the bottom fell out of everything' haven't you?"

Ellen nodded. She recalled how her grandmother was forced to sell her home and move to smaller quarters, no longer planning holiday baking and summer picnics. Now she rocks quietly, her faithful tabby at her feet.

The woman clasped her hands and continued. "My husband became quite ill. First I sold several acres of land, and that helped with the hospital expenses. When the doctor said he could do no more, I brought my husband home. I tended him until he mercifully passed away. Not wanting to be a burden to my son, I sold the farmhouse, including most of the furniture and personal possessions. I took up residence in a one-bedroom apartment near this mall. I can walk to the grocery and pharmacy in this building. Driving may not be a privilege I can enjoy much longer," she grimaced. "Now and then I just come to the mall and sit and observe the action around me, just as you are doing now."

Ellen smiled. "Would you tell me which slipper was your favorite; which miniature meant the most to you?"

"When we became engaged, my fiancé presented me

with a pearl-white shoe encrusted with lilies of the valley. It was not the most valuable miniature in the collection, but I treasured the memory of that night," she reflected.

Ellen rose and said, "Would you be so kind as to watch my package for a few minutes?" The woman nodded affirmatively.

Ellen sought the salesman behind the table and spoke to him. He stooped down out of sight and wrapped an item in white tissue paper.

Returning to the bench, Ellen handed the lady her purchase and grinned. "You remind me of my grandmother whom I dearly love. I have a little something for you."

The woman was flustered. "I don't know what to say."

"Don't say anything. Open it," Ellen admonished.

The woman tore away the tissue paper. Tears fell gently down her withered cheeks as she recognized the pearl-white shoe given to her many years ago.

Jacqueline Moffett

The $325 Salvation

I stood on tiptoe and handed the 3-by-5 card from the Help Wanted board at Fairfax High up to the tall, broad-shouldered, ruddy-faced man behind the counter of Mort's Deli at the Farmer's Market. He wore a starched chef's hat and a clean white apron over slacks and a sports shirt, and even before I opened my mouth to speak, he was frowning and shaking his head.

"This is a tough job for any high school kid," he said. "I need somebody big and strong."

At sixteen, I looked younger and was barely five feet tall. "I worked last summer washing dishes in a boys camp," I said. "Near Chicago. I'm not afraid of hot water, dirty dishes or heavy lifting."

"Florine, come out here a minute," called the tall man. In the kitchen doorway appeared an elfin presence, his dark skin mottled and wrinkled with age. He was even shorter than I was. Several long wispy white hairs sprouted from his chin. "This is Mr. Joaquin, the chef. He's eighty years old. He needs someone strong enough to lift great big pots filled with boiling water."

"I can do the job."

"Really, we need someone bigger. You'll find something

easier than this, kid," the tall man said in a kind voice. It was September 1957, and my family had just arrived in California. Without seniority in the local union, my father, a sheet metal worker, was lucky to get work two or three days a week. Our meager savings were gone, and I, the eldest boy among what would soon be six children, was the only one able to help. I'd applied at retail stores, but without local references shopkeepers were reluctant to let me handle cash, and everyone said I was too small.

"Tell you what," I said. "Put me to work the rest of the week, and if you don't like the way I do the job, don't pay me."

The tall man stared at me, then nodded. "I'm Mort Rubin," he said. "What's your name?"

The patio at Farmers Market, then as now, was a collection of small shops and about thirty highly individualized restaurants. All used the same crockery and silverware, retrieved from tables by busboys and returned for washing. At Mort's, a river of soiled utensils, trays and dishes flowed into my sinks. Huge pots and pans came off the stove and out of the ovens to be scrubbed. I washed and rinsed and scoured; by the end of my first after-school shift, sharp pains were shooting up my heels and lower legs from four hours of standing on concrete without a break.

My father suggested that I would get used to it, but as closing time approached on Saturday, I was in agony. I would need better shoes if I was to continue working here, but I had no money and no idea if Mort would pay me for four days of work. Near the end of the day he called me up front. "How much did that card at school say this job paid?" he asked.

"Dollar an hour," I murmured. "The minimum wage." I was willing to take less.

"That's not enough for someone who works as hard as

you," said Mort. "You start at $1.25."

Over the next few weeks I learned a lot about Mort. He was a few years older than my dad, was from Chicago and had a daughter my age. In about 1937, Mort had joined the National Guard's horse-drawn artillery because he loved horses. Early in World War II, he was nearly killed in a savage battle in the mountains of New Guinea's Owen Stanley Range. Recuperating from a terrible head wound, he was attached to General Douglas MacArthur's personal staff as a military policeman, where he cultivated an Aussie accent while tracking down GI black marketers. When things were slow at the deli, he often shared stories from his Army days. But things were never slow in the kitchen; there was always something to be washed or swept or scoured.

We were closed on Sundays, and so every Saturday evening Mort encouraged me to take home the leftover soup in a huge jar. A rich broth of turkey, rice and vegetables, it was a meal in itself, a treat for my struggling family. My father usually picked me up after work on Saturdays because the soup was too much to lug home on my bike. Then one Saturday about three weeks after I began working, my father was hired to hang gutters at a neighbor's house and I took the family car to work.

After work I drove home and parked on 6th Street, a few doors from Sweetzer Avenue, and, with the warm jar in my arms, crossed the lawn. As I passed the living room window, I glanced inside and almost dropped the jar. In my father's chair was a large, heavy bald man. He was cursing my father, flinging the most obscene words in a voice dripping with contempt. My brothers and sisters sat like statues. Dad's face was stone; Mom wept.

I crept into the darkened kitchen, carefully set the soup on a counter and listened through a crack in the swinging door. The bald man wanted to take our 1952 Chevy. Dad offered to pay the three weekly payments that were in arrears, but the man demanded the entire sum—$325—or the car.

I had been in Los Angeles just long enough to understand how essential a car is. I slipped out the door, pushed the Chevy down to the corner, then started the engine and circled the neighborhood, thinking furiously. Who might have $325? Who would even consider loaning me such a princely sum?

The only person I could think of was Mort. I drove back to Farmer's Market, rapped on the rear door, then waited until the window shade went up. I found myself staring down the barrel of an Army .45. "What do you want?" growled Mort, lowering the gun but peering behind me into the darkness.

I stammered out my tale; the bald man, his foul cursing, the outrageous demand. "So, could you possibly loan my father $325?" I finished, realizing how absurd it sounded.

Mort's eyes bored holes in my face. His cheeks began to purple, and his lips quivered. I realized that he was still clutching the gun, and took an involuntary step backwards. At that, he smiled. "I'm not going to shoot you," he chuckled, placing the pistol on his tiny desk. Abruptly he knelt, pried a worn red tile from the floor to reveal a safe and began to twist the dial.

He counted the money twice, placing it in an old envelope. "This is $325," he said. "When school is out this summer, you'll work full time. I'll take back half your wages until it's repaid."

"Thank you," I said, trembling at this responsibility. "Do you want my father to come over and sign something?"

Slowly, he shook his head. "No, son. I'm betting on you."

I went in the back door like the lord of the manor, and Dad came rushing into the kitchen, the bald man on his heels. "Quick! Drive away, take the car away!" cried my father. I calmly handed the repo man the soiled envelope. "Count it, give my father a receipt, and get out of our house," I said, a speech I'd rehearsed all the way home.

That night I was a hero to my family. But the real hero was Mr. Rubin, who not only saved us from certain penury, but also quickly raised my salary every month or so until, when summer came, I was earning $2.50 an hour, double the original wage. I worked for Mort until I graduated in 1959 and joined the Army. We stayed in touch for many decades, but I lost track of Mort several years ago and don't even know if he's still alive.

But this I know: Mort Rubin made Los Angeles a better place.

Marvin J. Wolf
Submitted by Willy Ackerman

Los Angeles Gets It Together

Very few burdens are heavy if everyone lifts.

Sy Wise

Some reporter.

I didn't get one piece of information.

Not one name, no job titles, no whos, whats, whys, ages or telephone numbers.

There simply wasn't time; not a moment for anything but quick decisions with hopes tight and fingers crossed among the blood, pain and anxieties of triage in the fast lane.

I'd been southbound on the Hollywood Freeway, coming up on the Four Level as gray minutes passed dawn, when a big dog was slammed by a car and tossed airborne, twisting and falling two vehicles ahead of mine.

Dammit. Across three lanes, wheels turned and locked in concern, as a half-dozen commuters stirred enough reflexes to get out of the way without rubbing fenders. The dog was left directly in front of me. With one foot deep into the antilock braking system, I stopped, my car shielding the animal.

I hunkered down and whispered inside: *If nothing happens in the next 4.7 seconds*—no crashing of bumpers, no sudden and involuntary acceleration of my precious body parts—*we might be able to help out here.* Nothing did happen.

The golden dog—born a little of this, a little of that, but a really handsome guy—had been smacked half-senseless. He was awake, head turning and eyes alert, but his haunches and back legs weren't moving much beyond an occasional quiver.

There were good signs. Only a little blood from one ear, and that had stopped. No bones piercing the skin. Better yet, he allowed me to smooth his head and feel gently for obvious damage, without showing any upset or teeth.

Commuters weren't quite as agreeable. Torqued by this Honda Accord of mine flashing in the fast lane, they unloaded everything but gunfire. Truck horns, fingers, references to my intellect, my anatomy, even my mother. You've got to love Los Angeles.

I called 911 on the cell phone and told the dispatcher I was on the Hollywood Freeway, in the fast lane, protecting an injured dog. She did not consider this a communiqué from St. Francis of Assisi.

"Sir, you can't block the fast lane."

"Right now, my blocking the fast lane is the only thing keeping traffic from turning an injured dog into a pizza," I said.

"Sir, you have to move your car out of the fast lane."

"Sorry," I replied. "But if it is any consolation, the fast lane really isn't moving that fast anymore. Matter of fact, it's kinda stopped."

"Sir, you could be putting others in danger and you'll have to move."

"Not until someone gets here to help me lift this big dog without hurting him. Here's my name and cell phone number if you need to reach me."

I called KFWB.

"This is Phone Forcer St. Francis," I said. "If you're getting reports of a stall in the fast lane, southbound on the 101, near the Four Level, that's me. I'm trying to keep cars off a hurt dog, and I'd consider it a huge favor if you told people to stop flipping me off."

Then the cavalry arrived.

I don't know if it was by accident, by the 911 dispatcher or if those guys stay tuned to KFWB and Jeff Bought in Jetcopter 98. But a pair of knights in Day-Glo vests arrived aboard a brace of Metro Freeway Service Patrol tow trucks.

They had it all figured, fast and efficiently.

They coned off our little emergency, front and back, and spoke confidently. Get the dog in the rear of my car. Put front floor mats on the backseat in case anything leaks from the pooch. Guy with the heavy gloves, get the front end, in case dog bites man. All together. Lift.

Now where?

"To the animal shelter," said one of the drivers whose names I will never know. "My buddy will stay on patrol. You follow me."

He headed through traffic east on the Pasadena Freeway and off at Avenue 26 to the city's North Central shelter. I followed. Damned if the dog didn't lift his head and whimper, and it didn't seem like any cry of pain.

The tow trucker couldn't stay. He had yet another call. No matter. A shelter worker wheeled a case to the car, gently lifted the dog and took him inside for treatment.

I told him I'd pay any veterinarian bills, and most certainly would adopt Freddy the Freeway Survivor when he was well.

It was not to be.

Freddy died of internal injuries while in surgery.

Yet there was a small, shining side to the sadness.

Because for one brief moment, one morning in this overworked, supposedly dysfunctional, certainly tough-talking city of ours, the right people cared, and all our systems worked.

Paul Dean
Submitted by Willy McNamara

A Simple Act

When our family—my wife Maggie, our four-year-old Eleanor, and I—drove through Messina, Sicily, to our hotel in the early hours of the morning one day last September, I felt I had never been in a bleaker place. We didn't know a soul, the streets were deserted, and we were leaving the hospital where our seven-year-old son lay in a deep and dreadful coma.

We wanted only to go home, to take Nicholas with us, however badly injured, to help nurse him through whatever he faced, to hold his hand again, to put our arms around him.

It had been the worst night of our lives.

The next morning we took a bus back to the hospital. There had been no deterioration but no improvement either. "You know, there are miracles," said the man who had been appointed to act as our interpreter, but the doctors looked grave. In lives that only a few hours before had been full of warmth and laughter, there was now a gnawing emptiness.

Within days our intensely personal experience erupted into a worldwide story. Newspapers and television told of the shooting attack by car bandits, Nicholas's death and our decision to donate his organs. Since then streets, schools, scholarships and hospitals all over Italy have been named for him. We have received honors previously reserved largely for kings and presidents, prizes that go mainly to Nobelists and awards usually given to spiritual leaders of the stature of Mother Teresa. Maria Shriver, who all her life has been told by people where they were when President Kennedy was shot, told us where she was when she heard about Nicholas. Strangers come up to us on the street still, tears in their eyes.

We have received letters from about a thousand people around the world, written with a simple eloquence possible only when it comes straight from the heart. A forty-year-old American, who recently became blind, said our story had given him the strength to resist despair. One man who was close to death now has a new lung because someone was moved by what happened to Nicholas. A woman who lost her four-year-old daughter imagines the two children playing happily together in a place where there is no violence.

All this for a decision that seemed so obvious we've forgotten which of us suggested it.

I remember the hushed room and the physicians standing in a small group, hesitant to ask crass questions about organ donation. As it happens, we were able to relieve them of the thankless task. We looked at each other. "Now that he's gone, shouldn't we give the organs?" one of us asked. "Yes," the other replied. And that was all there was to it.

Our decision was not clouded by any doubts about the medical staff. We were convinced they had done everything in their power to save Nicholas. To be sure, we asked how they knew his brain was truly dead, and they described their high-tech methods in clear, simple language. It helped. But more than that, it was the bond of trust that had been established from the beginning that left no doubt they would not have given up until all hope was gone.

Yet we've been asked a hundred times: How could you have done it? And a hundred times we've searched for words to convey the sense of how clear and how right the choice seemed. Nicholas was dead. He no longer looked like a sleeping child. By giving his organs we weren't hurting him but we were helping others.

For us, Nicholas will always live, in our hearts and our memories. But he wasn't in that body anymore.

His toys are still here, including the flag on his log fort, which I put at half-staff when we returned home and which has stayed that way ever since. We have assembled all his photographs, starting with the blur I snapped a few moments after he was born. Nicholas now lies in a peaceful country churchyard in California, dressed for eternity in the kind of blue blazer and neat slacks he liked and a tie with Goofy on it.

Donating his organs, then, wasn't a particularly magnanimous act. But not to have given them would have seemed to us such an act of miserliness that we don't believe we could have thought about it later without shame. The future of a radiant little creature had been taken away. It was important to us that someone else should have that future.

It turned out to be seven people's future, most of them young, most very sick. One nineteen-year-old within forty-eight hours of death ("We'd given up on her," her physician told me later) is now a vivacious beauty who turns heads as she walks down the street. The sixty-pound fifteen-year-old who got Nicholas's heart had spent half his life in hospitals; now he's a relentless bundle of energy. One of the recipients, when told by his doctors to think of something nice as he was taken to the operating theater, said, "I am thinking of something nice. I'm thinking of Nicholas." I recently visited him at school; he's a wonderful little fellow any father would be proud of and, I admit, I did feel pride. The man who received one of Nicholas's corneas told us that at one time he was unable to see his children. Now, after two operations, he happily watches his daughter fencing and his son play rugby.

We are pleased the publicity this incident has caused has led to such a dramatic arousal of interest in organ donation. It seems unfair, however, to the thousands of parents and children, who, in lonely hospital waiting rooms around the world, have made exactly the same decision. Their loss is indistinguishable from ours, but their willingness to share rather than to hoard life has remained largely unrecognized.

I imagine that for them, like us, the emptiness is always close by. I don't believe Maggie and I will ever be really happy again; even our best moments are tinged with sadness. But our joy in seeing so much eager life that would otherwise have been lost, and the relief on the families' faces, is so uplifting that it has given us some recompense for what otherwise would have been just a sordid act of violence.

Reg Green

Hope

*Someday all you will have to light your way will
be a single ray of hope and that will be enough.*

Kobi Yamada

The air was thick with heat and the whimpers of children as Lori Weller, nineteen, stood in an orphanage far
away from home.

"Bonjour," voices chimed as Lori reached for small
hands. Then her eyes met those of a little girl seated in a
corner. *God brought me here for a reason,* she thought. *Is that
reason you?*

Growing up in Walnut Bottom, Pennsylvania, Lori had
a typical life: school, friends, church on Sundays. But it
became a little less typical when she joined her church
youth group on a trip to build a new church in Honduras.

"I felt so *good* being able to help," Lori told her parents. But
even more than that, Lori felt different. *It's as if my heart is wide
open,* she thought. This is what I want to do—help people.

So when, in nursing school, Lori heard of a semester-
break trip to work at a medical clinic in Haiti, she leaped
at the chance.

Each morning, braying donkeys woke her. Then she'd climb onto a flatbed truck and ride a bumpy path to spend her day taking blood pressure readings and bandaging scrapes.

But it was the orphaned children who tore at her heart. "They will never be adopted," she was told at one orphanage. "They're just too sick."

The walls there were bare, the few toys, broken. There were so many hands reaching up—and too few caretakers to reach back.

Then her eyes fell on a child of about three who was alone, with cereal smeared across her cheeks. Below a tangle of black curls, Lori saw her forehead pulsating. "She was left with us when she was about six months old," the orphanage director said. "She has a hole in her skull from abuse. One fall could kill her."

"Poor baby!" Lori gasped. "Nothing can be done?" she asked.

"We don't have the money, the equipment . . . or the experience," the director answered.

"What's her name?" asked Lori.

"Agat Espoire. In Creole, her last name means 'hope.'"

The child with the least *hope,* Lori thought sadly. A child beaten and abandoned. But when Lori pulled Agat into her lap, the toddler surveyed her with dark, soulful eyes. *You deserve someone to love you, Agat,* she thought.

Day after day, Lori made dolls dance for Agat. But Agat was unresponsive. *If only I could see her smile,* Lori thought.

On her last night in Haiti, Lori lay sleepless. *How can I leave Agat here, where no one has the time to sit for hours and tell her stories? Where no one can afford to help her heal? How can I leave her . . . when she's already in my heart?*

Back at home, Lori couldn't stop thinking of the sad-eyed little girl. *If I never try to help,* she thought, *I'll never stop worrying about her.*

She called doctor after doctor, saying, "I have a child who needs surgery, but there's no money."

"Why don't you call . . ." came the usual reply. Finally, she was directed to neurosurgeon Joel Winer. "When can she get here?" he asked.

Lori couldn't believe her ears. "I want to repeat: There is no money," she said.

"I went into medicine to help," the doctor explained softly.

You sent me to Dr. Winer, Lord, didn't you? Lori silently asked.

And as she dialed the orphanage, she looked up to see her mother smiling. "I'm proud of you, honey," she said.

Lori's church friends were proud, too. "You're doing a wonderful thing," they said, digging into their pockets to help. A month later, with Agat's medical visa in hand, Lori flew back to Haiti.

Her heart pounded as she neared the orphanage. "Agat!" Lori called, scooping her up as the director explained to the little girl that a doctor far away would make her better. Agat looked at Lori, her wide eyes full of hope.

"I'll take care of you," Lori cooed. As Agat smiled, Lori's heart melted.

At home in Walnut Bottom, Agat was so overwhelmed by all the strange sights that she clutched the ragged toy she had brought with her. But by the second day of songs and stories, Agat—giggling—knocked down a castle Lori's dad had built from blocks.

"Listen!" Lori marveled. "She's *laughing!*"

Soon, Agat was full of laughter—until the day Lori handed her to the doctor. Agat shrieked in fear as he listened to her heart. *She thinks I'm betraying her!* Lori thought.

During a six-hour operation, Dr. Winer closed the fracture in Agat's skull. And though she woke from anesthesia crying, the moment she heard Lori, she stopped.

Soon, Agat was healing at home with the Wellers.

"Apples," Lori taught Agat, pointing to the fruit. "Bicycles," Lori said as kids rode by. "Mashed potatoes!" Agat said herself. "I . . . like mashed potatoes!"

Then one night, tucking Agat into bed, Lori said, "I love you." And a sleepy little voice echoed back, "I love *you!*"

Tears spilled down Lori's cheeks. She wished she could keep Agat forever. *But, I'm not even out of school yet.* She sighed. *Agat deserves a family.*

And that's exactly what Agat got. A few days later, the Wellers' phone rang. There had been a newspaper story about Agat's surgery. Looking at her smiling little face, a family who'd read the story said, "We'd love to open our hearts and home to her."

"They want to adopt her!" Lori cried jubilantly. And best of all, they lived only two hours away!

The day Lori finally had to say good-bye, she held Agat close. "I'll always love you," she promised. Today, Lori spends weekends sharing mashed potatoes and music with Agat's new family.

"Now Agat is going to grow up happy, healthy and loved," beams Lori, who's still in nursing school. "And I know I'll always keep in touch with her, wherever our lives take us."

Meg Lundstrom
Excerpted from Woman's World

My Father's Gift

Long winters and loneliness aren't good for any man, especially a seventy-five-year-old who has lost his wife. That's why several times a week I call my father in Montana and pepper him with questions: How's the weather? What's for dinner? When are you coming to Tucson? The answers seldom vary: cold, beef, soon.

Weeks go by until one day in February he calls to say that he has booked a flight. "No need to pick me up," he says. "I'll take a cab."

I don't argue. He likes being in charge. Whether I am suffering from a broken heart or a broken leg, I know that I can count on him for a strong cup of coffee and a strong piece of advice. I don't always want either one of them, but I swallow them anyway.

The day of his arrival, I head for the airport. By the time I arrive, the other passengers are walking into waiting arms. At any moment I expect to see Dad charging out of the gate just as I remember him charging his horse straight up Bull Mountain, hat pulled down low, reins held tight. The crowd thins to a trickle and then stops. I worry that he missed his connection, changed his mind, when I see him wander out of the tunnel.

"Dad," I call, waving above the crowd. He blinks in the sunlight. "Dad," I call again, making my way toward him. I stand in front of him, touch his arm and say, "Dad, it's me."

He puts his arms around me as if I'm a life preserver on a rough sea. "Oh, honey, I'm so happy you came."

"Of course I came," I answer, hugging him back, my arm registering the change in his appearance before my eyes have a chance to.

He's leaner than he was last summer. His red rag-wool sweater, too heavy for the desert heat, pads his narrow frame. Instead of a cowboy hat and boots, he's wearing an Irish tweed cap and black running shoes.

We drive north toward the foothills, straight for the Catalinas. The desert is foreign to him, but when we get close to the mountains, he relaxes as if he knows we're almost home. As we turn into my driveway, where bougainvillea cascades over a stucco wall, he shakes his head. "Your mother would have loved this place," he says.

When my husband comes home, he grills steaks. Afterward we sit outside and Dad smokes a cigar. The talk is general this time—no one mentions my mother. Dad insists on doing the dishes, stacking them helter-skelter in the dishwasher. I resist the urge to rearrange them.

The next morning, when I'm making coffee, I hear him whistling in the bathroom.

"Any horse races today?" he asks, coming down the stairs. "Let's go look at horses."

After checking the paper, we drive through South Tucson toward the fairgrounds. When he sees a sign for a pawnshop, he orders me to pull over. There are steel bars over the doors and windows, like a small-town jail. He pushes open the door and we walk inside. The back wall is lined with rifles, more rifles than I've ever seen. Simply being inside this secondhand arsenal makes me nervous.

"Dad," I whisper. "Let's go."

"Slow down," he says, draping his arm around my shoulder.

A man wearing a vest, possibly bulletproof, walks over to us. The scent of cigarettes and gunpowder hang in the cold air. "Let me see your diamond rings," Dad says.

I stop short and echo, "Diamond rings?" *Does Dad have a girlfriend?* I ask myself. I can't remember him mentioning any names.

"For my daughter," he adds, gesturing me.

"For me?"

"Come on," he urges. "I want to buy you a diamond ring." He casually leans one elbow on the counter as if he is used to shopping for jewels.

In an instant a black velvet tray of rings rests on the counter in front of me. "I don't want a ring," I tell him.

Ignoring my response, he points to one. "That's pretty," he says.

I look at the glittering rows of rings, symbols of weddings gone sour, marriages gone bad, promises broken. Some are the size of bullets, some the shape of tears. I finally slip a ring on my finger and hold up my hand. It's a gesture I learned from my mother. Every now and then she held up her hand to admire her diamond solitaire in its Tiffany setting. "Let me try it on," I would say, knowing what the answer would be. I never saw her take it off.

When she was dying, she asked each of her five children to make a list, tell her which of her belongings we wanted. I usually did what she asked, but this time I didn't follow through. I didn't want her Limoges china or string of pearls. I wanted my mother.

"Pick whatever one you want," my father offers.

The ring winks on my finger; another woman's ring. "You don't need to buy me a diamond ring," I tell him.

"I want to," he says.

"Let's go eat and think about it," I whisper. "We'll be back," I call over my shoulder to the man in the vest.

Later, as we spoon tortilla soup and listen to Mexican love songs on the jukebox, Dad clears his throat. Then he confesses, "I gave your mother's ring to Sheila."

Suddenly the shopping trip makes sense. Sheila is my younger sister, my only sister. Before our mother died, Sheila told me that she wanted Mom's ring, that to her it represented maternal love. She cried when she said that.

Just as he never lost hope, my mother never got around to dividing up their things. While my lawyer brothers worried how to disperse her estate, my Aunt Bern suggested that I should inherit her ring. "You're the oldest daughter," she reminded me. "You should insist."

That planted a seed, made me greedy for a while. But over time, I saw the irony. Bern, my mother's youngest sister, complained often and loudly that her mother favored the older girls. Each time I imagined Mom's ring on my finger, I couldn't get the picture of my little sister out of my mind: the middle of five children, growing up wearing my hand-me-downs, inheriting my old teachers who called her by my name.

"I hope you're not upset," Dad says.

"It's okay," I answer. I just wish that Sheila herself had told me.

Two daughters. One ring. Two possibilities. Or neither one of us could have it. The ring could be sold and the money divided. Remembering the rings at the pawnshop, sparkling beneath the guns, I close my eyes tightly so no tears leak out. Specks of sunlight filter in, sparkle like tiny diamonds. I say good-bye to my mother, happy that her ring is on my sister's finger and not in a black velvet tray.

I think about the gifts passed down from mother to daughter, gifts that don't have to be divided. The way she pinched the crust on an apple pie. Where to look for wild asparagus. The way to hold a watercolor brush. Firstborn, I made her a mother. She fine-tuned her mothering on me. Sheila her middle child, she held right in the middle of her heart. I suddenly realize that she didn't want to choose. That she loved each of us, all of us. Dad did the choosing, gave my sister what she wanted, her symbol of a mother's love. Now he wants to give me a ring so that I know I, too, am loved.

As we walk to the car, kicking up dust in the unpaved parking lot, I keep my eyes on the ground. "You're not wearing your boots," I point out. Back home in Montana, my father rides horses almost every day. "They hurt my feet," he admits.

Suddenly I have an idea. I drive a few blocks south to Stewart Boots, a tiny shop in an adobe house with cowboy boots as soft as caramel. After looking around at the leather uppers stacked like loaves of bread in bins around the room, Dad peels off his shoe like a boy and wriggles into a tall cowboy boot with a pointed toe. "It's too tight," he says.

Victor, the owner, caresses Dad's instep and recommends a wider size. Within minutes my father is standing tall in a pair of boots the color of walnut bark, made by the wise hands of old men, men who learned their trade from their fathers.

"Why don't you get a pair?" Dad suggests. I already have an old pair of Stewarts on the floor of my closet, but this time I don't refuse his offer. Now we stand together in front of the mirror, one of us old and the other no longer young. I think of the ties that bind us: our sense of family, our sense of place, our sense of fairness. The old man next to me stands tall, walks softly and says nothing, even when his heart is full of feeling.

"I want you to have them," he says with a grin. I smile back at him, thinking of the gifts that he's given me that I can't hold in my hand, can't wear on my finger, but hold in my heart. When he is gone, as I know he one day will be, I will have my boots, a symbol of a father's love, and the memory of a day he set out to make things right.

Michele Morris

Sprite

I was beside myself with frustration and annoyance at the little foal, curled up in the corner of the small stable where she had been born two nights before. The delivery had been a difficult one for the mother, and, in the end, she succumbed to heavy bleeding and died.

I felt for this little animal, so all alone in the world and without a mother to show her the ways of being a horse. But after three days, she still refused to venture outside her little nest on her own. Even the veterinarian, who found nothing physically wrong with her, could not motivate her.

Day after day the little horse, which I named Sprite in hopes that she would aspire to her name, moped about, sniffing out her mother's scent and eating enough to sustain her, but without the usual gusto of a growing animal. Sprite seemed determined to be miserable.

There were other horses and their infants on our ranch, and Sprite sometimes watched them, on one of her forced outings into the field, with a look of longing. Then she would sigh, a long, plaintive snort, slowly turn her head away and refuse to look until we delivered her back to her stable.

Weeks passed with little change in the foal's disposition. She ate and slept and complied with daily walks outside but never seemed to aspire to do the things that the other horses did, neither running nor prancing about with the simple delight of being alive.

Then one day, something changed. Not in Sprite, but in me. It happened one distressingly hot, summer day when I had retreated to the relative coolness of my home. Not knowing what to do with the hours stretching out before me until the sun disappeared behind the horizon, giving relief to blistering air, I perused one book, and then another, of old and yellowing pictures.

There were many pictures of my mother in those books, given to me by my father before he died an old man just a few years ago. I had barely known the woman on those pages and only imagined that she must have loved me. She, too, had died, when I was very little, leaving me to miss the presence of a relationship that seemed so innate, so necessary.

I remembered being a small girl at school picnics, watching other children and their mothers. It was often so painful that I had to turn away. It wasn't until a kind and understanding young teacher took it upon herself to be my friend, and became a kind of surrogate mother to me, that I began to blossom. After that I grew faster, my grades were better and I felt alive inside.

Now I understood.

With renewed determination, I headed out to the stables under the oppressive noonday sun. I didn't care. All I knew is that I had to try.

For the next few days, I all but lived within the tiny four walls that had become Sprite's safe haven from the world. Chores were hired out to a young boy who lived nearby, and my husband was instructed, via cellular phone, to bring me the necessities of life.

All that time, I talked to the sad animal, telling her about my life and her mother and anything I could think to say. When my throat was dry from it, I simply stroked her white muzzle, or brushed her chestnut brown coat until we both slept.

On the fourth morning, when my own odor had become indistinct from the smell of the horses, I woke to a beautiful sight. There was Sprite, standing on her own spindly legs, nudging me gently with her nose to get up.

Without a word, I opened the gate, and for the first time since her birth, she led me outside into the cool morning air, where she began to bounce and kick and just be the baby that she was.

Something in her eyes had changed, too. They were brighter and filled with the wonder of being alive. It was as though that empty place in her heart had been filled.

From then on, Sprite lived as though she was making up for the time she had missed. She ran as though she had wings and, when she was big enough, let herself be rode with a gentleness I had seldom seen. And every morning, she reminded me of our special bond. Though I no longer slept in the stables—much to my husband's relief—Sprite slipped her restraints and waited by my window until I woke up to greet her.

Darcie Hossack

First-Day Employee

There are only two lasting bequests we can give our children. One is roots, the other wings.

Hodding Carter

My father had a small business, employing approximately fifteen people at any given time. We pasteurized and homogenized milk from farmers each morning, and put it into bottles for home use and for restaurants. We also put the milk into small containers for the school kids everyday. We also made a wonderful little thing called homemade ice cream.

We sold all of these milk products, and many more, in the front of a dairy building, which had been fashioned into a small store with a large soda fountain. During the summer months, there were rows and rows of eager tourists lined up at the ice cream counter, waiting for their daily indulgence of my father's most exquisite recipes of some twenty-seven flavors of homemade wonder.

Being such an extremely busy little store meant that the employees had to work fast and furious for hours at a time, with little rest. The swarm of tourists never stopped and our "rush hour" lasted many hours on hot days.

I had worked for my father since I was young, as did all seven kids in our family. So I had seen many new employees come and go due to the fast and frenetic pace.

One day, in 1967, we had a new employee, Debbie, who wanted to work in the store for the summer. She had never done this type of work before, but planned to give it her all.

On her first day, Debbie made just about every mistake in the book. She added the sales wrong on the cash register, she charged the wrong prices for items, she gave the wrong bag of food to the wrong customer, and she dropped and broke a half gallon of milk. The torture of watching her struggle was too much for me. I went into my father's office and said, "Please go out there and put her out of her misery." I expected him to walk right into the store and fire her on the spot.

Since my father's office was situated within view of the sales counter, he had no doubt seen what I was talking about. He sat, thoughtful, for a moment. Then he got up from his desk and walked over to Debbie, who was standing behind the counter.

"Debbie," he said, as he put his hand gently on her shoulder. "I have been watching you all day, and I saw how you treated Mrs. Forbush."

Debbie's face began to flush and tears began to well in her eyes as she struggled to remember Mrs. Forbush from the many women she had given the wrong change to or spilled milk on.

My father continued, "I've never seen Mrs. Forbush be so polite to any one of my employees before. You really knew how to handle her. I am sure that she is going to want you to wait on her every time she comes in. Keep up the good work."

In return for being a wise and compassionate employer,

my father got a loyal, and hardworking employee for sixteen years . . . and a friend for life.

Mary Jane West-Delgado

First Night

The knock was so soft that I might not have heard it at all if I hadn't heard the footsteps on my wooden front porch immediately before. I wasn't asleep yet; I had been told that I might be needed this night, and I was waiting.

I'm one of the camp moms at a summer camp nestled deep in the northern Wisconsin pines. One of the campers who had just arrived this day was having trouble falling asleep. The little boy who stood on my porch said softly as I opened the door, "I'm not homesick, you know. I just can't seem to fall asleep. My counselor said I should come talk to you."

He shuffled his feet a little, looking down at them, but made no move to come in as I held the door open.

"I don't want you to think I'm scared," he said. "I'm not ... it's just that this is ... different for me."

"I know," I said gently as I stepped out onto the porch and closed the door quietly behind me. "Why don't we just sit out here and talk for a while?" He took the chair I offered and we both sat and looked up at the beautiful, star-filled sky. I caught my breath. Living in the city, I never appreciated the magnificence of a night sky filled with a million twinkling lights. Maybe I was always too busy to notice or the sky was never clear enough, but I didn't think summer nights back home in Chicago ever looked like this. I shared my thoughts with my young friend.

"My brother got a telescope for his bar mitzvah," he said. There was the smallest catch in his voice, but I couldn't see his face in the darkness. "He lets me look through it and he knows the names of all the constellations. That one there is the Big Dipper and that one is the Little Dipper. You can tell by the North Star—Polaris."

"You know a lot about astronomy," I said appreciatively.

There was a long pause. "My brother is leaving for Israel for a whole year after I get back from camp. I'm going to miss him . . . a lot."

Ah, I thought.

Now, when a child—any woman's child—is in pain, a mother—anybody's mother—responds. But I thought hard about exactly the right thing to say to this little boy. I didn't know him. I didn't know the things to say or do to comfort him as I would with one of my own children. But I clearly saw that he needed comfort. And even though the night was dark, I saw something else. It was very important to him that I not baby him or intimate in any way that his feelings were childish or misplaced. He needed to hear that it was okay to feel as he did; he needed to feel respected. I could not let him think that being homesick his first night at camp was, in any way, abasing. After all, he was nine years old.

So, I asked him questions about his brother—what he was going to do in Israel, whether he would get to visit him there, whether he has any other brothers or sisters, or any pets. He talked a lot—happily.

Finally, he asked me to walk him back to his cabin. I did. But he stopped me at the door. He did not need me to walk him in, even though it was late and all the rest of the campers were asleep.

"I can put myself to sleep," he said. Then, looking up at the stars once more before he closed the cabin door, he said, "It's the same sky."

That was all.

And that was everything.

Marsha Arons

HUGS –
50¢

Reprinted by permission of Jonny Hawkins. ©1998 Jonny Hawkins.

Missing Pieces

When I got pregnant at seventeen, the circumstances could not have been worse. The father was a thirty-eight-year-old police officer. He was furious at the news of "my" problem. Life at home with an alcoholic parent and abusive stepparent was lonely and precarious.

Childishly, I tried to ignore these facts. I crocheted small pink blankets (I knew the baby was a girl) and scoured yard sales for tiny dresses and parenting books, determined to be a "good" mother. *My* daughter would be loved, and I, at last, would have someone to love me.

Reality reared its ugly head. Nights I didn't work were spent in my car or at a movie to avoid my parents' drinking and the fighting that ensued. Finally, I could no longer push away the thought that tormented me: My child could not live like that. The mere thought of bringing her into that house made me physically ill; the idea of losing her broke my heart. My only other family was a grandmother who refused to have anything to do with me once she found out I was pregnant. There was no way to escape *with* the baby. There was no place to go.

But there was a way out for her.

Not surprisingly, my OB/GYN knew an attorney with

clients waiting for a baby. His clients had enough money to smooth out any obstacles in a child's life. He met me at a pie shop, carrying a sheaf of papers for me to sign. I had no idea what they said, tears blinded me and I was sure I was going to throw up. Obediently, I signed every place I was told to. He paid for my pie and left.

Hours after I delivered, the new parents arrived at the hospital. "No need for you to hold her," said the nurse, whisking the baby from me.

Alone in the hospital room, I called my mother. Angry at being deprived of the welfare check the baby would have "entitled" us to, she told me never to come home and hung up. Somewhere in the plastic hospital bag that contained my clothes was my worldly fortune of thirteen dollars and twenty-eight cents.

The parents stopped by my room the next day. They were smiling and happy, just popping in for a quick visit to let me know they were grateful and in a hurry. Then they were gone, taking my daughter to a better life.

In desperation, I called a coworker who took me in. That night, I stood in the shower, watching the water, blood, milk and tears swirl down the drain and wishing the rest of me would go, too.

But the heart lives on hope. No matter what those papers had said, I was convinced I would see her again. Clinging to that, I let time propel me forward. The bleeding stopped, the milk dried up, the tears slowed and hardened into a lump that settled in my chest.

The loving logic that forced the "right" decisions for my child did nothing to heal the shambles of my heart. The loss remained with me, a discreet open wound that bled quietly, steadily through the years.

Life went on. I went to work, married, had five more children and, eventually, divorced.

The children have always known they have an older

sister. Although they watched me send out information to reunion organizations and conduct searches on the Internet for her, they never knew that I choked inside whenever someone asked how many children I had. The socially acceptable lie, "I have five," brought a wave of grief every time it left my lips.

"My" children are seventeen, twelve, eleven, ten and eight. At thirty-seven, my life appeared rich and full. So, how do I make sense of the fact that I have lived with a hole in my heart these many years, that nineteen and a half years ago I swallowed my screams and they still echo inside?

Since the birth of my first child, a shadow person accompanied me, an infant that grew through the years, a blurry outline with a face that I could not see, a face I was sure I would recognize if given the chance. She stood just out of sight at every birthday or holiday and as I dried dishes or washed my face. And she took from me any sense of completeness, for she held a piece of my heart.

Every year on November 27, her birthday, I wrote her a letter and then threw it away. I wondered and grieved. Before she turned eighteen, I registered with every adoption reunion service. Perhaps she would not want to find me; maybe she didn't know she was adopted. Maybe she knew and would hate me forever. So I waited, with the knowledge that any phone call, any knock on the door could heal my heart or break it again. Worst was the thought that I might wait forever.

On April 19, we were leaving for church. The flag on the mailbox was raised, which was odd for a Sunday. Inside lay a small piece of lined paper torn from a notebook.

"Lizanne S.: The daughter you gave up for adoption, Aaron [sic], is looking hard for you. Her number is . . ." A North Carolina phone number followed. Below that was printed a man's name and a local phone number.

Sure that this was a cruel hoax my first reaction was grief and fury. In tears, I called the local number. The writer lived on the same country road as we do. All he could tell me was that a young woman had called him from North Carolina, saying she was my daughter and that she could not find my phone number. So she pulled up listings for all numbers on the same road and began calling them to ask for help in contacting me.

I was stunned. My stomach knotted as hope and fear battled within. The six of us continued on to our church in complete silence.

Our service had guest musicians that day. We sat down as a woman's clear voice began the first song: "I will never forget thee, I will never forsake thee." In the instant her words hung in the air, my fear and doubt vanished.

There was no answer at the Charlotte number, so I left a message on the answering machine. I waited for two long hours before the telephone rang. "Mom . . . ," the voice said hesitantly, "Mom," and she began to cry. My daughter had found me.

Over the next hours, we boosted profits for AT&T and the makers of Kleenex. Her summer break was four days away, and she would leave for a monthlong internship in Central America in nine days. Unable to wait so long to meet her, I was on a plane from Portland to Charlotte the following day.

During the interminable flights and layovers, I sifted through years and memories, searching for the pieces she would care about, weaving a chain of my life to give her.

Erin stood, tall and blond, at the gate, holding a teddy bear and balloon. Hugging and crying, we held on to each other, trying to make up for almost twenty years in one fierce embrace. Over the next few days, we talked, laughed, hugged, stared at each other and cried more.

Piece by piece, we filled in details of the shadowy picture we had of each other.

We share the same coloring, fierce competitive drive and anger at any injustice. Both of us have cold hands and feet, skin that burns at the first ray of sun, and an addiction to caffeine. Given an option, neither of us believes in mornings that start before ten. Currently, each of us is enrolled in a Spanish class, studying law and spending time weight training. However, the saddest commonality is the core of hurt, the sense of incompleteness and the "missing piece" in our hearts.

For the last month that I carried her, when I knew I would lose her, I grieved. And that was part of the legacy she carried away. No legal paper could sever that tie.

Erin has a good life with parents who love her and have given her everything money could buy. She is happy and healthy. For that, I am grateful.

This summer she is spending time with me and her newly found siblings. Her five brothers and sisters are ecstatic, stunned, confused and sometimes, I suspect, a bit jealous. So they talk about it, ask questions and adapt, throwing open their hearts to a stranger who has always held a place in mine. I watch them play and wrestle together, a jumble of arms, legs and giggles. Late at night, I creep down the hall and watch her sleep.

As she fills out the application to transfer from college in Charlotte to Oregon State, I can feel my heart relax. For nineteen and a half years, I have held my breath, held my loss, held my tears. Now, I can let it all go.

All our lives are better now that we can share them with each other. The core of heartache is gone. Our shadows have faces—familiar, tear-streaked, laughing faces. The search for the missing part of us is over.

Lizanne Southgate

"Mom, was I adopted or made from scratch?"

A Christmas Adoption Miracle

The Christmas tree lights twinkled as Terri Roy affixed a stamp to the very last envelope. On the table before her lay two thick piles of holiday mail. The first was a collection of Christmas cards going out to all her friends and relatives. The second contained forty-one letters—all of them addressed to perfect strangers who lived in Mississippi and who happened to be named Shearer. Terri didn't hold out much hope, but maybe, just maybe, one of these strangers could tell her something about Bernice Shearer, the woman who had given Terri up for adoption thirty-four years ago.

Terri was only three when she learned that her brother Neal, her sister Mindy and she were adopted. "I used to tell anyone who would listen about how my mom and dad had picked me out because they wanted me so much. I felt so special, so loved."

When she turned thirteen, Terri's parents gave her some papers from the adoption agency. From them she learned that her birth mom's last name was Shearer, that she was forty-one years old when she gave birth to Terri, that she weighed 135 pounds and had brown eyes and dark auburn hair.

Terri loved her adoptive parents deeply, but she was also curious about her birth mom. Lying in bed at night, she would wonder, "Why did she give me up? Was she pretty? Do I look like her? Act like her?"

In 1987 Terri and her husband, Doug, gave birth to their first son, Doug Jr. "He must take after your side of the family," people told her, but all Terri could do was shrug and say, "I guess so."

A few years later Terri's mom and her mother-in-law both died from cancer. "I felt cast adrift," says Terri. "Now more than ever, I wanted to learn about my roots, about who I was and where I came from. And so I contacted the adoption agency to see what I could find out."

Much of the information on the papers the agency sent Terri was blacked out, but they left in her mom's first name, which was Bernice. Terri also learned that her mom was single when she got pregnant, and that her father was a married man. Bernice had kept her pregnancy a secret from everyone, including her conservative Baptist family in Mississippi. She'd worn girdles to hide her growing belly, and took two months off from her job in a Denver department store so she could have her baby in secret.

And then last fall Terri joined America Online. "I've always enjoyed working on our home computer, and I was curious about the information superhighway everyone was talking about."

One evening when Terri was exploring the various services offered by AOL, she idly typed in "adoption" as a search word. She was startled to discover an entire forum devoted to adoptees and their families. Excited, Terri logged onto this forum immediately. There, she dis-covered hundreds of e-mail messages being passed back and forth between people who were searching for their own birth parents, or for the children they'd put up for adoption many years ago. "At last, people who understand why I feel I have to do this," Terri realized, and eagerly began to type in her own story.

Almost immediately Terri received an e-mail message from one of the forum's hosts. "Since you know your mom's name, and where her family is from, you should also post the information on the genealogy forum." Terri did this right away.

Other forum members offered Terri helpful advice and support. One member who lived in Denver even offered to visit the hospital where she was born to search any records that might still be there.

Terri also received several replies to the message she'd posted in the genealogy forum. One user sent her a list of everyone named Shearer who lived in Mississippi. "Can one of these people possibly be related to me?" Terri wondered, addressing a letter to each of the forty-one names on the list.

Another genealogy forum member with a computerized telephone directory e-mailed Terri the numbers for four different Bernice Shearers who lived scattered across the United States. "I was too nervous to pick up the phone. What if one of them was my birth mom? She was old. Hearing from me might give her a heart attack. Or what if she hated me so much, when I told her who I was, she hung up on me?" Doug finally had to make the calls for his wife, but sadly, none of the women he reached turned out to be the right Bernice Shearer.

It was Christmas Eve morning, and sixty-eight-year-old Ben Shearer was showing his daughter-in-law, Kim, how to use America Online to help research her family tree. He was teaching her how to use the genealogy forum, when suddenly they spotted a message from someone looking for a Bernice Shearer who was born in Mississippi back in 1919.

"My sister Bernice was born in 1919," Ben said to Kim.

He pressed the reply key, and posted a brief message back to Terri.

Later that same evening, after tucking their two boys, D. J. and Nathan Alan, into bed, Terri and Doug finished putting out presents. "Merry Christmas," they wished one another, and then while Doug relaxed with a book, Terri slipped upstairs to their bedroom to check her e-mail.

A few minutes later Doug heard an excited scream. Then Terri came hurrying down the stairs, a piece of paper clutched in her hand. "I found her!" she exclaimed, handing Doug a printout of the e-mail message from Ben.

Doug scanned the brief message, and when he read that Bernice had died of lung cancer in 1983, he said, "I'm sorry, Terri. All this searching, only to discover she's gone."

"For a long time I've had a feeling she was dead," Terri told him. "But that's okay. At least now I can find out who she was, what she was like."

Early Christmas morning something told Ben he needed to go online. Waiting for him was an e-mail message from Terri. "Ben, I really don't know how to start this," it read. "But thirty-four years ago your sister Bernice got herself into a little bit of trouble, and I was the result of that."

Ben was thunderstruck. "Imagine that," he said to his wife, Jimmie. "None of us ever knew. Bernice never told anyone." Terri's phone number was at the bottom of the message. Ben picked up the phone and dialed. "Hi, this is your Uncle Ben," he greeted his brand-new niece, and hearing Terri's voice was like turning back the years and speaking to his beloved sister once again.

D. J. and Nathan Alan were playing with their Christmas toys when Terri logged on to AOL a few hours after her conversation with Ben. A brief message from her uncle was waiting for her online, along with a special Christmas surprise.

"I have my mother's nose!" Terri laughed and sobbed as a digitized photograph of her birth mother appeared on her computer screen.

"You have her eyes, too," said Doug, giving her shoulder an affectionate squeeze.

Ben sent four photos of Bernice that day. "Who's that?" D. J. asked as the last of them was transmitted to her PC.

"That's my mother," Terri told him. "You look exactly like her."

"You have two moms?" D. J. asked.

Terri nodded her head, no longer able to speak through the thickening lump that filled her throat.

Last April Terri and her two boys flew to Mississippi to help celebrate Ben's sixty-ninth birthday. Bernice never had any more children, so Terri had no brothers or sisters. But she did get to meet her Aunt Kitty, and three of her four cousins and their many children. "My cousin Steve has a son a year older than my youngest who's also named Nathan Alan. Both of them have blond hair and blue eyes."

"It's like we have a piece of Bernice back with us," Terri's Uncle Ben said as the gathered family sat reminiscing over a thick stack of old photo albums. "It's a gift from God, via America on Line."

Recently, Terri received a package in the mail, along with a letter from her Aunt Jimmie. "When your mom was nine, she cut little Dutch girls out of old sacking cloth and stitched them to quilting squares. The squares lay packed away in your grandmother's attic for decades, and when she died, they were passed along to me. I assembled the quilt, thinking I'd give it to one of our grandkids. There was one square missing, though, and now I know why."

Enclosed in the package was a beautiful, hand-sewn quilt. Stitched into the new bottom square was:

Pieced by Bernice Margaret Shearer at age nine years 1928
Assembled by Aunt Jimmie Shearer
Quilted by Aunt Kitty Shearer Booth
With love for Terri Mondschein Roy 1995

Today the quilt hangs on Terri's dining-room wall, "Where I can look at it and touch it every day. It helps me to feel closer to my birth mom, but also to my adoptive mom, too. I used to feel so guilty about looking for my birth parents. I felt like I was betraying the mom and dad I grew up with. But now that I've found my birth family, I can't help but love my adoptive family even more, and appreciate how very much they love me—not because they had to, but because it was what they wanted to do."

Bill Holton
Excerpted from Woman's World

The Storyteller

They stood on the edge of the sprawling desert, a very small girl holding a kitten in her arms and an old rancher so tall and frail he swayed like a cypress in the gentle wind.

"Boy calicoes are scarcer than a hen's teeth," I heard him say. "Musta been that unusual blue fur that made him a boy!"

From the glint in the old man's eyes, I could tell he was a spinner of tall tales—and children are believers because their world is still full of magic and miracles. I'd always heard, though, that because of a genetic flaw, male calicoes are very rare.

But this man could weave a spell, and I found myself believing him. A look at this very much alive kitten—and at the joy in my child's eyes—was all I needed to start doubting established fact. Maybe this calico was a boy.

Hugging the ball of fluff to her cheek, she studied the old man's face with the wrinkles pounded in from years in the sun and wind. "I'm going to name him Blueberry, Uncle Ralph," she said, "because blue's my favorite color."

"Mine, too," he answered.

From the moment Jaymee and Ralph met several weeks before, their hearts had instantly bonded. Our Arizona ranch was isolated among miles of yucca and mesquite beneath the vast blue sky, and now that Jaymee's sister, Becky, had started school, our four-year-old felt small and alone. Suddenly the coughing of a distant motor announced the approach of an ancient pickup crawling down the long, dirt road toward us. The vehicle rolled into a barnyard pothole and rocked to a stop.

"Mornin', ladies," the driver said, pinching the brim of his sweat-stained hat. "I'm Ralph Cowan. Bill around?"

"He's in the horse barn," I said, conscious of Jaymee's arms locked suddenly around my knees.

My husband, Bill, had told me about Ralph Cowan, owner of the NI Ranch bordering ours. A well-known figure among cattlemen throughout the state, Ralph had once owned a spread so vast that it took 150 horses just to keep his ranch hands mounted. The father of three sons, he'd also found time to serve fourteen years in the state legislature. But that had been decades before. Now, except for his niece, Edythe, who took care of him, a few pets and his old horse, Dodger, Ralph was alone.

He opened the door and untangled his long legs. Then, squaring his boots on the ground, he leaned forward and smiled into the solemn little face peeking out from behind me. "I'll bet you like calico kittens," he said.

Jaymee's head bobbed.

"Well, I've got a brand-new litter at my place, and as soon as they're old enough to leave their mama, how 'bout I bring you one?"

Jaymee looked up at me anxiously. "I hope it's a boy, Mama," she murmured.

Ralph cupped an ear. "A boy you said?"

The grip tightened. "Daddy says no more girl cats!"

Ralph's blue eyes disappeared into a mask of friendly wrinkles. "Well, you tell your daddy if it's a boy, it's worth five hundred dollars! That's more than he can get for a good yearling bull nowadays."

"Five hundred dollars!" Jaymee's eyes widened. She knew about money. She and Becky sold eggs and spent hours at the kitchen table counting and stacking coins in piles on the red-checkered cloth.

"Now, don't forget," Ralph cautioned, "a boy calico is hard to find. I've been lookin' for one . . . most of my life. But we'll see if we can't find you one." As he smiled at Jaymee, a sudden warmth tugged at my heart.

"Yep," he continued, "a blue calico is as rare as a white tarantula."

"A white tarantula?" Jaymee squeezed me harder.

"They're out there somewhere," he said. "You just gotta keep looking." I didn't think that white tarantulas existed, but who was I to break the spell that Ralph had woven?

Gripping the top of the door, Ralph hoisted his lean, six-foot-six-inch frame from the truck and struggled to steady himself. Afraid he might fall, I wanted to reach out and help—but right away he headed toward the barn. To my surprise, Jaymee let go of my leg and tiptoed softly in the long shadow trailing behind him

During the weeks that followed, Ralph visited often to "talk cattle" with Bill. Sometimes, listing like a mast on a sinking schooner, he arrived on Dodger, his legs so long he could almost wrap them around the horse's middle. But most of the time, he came in his truck, and it wasn't long before we realized it wasn't Bill he really came to see.

"Where's the little gal?" he'd ask. It didn't matter that sometimes he couldn't remember her name. It was the chuckle in his eyes each time he saw her that made the difference.

Then came the day when he brought Blueberry—pink nose, buttercup eyes and frosted silvery-blue fur. Ralph told Jaymee that Blueberry was a male. But it later dawned on me that he probably said this because he wanted it to be a male for Jaymee's sake. Since Bill didn't like cats in the house, Jaymee arranged a box for the kitten on the back porch. There he could come and go as he pleased at night, and light up her world by day.

Ralph, however, became the real flame for Jaymee. At the first sound of his pickup, she cried, "Uncle Ralph's coming to play!" and dashed to the end of our long driveway, Blueberry flailing like a mop in her arms. When they returned in Ralph's pickup, the calico cat would be reclining on the dashboard amid rusty spurs, fence pliers, bits of wire and assorted hardware, while Ralph and Jaymee, seated among springs escaping the worn seat cover, would be making plans. Soon they were searching for secrets among fallen cottonwoods and twisted mesquites and poking sticks into forbidden lairs.

"What do you and Uncle Ralph look for?" I asked Jaymee one hot afternoon as she and Blueberry shared a dripping Popsicle.

"White tarantulas." She sighed heavily. "But we can't find one anywhere."

"What does Uncle Ralph say about that?"

"He says we gotta keep looking, that's all. He says that's the only way you find things in life—by believing and looking." Her face brightened. "So we find other things."

"Really?"

"Yep. Dead baby doves, all over the place." She frowned. "Dumb, lazy birds. They can't even build a nest right. Three twigs! That's all they use. Then the poor little babies fall through and get killed, and the mamas and daddies cry all the time. That's why they're called mourning doves. Uncle Ralph said so."

One day she dashed into the house, eyes sparkling with excitement. "Mama!" she cried. "Chickies play songs before they hatch!"

I raised an eyebrow.

"Uncle Ralph took an egg out of the incubator and pressed it against his ear. Then he let me listen. He said it was tapping 'Yankee Doodle,' and I could hear it, too!"

Later that night after the children were asleep, I asked Bill, "Can you believe all those stories Ralph tells her?"

"Can't hurt her," he said. "It's all good stuff. Better than sitting in front of the TV all day watching things she's far too young to understand."

One morning, I caught the unlikely pair crouched over an anthill, heads nearly touching as though there was a conspiracy between them. Blueberry, eager to pounce on anything that moved, twitched his tail nearby. "When ants build a hill around their house," Ralph began, "it means it's going to rain."

"Does Daddy know that?" Jaymee asked loudly. She had learned to speak up because Ralph couldn't hear too well.

"Maybe not, sweetheart," he said, "but next time he goes out to bale hay, you check on the ants first. If they're buildin' a hill, tell him to wait a day." He winked at me, but Jaymee believed him.

Next to Becky, Ralph was Jaymee's best friend. But he was ill, and even at four, a child can worry. "He hurts, Mama," she said. "I can tell." To Becky she confided, "Uncle Ralph's going to be an angel soon. He told me so." *What will happen when he's gone,* I wondered. *What will she remember?*

Meanwhile, Jaymee absorbed his wisdom like alfalfa soaks up rain, and in subtle ways we all became victims of Ralph's stories. From Ralph, Jaymee learned to whistle "Yankee Doodle," and Becky joined in. Hours and days of the same tune trying to be whistled can be nerve shredding. "Can't get that darn sound out of my head," Bill grumbled. "It's driving me nuts!"

Then came the migration, a yearly event that prompts hundreds of huge, black, hairy tarantulas, some the size of my hand, to cross sparsely traveled Route 666 in quest of mates. Ralph had planted the seed with Jaymee—and that's all it took. "We have to go watch!" She jumped up and down. "Maybe there'll be a white one!"

So off we went in the pickup: Becky, Jaymee, Blueberry and I, with a three-pound coffee can to put "Whitey" in. Parked on the side of the road, we watched the phenomenon as Becky counted, ". . . 307 . . . 308 . . . 309 . . ." and Jaymee kept "almost" seeing one—while I prayed and prayed there was no such creature, knowing in my heart that nothing would make me get out of the truck. In the Southwest, tarantulas can live to be over seventy-five years old, and they can actually jump two feet—or more. Thankfully, I was spared.

Then the monsoon season arrived, bringing torrential storms and toads and frogs by the thousands. Puddles simmered with tadpoles. Then, gradually, the water dried up. "The pollywogs are dying, Uncle Ralph," Jaymee said, full of sadness.

"Can't let that happen," he said. "There'd be nothing around to catch the mosquitoes—and we'd all be eaten alive!" For the rest of the day, Jaymee scurried back and forth with coffee cans full of water to keep the puddles full.

Why, I wondered, did Ralph spend so much time with Jaymee? The day she found an old box turtle living under the log pile offered a clue. "I'm going to feed him tomatoes and lettuce every day," she told Ralph.

"I'll bet he'd like Oreo cookies better." Ralph spoke slowly as he leaned down to pick up the turtle. Suddenly, he paused—then ran his stiff fingers over the worn letters carved on its ancient shell. "RC," we heard him whisper.

Of course! I thought. *Ralph Cowan.* Had he been the one to carve those initials years and years before? But the gentle voice of the storyteller soon rearranged my thinking.

"His name was . . . Running Coyote!" Ralph began, his eyes misting. "He was an old Indian friend of mine. He had a little girl . . . just like you." He looked down at Jaymee. "And he carved these initials into this shell some fifty years ago—just for her. He loved her very much."

Running Coyote? Ralph Cowan? My heart softened. *Was this another tall tale? But what does it matter?* I thought. The important thing was that he had awakened in Jaymee a curiosity and love for the world around her. In her bright-eyed innocence and enthusiasm, she had touched his heart and brought him back to the wonders of life. And yet, I couldn't help thinking about those initials.

Ralph's visits suddenly stopped. A phone call from Edythe confirmed our fears. He was laid up—badly injured by a bull. "It will be a while before he can drive again," she said.

Jaymee missed him. "Can we go visit Uncle Ralph?" she asked me one day.

When we arrived at the NI, Ralph was sitting on the porch steps patting a dog so old not even a thump was left in its tail.

"Why did the bull hurt you, Uncle Ralph?" Jaymee asked.

As frail as the storyteller was, he still spun his magic. "He's old, sweetheart," Ralph said, "and his skull's getting so thick, it's squeezing his brain. It hurts. So he got mean." Jaymee nodded sadly and put Blueberry on Ralph's lap, while I went inside to talk with Edythe.

Over a steaming cup of coffee, we watched the two through the kitchen window. "Wouldn't you love to hear that conversation?" I said.

Edythe smiled. "Ralph has always loved children," she said softly. "Did you know he lost his own little girl when she was about Jaymee's age? Her name was Ruth. . . ."

Ruth Cowan. RC. Suddenly, my mind filled with the vision of a young father scratching those initials on a box turtle for a very small girl. I pictured the two rescuing baby birds, saving pollywogs and searching for blue calico boy kittens. And just as suddenly, I knew that it was one of life's quirks of timing that had brought Ralph and Jaymee together when they were both lonely and needed a kindred spirit.

Heading home, I noticed Jaymee squeezing Blueberry much too tightly. A tiny furrow creased her forehead. "What's wrong, honey?" I asked.

"Uncle Ralph told me Blueberry's going to have . . . babies!" she said, her lip trembling. "Uncle Ralph says it's a miracle, Mama . . . and since only God makes miracles, to tell Daddy Blueberry's worth a lot more than five hundred dollars."

"Of course he is, honey." I hugged her close.

When Becky started school again, Jaymee didn't seem so alone anymore. She spent hours feeding cookies to RC and searching for white tarantulas. And soon she was caring for the "boy" calico's nine "miracle" kittens.

The next time we visited the NI Ranch, Ralph sat huddled in an old leather chair. Edythe had arranged a wool blanket around his shoulders. Orange coils glowed from an electric heater near his feet. He smiled and talked with Jaymee and Becky. When we got up to leave, he insisted on seeing us to the door.

"Did I ever show you my cattle brand?" he asked pointing to an empty hole in the living-room ceiling. "There used to be a neon light hanging there, molded into the letters *NI*." His hand trembled as it covered the wall switch. "I lit it every night," he said, "a long, long time ago." His eyes sought Jaymee's. "It was blue," he murmured, "just as blue as your calico."

Jaymee stared upward at the hole, mesmerized. In her mind's eye, I could tell she saw that calico-blue light just as though it were shining down on us. And I could tell that Ralph, too, sharing Jaymee's excitement, could also see it. As ill as he was, he still loved journeying into this child's imagination.

Uncle Ralph disappeared from her life as quietly as he'd entered it, dying peacefully in his sleep. Years passed before we witnessed the absolute power of storytelling.

Almost everything a small child hears and sees is tucked away in the memory. There it can hide undisturbed for years, perhaps forever—sometimes resurfacing just the way it really was—or as the heart wanted it to be.

Jaymee and Becky were in their teens, and Bill had just rewired the wagon wheel chandelier he had made for me so many years before. This time he added seven blinding-white light bulbs. "Gosh, Daddy," said Becky. "You better invest in a dimmer switch. That's so bright it's like hanging the sun in the house." She turned to Jaymee, who was sitting on the floor. "Don't you think he should?"

But Jaymee's thoughts were elsewhere. Smiling, she wrapped her arms about her knees as though hugging the memory that came drifting back. "Do you remember Uncle Ralph's chandelier, Beck? The one with the NI brand on his living-room ceiling?"

Becky looked puzzled. "No ... I ... I don't remember."

"Well, I do." Jaymee's brown eyes shone. "And when Uncle Ralph clicked the switch and turned it on, it glowed—the prettiest, warmest shade of blue I ever saw—just like my blue calico."

Penny Porter

My Second Proposal

Have you ever invited someone for supper and then wished you hadn't? More than ten years ago, I answered a knock on my front door one evening to find A. K. on my doorstep. Clean-shaven, sporting a red-and-black plaid shirt tucked neatly into pressed khakis, and smelling of Aramis cologne, he held a package of hamburger buns in his hand.

"I need to talk to you," he said, pushing his way into the front hall. "I have something to say. If you don't like it, all you have to do is tell me to leave, and I'll never bother you again."

He dropped the buns on the hall table, squared his chin and said, "I think I love you."

The next few moments blurred as thoughts whirled through my head. I had been a widow for two-and-a-half years after having been married for thirty years to the only other man in my life.

I was sixteen when we married; Bill was thirty. For most of those years I never bought groceries, paid a utility bill, or went anyplace by myself. I was loved, protected and cherished, but I had to ask for and account for every penny I spent and then give back the change.

Bill took care of our business. But, except for our

financial disagreements, every day of our thirty-year union was sunshine, security and love.

Then one day, I came home from work to find a note on the kitchen table: "Gone fishing. Be home for supper. Get the skillet ready." But he didn't come home. He drowned.

How that happened, I'll never know. But I do know that for the next two years, every day was a shadow and every night a nightmare.

Then, one Saturday morning in early spring, I was washing dishes at the kitchen sink and watching bluejays test the branches of the nonbearing mulberry in my back yard. From out of nowhere came the thought: *This day is beautiful, Father. Thank you! I'm glad to be alive.* At that moment, I began to heal.

Ten months earlier, A. K.'s wife, a good friend of mine, had died. I had checked on him and had taken food a time or two to "do my thing" to help him through the aftermath of death. Now that I was alive again, however, I wanted to encourage him, to assure him that "This, too, will pass away." So I stepped up my baking and taking.

It wasn't long before this forty-nine-year-old Good Samaritan became a silly, lovesick teenager. Whatever food A. K. mentioned he liked, I cooked it and took it. I went to him for help and advice—help in mending a chair I never sat in, advice for pricing my house for sale when I knew I would never have the courage to move away and start over. I kept a list of topics by the phone so that when he called me or I called him I wouldn't stammer around, trying to keep him on the line.

If I didn't see him or his truck when I passed through town on my way home from work, I panicked. I couldn't concentrate on the homework I needed to grade, because I was listening for the phone and planning what I would say.

Finally one Sunday afternoon, I said a quick prayer, called him, and told him if he had the buns, I had the barbecue.

Now here we sat in my kitchen, the sound of his "I think I love you" echoing in my brain, while he munched scorched barbecue and talked about how wonderful Bill and Jayne had been.

Suddenly, A. K. stopped chewing and asked, "Well, are you going to marry me or not? If you're not, there's no sense in going on with this."

I looked at him—a man I had known for thirty-two years, a man I knew to be independent, hard-working, brusque and a little intimidating; a man who, as far as I knew, had been a good father and a good husband. I couldn't swallow. The only thing I could think of was: *I started this, God. Now what do I do?*

The great comeback of the year fell trippingly from my tongue: "If all my children say it's all right."

Less than three weeks later, we married. Our five children attended, a little hurt, a little embarrassed—a great deal shocked. Everybody smiled a lot, ate a little, and (I heard later) sat around saying over and over, "I didn't even know they liked each other."

It hasn't always been easy combining two families. It hasn't been easy sharing an intimate life with another person, but A. K. and I have been married ten years now. And every day has been lightning in a bottle—bright, exciting, intense, and sometimes filled with thunder. He insists I pay the bills and keep the checkbook balanced. He encourages me to read about insurance and health care, but he buys the groceries and programs the VCR.

Sometimes, when I turn a calendar page and find a note, when I open my desk drawer and find an inscription carved into a pencil, when I find a note taped to the steering wheel of my car, when I hear A. K. say, even in his sleep, "I love ya, Babe," I thank God for a second chance at love. I thank God for giving me the courage to invite A. K. for supper . . . and for giving me the courage to answer that knock at my door.

Donna Smith

The Swordsman

When I was about ten, there were a million things that I wanted to own. But it was in the 1930s and money was scarce. First and foremost, I wanted a black hat and mask like my hero, Zorro. I already had a sword. I made it out of a wooden slat, and it was always ready, jammed under my belt. I never went anywhere without it. I also wanted baseball cards, a six-shooter with a yard and a half of live caps and a crystal-clear marble to use as a shooter. My spending money was a penny a day for candy, but even if I gave up eating Tootsie Rolls, I'd never have enough money for all that stuff. Al and Maxie, my two best friends, came to my rescue though and showed me a way that might do the trick.

"Best bet for dough, Harry, is getting a magazine route," Maxie suggested.

"Yeah, Harry," Al chimed in, "go see my cousin Vito. He'll give you a tryout."

"I need a tryout, like making a team? For a magazine?"

"Well, kinda. Just go see him if you want the route."

Out of the corner of my eye, I saw Maxie pulling his sword out of the belt on his hip.

"Señor, you must fight for the information you just received. . . . *En garde!*"

This week it was my turn to be Pancho Romero, the bad guy, and for that favor I knew I'd have to die like a dog. I whipped out my trusty blade and met the challenge with fury, but in seconds Maxie plunged his Zorro sword through my heart. I staggered and fell to the ground, dead.

The next day, still armed with my weapon, I went to the Paradise Magazine Company and was interviewed by Vito, the sales manager, seven or eight years older than I. He was still young enough to recognize the danger that I wore at my side.

"I see you're armed, kid. Is it okay if I ask you a few questions?" I nodded okay.

"You got any selling experience? No, huh? Well, here's your first lesson. In the magazine business, the big dough is with *Good Housekeeping*. You make a nickel a copy for a sale, and I get points from Paradise. Got it, kid? *Good Housekeeping!*"

"How about *Liberty* and *Colliers*, Vito?"

"Not enough dough, Harry. They sell for a dime a copy. You get a cent and a half, and I get bupkis! By the way, Harry, you Jewish?"

"Yeah, Vito, does that help?"

"Sometimes it works like a charm, especially in Jewish and Italian neighborhoods. Remember you're only ten, and you're making a living. They'll eat it up. Just remember one thing, kid: Stay away from Locust Avenue."

"How come, Vito?"

"They hate Jews."

"Why?"

"Got me, Harry. Just stay away. We're poison to 'em. Jews, Italians and Irish—they hate our guts."

I guess I passed Vito's test, for he placed a brand-new magazine bag over my shoulder and adjusted the straps to my size. When I brought it home, my mother's eyes were glued to it. In her old neighborhood, the Transylvanian Mountains, kids my age didn't sell books with recipes and directions on hemming skirts.

After three weeks of sales, my record wasn't too good. I sold one *Good Housekeeping* to my mother, one to my aunt, and a *Liberty* magazine to a neighbor who hadn't learned to speak English yet. Boy, did I need sales! How did it look, walking around without a black hat or a mask on my head? I had to live dangerously and get out of the neighborhood. I made a big decision and decided to cross over to the forbidden land—Locust Avenue!

The scenery changed. I left behind tenements and entered a section of beautiful private homes with big lawns and strange flowers. They loved lilies. Tiger lilies, daylilies, even those great big calla lilies. Everything was so different from what we grew. Our stuff sprouted from fire escapes, in barrels, washtubs . . . tomatoes, eggplants, cucumbers . . . and who could pass an Italian fire escape without smelling basil, parsley and oregano? Flowers? Nah, I don't think they'd survive on our block.

I went from house to house, ringing bells, but no one would answer. Finally, a door opened, and a tall gray-haired lady asked, "What do you want, young man?"

My hand gripped the handle of my sword; she sounded a little too angry.

"I'm selling magazines. Would you like to buy a *Good Housekeeping?*"

"It depends. Come inside and we'll talk about it."

My hand gripped the sword handle so tight I thought I'd crack the wood. I was going into her house. I had to be ready for anything!

"What's your name, young man?"

"Zorro, er, I mean Harry."

Now her questions came flying at me.

"How old are you, Harry? What grade are you in?
Where do you live?" And then the one I was expecting:
"What church do you belong to? Answer that one first,
Harry."

"The one on Tenth Street."

"What's it called?"

"Saint uh . . . Saint uh . . . I can't remember exactly."

"Is it called St. Agnes, the Catholic Church?"

"Yeah, that's it."

"You're lying, Harry, aren't you? You're a Jew. I can tell."

This time my hand almost withdrew the sword—I had
to defend my faith. But I let it rest in the invisible scabbard under my belt. My sale was slipping away, and my
answer was crucial. Didn't I want the black hat, the mask
and the new shooter? Shouldn't I just lie and sell her the
magazine? Before I knew it, words that shocked me came
tumbling from my mouth.

"You're right, lady, I'm lying. I'm a 100-percent Jew!"

She gasped and said, "Why didn't you lie, Harry? I
would have bought all your magazines. Just one little
white lie, one lie and you could have sold your whole bag!"

My eyes were blinded by tears, as I walked out of the
front door. Even gripping the sword didn't help; the hurt
was too deep. She called to me at the curb to come back,
but I didn't answer. I was in a hurry to get back to my part
of the world on the other side of Locust Avenue.

Vito, who was Italian just like my pal Al, was so mad
when I finished the story that he got on the phone and
arranged a brand-new job.

I was to be the out-of-town delivery boy for Ryan and
Steinberg, the biggest florists in Brooklyn.

"None of that kind of stuff on this job, Harry," Vito said.

In the morning, I reported to work and had a two-
minute interview with Ryan.

"You ever deliver stuff, kid?"

"Sure."

"Is the sword for protection?"

"That's right, Mr. Ryan, no one will ever steal the flowers."

"That's great, Harry. Thanks for the protection, and by the way, do you know how to use the subways and trolleys?"

"Sure."

"How old are you?"

"Thirteen," I lied.

"Kinda small, aren't you? You been bar mitzvahed?"

I didn't answer him. I was too scared about the subways. I was never on one in my life.

"Here are your first deliveries, kid. A dozen roses to Eastern Parkway and three bunches of violets to Lenox Road. I supply the subway fare, and you keep the tips. You know how to get there?"

"Well, not exactly."

Ryan was a swell guy. He explained the subways and even gave me some pointers on getting tips.

"Harry," he said, "take the roses out gently and fan them like this." He shaped them into a perfect fan and swished the air.

"Do that, kid, and you'll clean up on tips."

"How about the violets, Mr. Ryan?"

"You can't fan those; just make sure you get there before they wilt. Fresh violets are like money in the bank."

I went down under the ground and waited for the Brighton train, which roared in and scared the wits out of me. I followed the subway map glued to the window and found the place on Eastern Parkway where the roses went. It was an anniversary present, and the woman I delivered them to cried when I spread the roses into a fan. What a tip I got—*twenty-five cents!* I could buy a black hat, a mask and shooters in every color of the rainbow!

Now for Lenox Road. The doorman said it wasn't too far, and I could walk to the violet delivery. I followed his instructions and was lost in fifteen minutes. I didn't know where I was.

The only thing in sight was a big church with huge doors that were wide open. Could I trust them with directions, or would I get that Jewish stuff all over again? I had no choice; the violets were wilting, and I had to find the address in a hurry. I walked into the church and was met by a lady in a nun's outfit. She frightened me at first, but when she smiled, my fears melted away. Even my palm relaxed squeezing the sword. "I'm Sister Marianna. Can I help you?" she asked.

All my bravado left me, and the words I blurted out seemed to shake her as much as they did me.

"I'm Jewish, Sister. Is it okay if I ask directions? My violets are going to die."

"Oh, so you're a delivery boy. How old are you, son?"

"Going on eleven, and I'm Jewish, Sister. Is it okay?"

Sister Marianna restored my faith in humankind right on the spot.

"Stop worrying about being Jewish, and let's try to fix those violets."

She left for a few minutes and returned with the violets soaked in cold water and wrapped in wax paper. Not only that, she located Lenox Road and walked with me to the exact address.

I was overwhelmed. How could I ever repay this kind lady? She smiled at me and said, "Get going, before the violets wilt again."

Suddenly, I unsheathed my sword and held it high in the air. She was startled.

"What are you doing, Harry?" she asked.

"I'm knighting you with a touch of the sword on your head."

"But I thought you were Zorro. Isn't knighting King Arthur's job?"

"Sometimes I'm a king, especially when people are so nice like you."

She bent her head down to be knighted, and a tear ran down her face. As the sword touched her head, she rose slowly and in a soft voice said, "Thank you, Your Majesty, for the honor bestowed."

As I put the sword back in its scabbard, Lady Marianna leaned over, planted a big kiss on my cheek and said, "Hurry up, Harry, or those violets will wilt again."

Mike Lipstock

2

ON
PARENTING

*The ordinary acts we practice every day at
home are of more importance to the soul
than their simplicity might suggest.*

Thomas Moore

The Bus Doesn't Stop Here Anymore

I remember leading my oldest to the big yellow school bus, name tag pinned to his striped shirt, which was tucked in and matched perfectly with his cotton pants. With a new backpack over his shoulders, he turned to glance at me before heading up the steps.

"It'll be fine," I said. "You'll make lots of new friends, learn wonderful things and have lots of fun." As I gave him a hug, he looked up at me and asked what time he would be back. I tried to assure him as I sent him up the steps. "You'll be home at lunchtime. The bus will bring you right back here, and I'll be waiting for you, and you can tell me everything." It happened just that way. Not long after that I sent my youngest on the big yellow bus, and when it brought her back, I was there waiting for her, too.

As our lives changed, I acquired a full-time job and could no longer wait for them as they arrived home, but the big yellow bus still stopped in front of my house each and every day to bring them safely back. In the evening as we sat for dinner, they were anxious to share their day with me. We talked about friends and recess, teachers and books. My refrigerator became a gallery full of "star" papers, pictures and report cards. Every Mother's Day they planted marigolds in milk cartons decorated with crayons and construction paper and carefully carried them home accompanied with the most beautiful cards. I wore priceless macaroni jewelry and paper corsages. As my children grew over the years, I still counted on the bus to bring them safely home each and every day, and it continued to do so school year after school year.

Before I knew it, they were talking about driver licenses and part-time jobs, dances and dates. They no longer made Mother's Day cards; instead they borrowed the car and drove to the store to purchase them. Marigolds in milk cartons turned into hanging planters or small bouquets, which they purchased with the money they had earned. They wore what they wanted whether it matched or not, and the macaroni jewelry found a permanent home as a decoration on our Christmas tree.

Their backpacks grew heavier as the books they carried got thicker. The refrigerator now held a calendar, which was necessary to keep track of their busier schedules, and a dry-erase board so that we could communicate our whereabouts to each other when we weren't at home— which by now was most of the time. They were once small children, and now they were young adults who were quickly becoming more and more independent. The big yellow bus no longer stopped each day in front of my house.

High school had gone by quickly; and before I could turn around, my daughter, the youngest, was investigating colleges, and my son had graduated. He pondered his future and opted to join the military. He was ordered to report to his station one sunny, August morning to be sworn in. I went along with other proud parents to witness the beginning of their new lives. I caught a glance of him when I was leaving, just as he was swinging his backpack over his shoulders. Although I had seen him do this hundreds of times, it was somehow different this time. I looked around at all of them, these fine young men and women lined up, one foot over the threshold of their bright futures, backpacks over their shoulders and waiting for—what else—a bus! I walked over to my son and reached up to give him a hug, and he looked down at me. I had done this before, I thought, but where had the years gone?

He was suddenly five years old again, and I asked him if he was nervous. "A little," he said.

"Don't be nervous," I assured him. "It will be fine. Think of all the opportunities you'll have and all the new people you'll meet."

I hugged him again and sent him on his way. I could barely get the words out of my mouth as he walked forward, but I did manage to whisper, "When you come home, I'll be here waiting for you, and you can tell me everything."

Denise Syman

Crossing Over

It was a cool autumn day. Clouds overshadowed the canopy of blue, as if God wanted to hide the sun's great splendor. The winds whispered by as leaves rustled to the ground.

A day to remember, that was. The day young women everywhere wait their whole lives for, and I knew in my heart I would treasure those moments forever.

Before me stood a young man with whom I had shared my vast secrets and enchanted moments. I had whispered promises in his ear and did my best to fulfill them. I had never trusted anyone with the key to my heart until he entered my life. Now, I knew the only safe place for this key to remain was with him.

This was a first for both of us. We gazed nervously in each other's eyes, waiting for the other to make the first move. I was unsure if we were ready for this. Making a hasty decision like this could be so devastating to our lives.

We stood there in silence for what seemed an eternity. Echoes from the past rang endlessly in my mind. The laughter and tears we had shared will forever be held in a special place in my heart. My emotions were so vulnerable at that point. Part of me wanted to run and hide, and the other said, "Go ahead. It's time."

Then just as if he were reading my mind, he gently grasped my hand, sending a cold chill up my spine and erasing all my doubt. With his soft voice, he whispered, "It's time."

I stood back to take one last glance at him to remember how he looked before we took this major step. Never again would I look at him as I do now. Things would be different once we crossed over; we couldn't look back.

Once again our eyes met. If only we could cease time and steal those moments away in our hearts forever. Neither he nor I would ever feel as we did then. There's only one first time for everything, and this was it.

I wrapped my arms around him and playfully kissed the tip of his nose, then I whispered softly in his ear, "I love you." Then it happened—the moment we both had been waiting for.

I'll never forget that day or the silly grin on his face afterward. Tears streamed down my face as he crossed the street to step onto the big yellow school bus. Then he turned to me and said, "Bye, Mommy. I love you."

Angela Martin

Through the Years

My mother, Hazel, sits peeling potatoes. Dressed in Mama's movie star coat with the real fur collar, high heels, and beautiful red velvet hat, I shuffle elegantly into the kitchen and gleefully yell, "Look Mommy, I'm little Hazel!" Mama looks up and smiles with tears in her eyes. I am completely aware of how incredibly cute I am being. I am four years old, and Mama is my friend.

"Oh, Mom, it's so pretty! I love it! Thank you, thank you, thank you," I cry as I turn and rustle in my new party dress. My fingers touch the soft, peach satin, and I look up to see Mom smiling at me. I am nine years old, and, sometimes, Mom is still my fairy godmother.

"I'll be glad when I go to college next year and don't have to live here any more," I scream at my mother. "If you keep on acting this way," she says in frustration, "I'll be glad too." Hurt and shocked by this revelation, I storm out of the room, trying to hold back my tears. I am seventeen years old, and, too often Mother is my adversary.

"I did it! I did it! I got an A from Professor King," I shriek. I leap to my feet, waving my report card in the warm kitchen air. Mom tells me she's proud of me, and we dance around the kitchen in a wild victory jig. I am twenty-one years old, and Mom is my biggest cheerleader.

I am barely able to make out "Flight 405 to Great Falls is now ready for boarding" over the airport intercom. After all those times when it was me leaving and my mother was crying, it's now her turn to depart, and I am the one left crying. I look at Mama and do something I haven't done since I was four years old; I grab her hand and say "Don't leave." She touches my cheek and says, "But honey, I've got my ticket." Hugging her close to me, I say, "The only way I'll let you go is if you promise to come back for Christmas." Dabbing at her own tears, she says, "Oh yes, I'll be back." I am thirty-seven years old, and Mama is my friend. *This* time, it is forever.

Nancy Richard-Guilford

Leading with My Chin

When I was a teenager, I scraped up money to buy an old truck. Every day after school, I worked on it—sanding, painting, buffing. As a present, my parents got me brand-new upholstery for the seats.

Then once I slammed a door a little too hard, and a window shattered. I didn't have any money to replace it. I drove it anyway, including to school.

My high school was a big flat building, and you could see the car park from many of the classrooms. One day it began to rain. I sat in class and watched my truck—and new upholstery—get drenched through the broken window.

Suddenly I saw my mom and dad tear into the car park. They screeched up next to my truck and dragged a huge piece of plastic out of their car. Then, in the pouring rain, they covered up the truck.

Dad had left his office in the middle of the day, picked up Mom and bought this hunk of plastic to save my seats. I watched them do this. And I just began crying right there in class.

My parents were with me through every high and low in my life, always supportive and proud of my accomplishments. I never think of them as gone. I've got all their stories, and that keeps them nearby always.

Jay Leno

Why Monks Sit in the Snow

My six-year-old son and his friend have just left the dining room, where I am writing. The boys were wearing black sweat pants and black turtlenecks that they had pulled from Ryan's dresser. They cinched the pants at the waist with belts, through which they had slipped wooden swords. Then they crept up on me. When I looked up from my computer, they ran squealing from the room.

This stunt was repeated about ten times in eight minutes. The repetition did nothing to diminish the hilarity for the two boys (or increase it for me). The pirate-spy routine had been preceded by attempts to pogo in the family room, in-line skate in the kitchen, dribble a basketball down the stairs, burp the letters in their names (my son has shown genius in this area) and play catch in the stairwell.

I took away the pogo stick, put the skates outside, stored the basketball in a closet, told the boys I'd heard enough burping for one day and guided the game of catch to the driveway. Still ahead: the friend's anguished departure, subtraction homework, spelling flashcards, dinner, dishes, books and a pokey meander into bed. During this time I had to finish my column.

Two nights earlier I had dinner with a friend who was in town on business from Los Angeles. I drove into the city early so we could catch up, and we ended up walking through the shops around Union Square. She has a three-year-old boy and a baby due in three months. At the Banana Republic, she ran her hands over a soft throw blanket.

"Oh, isn't this wonderful?" she asked. Then she found a comforter. "Look at this," she said. At Saks, she found a flannel nightshirt. "Feel this," she said.

I looked at her. "Do you realize everything you've looked at has to do with sleep?" Once upon a time her shopping tastes ran to spike heels and miniskirts.

She laughed. "When I get up in the morning," she said, "all I think about is how many hours until I can get back in."

The next night I sat in a darkened room at a Zen retreat not far from my house. The room was packed with people who had come to meditate then listen to a lecture on spirituality. The teacher mentioned how he had traveled to Asia as a young man to learn the ways of the monks. He sat in a snowy forest for days with little food, drink or sleep. He sat like a yogi on the bank of the Ganges River for twenty hours at a stretch though his legs burned with pain and his eyes longed for rest. He explained that the effort of his mind to overcome the deprivation and distractions took him to higher states of clarity and vision and taught him patience.

I was thinking about this, and about my L.A. friend, as my son and his pal staged a sword fight in the hallway. The connections of the last few days began to fall into place. I thought about the repeated reminders and admonishments we parents deliver through the day, the noise, the lack of sleep, the long waits for our child to get dressed, clean his room or get out of the car. ("C'mon, we're going into the store now. Put down the soccer ball. No, we can't take the dog. What are you doing? That cookie's probably been under the seat for a month. C'mon. Now. I mean it. Don't worry about the cookie. We'll throw it out in the store. Let's go." The only things children do quickly are go to the bathroom, eat dessert, open gifts and climb fences separating playgrounds from deadly freeways.)

Suddenly it clicked. I understood why monks must sit in snow and on the banks of the Ganges. They don't have children!

It occurred to me that, in my search for self-improvement and spirituality, I had everything I needed in my own home. Every parent does. There are the long painful nights we sit without moving because one twitch might wake the (potentially) very loud baby in our arms. There is the excruciating mind and muscle control to stifle a smile when our child earnestly tells us he didn't pick up his toys because he got hit with a ball at school and suffered brain damage.

There are the tests of concentration when you're talking to a client on the phone and your child appears in the doorway in nothing but boots and a gun belt and acts out the final scene from *High Noon.*

There are the years on end of getting to sleep after midnight because only when the kids are asleep and the phone isn't ringing can you get your chores finished, then you're up at six to make lunches and get breakfast and shuttle them to school before you go, bleary-eyed, to work.

Religious students travel the globe to find tests of will, patience, deprivation and selflessness. Parents live them every day. Anyone looking for a mysterious, contradictory and fulfilling religion couldn't do much better than child-rearing. All the components are there: rituals, generosity, penance, guilt and desperate prayer, all punctuated by moments of transcendent clarity and unmatched joy.

I'm just thinking out loud here, but I'm wondering if we can get tax-exempt status.

Joan Ryan

Making Room for Shooting Stars

This was the big game. The bleachers were packed with parents and kids. Lights blazed down on the baseball field, giving it a real "big league" feel. The boys in the dugouts were nervous and excited. It was the bottom of the fifth inning, and our team was actually leading by one run. Andy, our son, was in right field, and behind him, at the edge of the lights, it was dark, with the black shape of the distant mountains rising up to the stars. It was a clear and chilly night, and Andy's Little League team, which had struggled all year and didn't even reach .500 in the final standings, had shocked two of the better teams by making it to this championship game. The mood was electric.

Only one out to go to end the inning. The other team's left-handed slugger, a big kid who always hit long balls and had that home-run swagger when he walked, was up. He was poised at the plate like a rattlesnake, dangerous and ready to strike.

Nervously, I looked out Andy's way. He had never really done well in the outfield. I was shocked to see Andy looking straight up at the night sky! It was obvious he wasn't paying attention to the game. I was horrified this slugger was going to launch the ball Andy's way and he wouldn't even know it was coming. They'd score a bunch of runs and break the game wide open.

"What's he doing out there?" I hissed to my wife, Mary.

"What do you mean?" she replied.

"Well, look at him—he's not paying attention; he's goofing off! This guy's gonna hit it right to him!" I muttered.

"Relax," said my wife. "He'll be fine. It's just a game."

"Come on, Andy. Wake up out there," I said more to myself than Mary.

I could barely watch. My body was tense. The pitch was on the way, a slow, enticing floater right in the middle of the strike zone. I squinted out at Andy, who was still gazing heavenward. *Maybe he's praying,* I thought. I heard the crack of the bat. "Oh, no," I said.

I was mostly worried that Andy would be really embarrassed, because he did take his performance seriously, and cared what his teammates thought of him. But I also realized I was worried that I'd be embarrassed, too. I prided myself on being a supportive and not-too-pushy dad. We'd go out and play one-on-one games and practice catching those high flies. I always tried to make it fun, yet pushed hard enough that Andy would improve. And I'd always say, "Just give it your best shot." So if Andy made a good try going after the ball and missed it—you know, stretched out with the glove and eating sod, or backwards over the fence—that was okay. But to miss it because he was off in a different dimension somewhere—that was embarrassing. Downright goofy. Not playing tough. Letting the guys down. I felt all that macho sports stuff churning around inside me like indigestion.

"Yes!" I shouted, as the play ended. Sluggo had grounded out to first. We (Andy and I) had been spared, and we still led by one run. It was imperative that I get Andy straightened out for the last inning.

We were sitting behind the fence near home plate, and

as the kids came in from the outfield, Andy ran up to us, breathless. I was about to start my "What-do-you-think-you're-doing-out-there speech" when Andy exclaimed, "Did you see that shooting star? It was beautiful! It was so great. It had a long tail, and I thought it might crash into the mountain. But then it just disappeared, like someone turned the lights off inside. I wonder where it came from. It was so awesome. I wish you'd seen it!"

Andy's eyes were glowing with excitement (after all, we had spent as much time looking for meteors as we had practicing baseball). I paused. "Me, too," I said. "Well, one inning to go. You guys hold 'em now. Hit a home run!"

"Okay!" said Andy, and he ran back to his teammates in the dugout.

Mary smiled at me. We were thinking the same thing—that it was nice our son would take time out to appreciate the wonder and beauty in life, and that it was important to him. There was plenty of time for Andy to experience the suffocating crush of team sports, the peer pressure, the "at all costs" mentality. He was still a kid, thank goodness. And I was a little chagrined that I had been temporarily caught up in the same vortex.

As we grow up, it seems we have less and less time to seek beauty and wonder. As adults, it's way down the list somewhere. For many of us, just keeping up with everything we have going consumes most of our time and energy, and sadly there's not much room for shooting stars. So every once in a while I take time out to look around, even if I'm in the middle of something I think is too important to interrupt. You might be surprised by the beauty you can find when you least expect it—on the street, in the sky, even in the corporate boardroom—and how it can make your day better. Andy hit a triple in that last inning. But I still wish I had seen that shooting star, too.

Mark Crawford

My Favorite Father's Day

We cannot tell what may happen to us in the strange medley of life, but we can decide what happens in us—how we take it, what we do with it—and that is what really counts in the end. How we take the raw stuff of life and make it a thing of worth and beauty—that is the test of living.

Joseph Fort Newton

The summer after my son Kotter's freshman year of high school, with the exception of senior league baseball, was spent home alone. He wasn't happy.

Without any malice on Kotter's part, he made a typical adolescent freshman mistake that caused the loss of his closest friends. Afterward, he called them on the phone, but they were always too busy to talk. He biked over to their houses, but they were always gone. He often walked with his head down or stared out the window at nothing. I watched the hurt overflow in Kotter and bled for him as well.

I decided to give up what I too often considered my own precious activities to become Kotter's summer companion and help him through this stormy, confusing period in his life. In earlier years, Kotter would often call me his best friend, and now I would work to earn that privileged title.

So I became Kotter's buddy during the summer ball season. I biked with Kotter to and from the games. I took him camping. We went to movies. I cheered Kotter's accomplishments and comforted him in his failures. In short, I became the father that I always should have been.

Little by little, as the senior league season moved deeper into summer, I saw signs that the ice curtain of lost friendship was starting to melt. First, it was his team- mates' handclasps after a good play, and then it was the shouts of encouragement from the dugout. I pointed these signs out to Kotter and encouraged him to hang in there. Kotter and I, each in our own way, used these proclamations as our banners of hope.

During the latter part of June, a senior league tournament was held on Father's Day weekend, and Kotter's team earned the right to play in the championship game, which was held on Father's Day. The evenly matched teams took turns taking the lead. Near the end of the game, Kotter's team was behind by one run with a man on base and Kotter at bat. Kotter walked up to the batter's box as tension filled the air. He would not be denied encouragement from his friends at that moment. "You can do it, Kotter" and "Come on, big boy" rang out from the dugout. Kotter fed on this affection as he stepped into the box. I cheered as well. I cheered to encourage Kotter, and I cheered inside for the affection I saw coming from the dugout.

CRACK!—The soft spot of the bat connected perfectly with the ball and sent it screaming out into left field! This ball was tagged. I gripped the edge of my seat and held my breath in disbelief. The left fielder stopped running, turned around and watched the ball sail over the fence! The home run sealed the victory for Kotter's team.

Pandemonium broke out in the crowd. Every spectator was standing up and celebrating, except for one. I remained seated, trying to control my emotions. The home run no doubt made me happy, but the scene I witnessed at home plate overwhelmed me. My son, whose heart bled so profusely those past months, was now being hugged by his teammates as they marched triumphantly back to the dugout.

Once I composed myself, I hurried to the fence near the dugout to celebrate the home run with Kotter and to celebrate something even deeper—to celebrate the resurrection of human spirit that was occurring within him.

When I got to the fence, I saw something else that tugged at my emotions. I saw an old friend and teammate hand Kotter the home-run ball that he had retrieved from outside the park. The gesture brought back memories of these same two boys riding their bikes together the previous summer. I turned from the crowd so my lips could quiver more freely.

After the victory celebration, I went for a long walk to collect my thoughts about the game. I thought about the home run that fulfilled, for my son, a dream that all senior leaguers have. I thought about the crisis that helped strengthen the relationship I had with him. Most of all I thought about the human spirit's ability to revive itself after letdown. This was truly the best Father's Day that I had ever experienced.

Yet the warmest moment was yet to come. When I got home that day, I spotted a baseball sitting on the table with writing on it. I picked up the ball, read the inscription and started to cry. The ball I held was my son's home-run ball, and the inscription read: "Happy Father's Day, Dad! Love, Kotter."

Jerry Harpt

Dear Old Dad

When the good Lord was creating fathers, He started with a tall frame.

A female angel nearby said, "What kind of father is that? If you're going to make children so close to the ground, why have you put fathers up so high? He won't be able to shoot marbles without kneeling, tuck a child in bed without bending or even kiss a child without a lot of stooping."

And God smiled and said, "Yes, but if I make him child-size, who would children have to look up to?"

And when God made a father's hands, they were large and sinewy.

The angel shook her head sadly and said, "Do you know what you're doing? Large hands are clumsy. They can't manage diaper pins, small buttons, rubber bands on pony-tails or even remove splinters caused by baseball bats."

And God smiled and said, "I know, but they're large enough to hold everything a small boy empties from his pockets at the end of a day, yet small enough to cup a child's face."

And then God molded long, slim legs and broad shoulders.

The angel nearly had a heart attack. "Boy, this is the end

of the week, all right," she clucked. "Do you realize you just made a father without a lap? How is he going to pull a child close to him without the kid falling between his legs?"

And God smiled and said, "A mother needs a lap. A father needs strong shoulders to pull a sled, balance a boy on a bicycle or hold a sleepy head on the way home from the circus."

God was in the middle of creating two of the largest feet anyone had ever seen when the angel could contain herself no longer. "That's not fair. Do you honestly think those large boats are going to dig out of bed early in the morning when the baby cries? Or walk through a small birthday party without crushing at least three of the guests?"

And God smiled and said, "They'll work. You'll see. They'll support a small child who wants to ride a horse to Banbury Cross or scare off mice at the summer cabin or display shoes that will be a challenge to fill."

God worked throughout the night, giving the father few words but a firm, authoritative voice and eyes that saw everything but remained calm and tolerant.

Finally, almost as an afterthought, He added tears. Then He turned to the angel and said, "Now, are you satisfied that he can love as much as a mother?"

The angel shutteth up.

Erma Bombeck

My Name Is Mommy

I've said it a thousand times and I'll say it again: There is no job more important than that of being a parent.

Oprah Winfrey

It's only been ten years. Yet, as I stand in the vestibule of the posh country club, staring at the picture, all I can think is *where did the time go?* The girl in the picture is smiling. A wide I'm-ready-to-take-on-the-world smile of an eighteen-year-old with her whole life ahead of her. I read the caption under the picture: "Cheerleading, Varsity Track, DECA, Choir." And under that, the phrase "In Ten Years I Will Be . . ." The handwriting that completes the phrase is still the same. It says, "I will have a doctorate in marine biology and be living in either North Carolina or California."

That's it.

Nowhere does it say, "I will be pregnant with my sixth child and getting ready to celebrate my tenth wedding anniversary." Yet, that's what it ought to say because that is where I am ten years after high school graduation.

The girl in the picture is me. A hardly recognizable me.
Over the years, I traded in the eighties "big" hair for a
more easily maintained style. I exchanged the now out-
dated, but then trendy, clothes for never-go-out-of-style
jeans and whichever-my-hand-grabs-first-out-of-the-
drawer shirts. I somehow lost the fullness to my face and
the tight skin around my eyes. As I creep toward
twenty-nine, these things don't bother me—the
inevitable, the getting older. But the caption does bother
me for some reason—"I will have a doctorate in marine
biology. . . ."

What was I thinking? Did I really think I could accom-
plish such an extravagant goal? I guess I must have. Ten
years ago. Funny, I remember loving science in high
school—anatomy, chemistry, botany, the whole nine
yards—but marine biology? I don't even have pet fish!

I enter the main room, where the class of '87 high school
reunion is already in full swing. I am wary, uncomfortable
in the outrageously expensive maternity outfit I bought
especially for the occasion. I search the crowd of some two
hundred people for a familiar face, but I moved six hundred miles away just after graduation, married and hadn't
seen these people for ten years. When I received the invitation, it hadn't seemed so long ago. For some reason,
now it feels like an eternity.

At first, faces look vaguely familiar, then names start
popping in my mind like kernels of popcorn. A girl from
my cheerleading squad, Debbie, yes Debbie! Gosh, she
looks so chic! And . . . It's all coming back to me now. Over
there is Brett What's-His-Name. He still looks the same,
just older, just like the rest of us. Somewhere in this crowd
are the girls I'd been best friends with, the girls I had once
confided my deepest secrets to, my dreams, my desires.
Here are the boys I once dated and fancied myself in love
with for a few days or weeks.

Memories I didn't know I remembered surface, one by one, dripping a name to match a face here, then trickling more there, then flooding me with snapshot memories of classes, football games in the rain, dates and dances, musicals and plays, lunches at McDonald's on one dollar and ten cents, my first car, parties and friends. Suddenly, I don't feel so out of place. I even see a few protruding bellies that rival mine.

I take a deep breath and smile at the first girl, or should I say woman, who catches my eye. I remember her. We never did get along well, but what the heck, it has been ten years. We are all grown up now, right?

I take a step closer and yell over the eighties music and chattering noise, "Hi, Kirsten!"

She searches my face, trying to place me in her own memories. Maybe I have changed that much. She finally gives up, and her eyes float down to my name tag, then snap right back to my face as her mouth drops open. "Oh, my gosh!"

I say, "How are you?" with a huge smile I practiced for just such an occasion as this.

"Oh, my gosh!" she repeats and calls me by my maiden name, a name I haven't thought of as belonging to me for nearly ten years. "You look *sooo* different!" she exclaims, looking me over, the way a female will do only to another female. "Are you pregnant?" she asks.

I nod and say, "Six months."

"Don't you already have like a *million* kids?"

Do I detect a condescending note in her voice? "Just five," I answer, my eyes dancing over the crowd for a more friendly reception. I spot a girl I'd known since grade school. "Nice seeing you again, Kirsten," I call over my shoulder as I move away.

I start having fun, reminiscing with old friends I'd once shared everything with. Each conversation started with,

"Oh, my gosh! You've changed *sooo* much, blah, blah, blah. You look *fabulous!*" And then, "What have you been doing?"

I listen as these once-great friends—now strangers— gush on and on about fun-filled college years, fantastic careers, outstanding salaries, dreams of corporate ladder climbing, travel, big-city life in Chicago, New York, Los Angeles, Atlanta. I am reacquainted with friends who have become doctors, lawyers, engineers, teachers, accountants, scientists, actors, etc.

And then they turn back to me and say, "What have you been doing? Where did you go to college?"

This is where my smile starts to feel forced. "I didn't go to college," I say. "I got married. We started a family right away." They tell me how great they think it is that I am what they call a stay-at-home mom. How they can't believe I have five kids, am expecting a sixth and still have my sanity. How I must really have my hands full and how busy I must be.

I smile and think, *They have no idea what they are talking about.* I smile through their caustic teasing about birth control and planned parenthood. I smile through their sly speculation of what a stud my husband must be. I smile and smile and smile. I feel myself sinking. I entered the room as a mom, but now I am nothing but a mom. I never thought of myself that way before.

I return to the vestibule and stare at the picture again. What happened to the girl I once was? Or better yet, where is the woman I almost was? The marine biologist, living on the ocean, sun-kissed face, salt-bleached hair?

At one time, I was filled with such dreams, such goals. I wanted to make a difference; I wanted to be successful; I wanted to be rich. . . . I wanted to have it all.

I think about this all the way back home on the plane to Maryland, where I now live, getting more of that awful sinking feeling in the pit of my stomach, the kind that makes you want to cry in self-pity. Then I see something.

I see a woman holding a baby.

The baby is not yet a year. He's wild-eyed, clutching his ear with one hand, the other hand wrapped around his mother's neck in a white-knuckled grip. The mother is rocking gently back and forth in her seat, singing softly, patting lightly, face calm, soothing her baby. I watch. I can't take my eyes off her. The baby's eyes begin to droop, then close; his body relaxes.

It's something I've done a hundred times, a thousand, maybe, rocking my baby, one of them, any of them, all of them. An earache, a stomachache, a nightmare, a boo-boo, a fight, something I could always fix with my rocking chair and my arms.

Suddenly, I realize I do still have dreams, just different ones. I dream of seeing the bottom of my laundry basket, an empty kitchen sink, a freezer that is always stocked, a toothpaste-free bathroom counter, a bathroom without a miniature potty right next to the big one, stairs that don't have a gate at the top and bottom, every sock in my house reunited with its mate. And I know when I have accomplished these goals, I'll sit down and cry.

It occurs to me that, over the years, I have gone through an unseen but tremendous transformation. I have learned to love construction paper; crayon-colored birthday cards; sun catchers made from wax paper; autumn-colored leaves; Christmas decorations of cotton balls, glitter and too much glue; Dixie cups full of dandelion tops and assorted weeds on my table; refrigerators covered in papers, and pictures with "I Lov U Momy" scrawled beneath.

I've learned to see swing sets as lawn ornaments, exclaim with genuine enthusiasm at the sight of a hot-air balloon or a helicopter flying low in the sky, offer up a cheek for a sticky-faced kiss and then beg for another.

I *do* make a difference—in the lives of my children. I have awesome responsibility—making major decisions that will shape the lives of five—almost six—individuals. I am rich—in love and family.

I do have it all. Or all I need to have.

The plane lands, and the passengers make their way down the gateway. I walk slowly, waddling really, lugging my carry-on, while my mind switches back into mommy mode, as my thoughts race through all I must do once I get home. The dishes and the laundry and the groceries and the . . .

"Excuse me, ma'am." I turn toward the voice behind me, a gentleman, his hand outstretched. He asks, "Can I give you a hand with that bag?"

I smile broadly. "I'd rather you carry this baby. My back is killing me."

He laughs. "Is this your first?"

We are coming through the gate now, and I spot my family waiting to meet me, five little faces lighting up at the sight of me, and my heart swells with love. "Not hardly," I say and gesture with my free hand.

He says, "Your life must be pretty hectic."

To this I respond, "It's pretty wonderful."

Stacey A. Granger

Mikey's Goal

*The greatest test of courage on earth is to bear
defeat without losing heart.*

Robert Green Ingersoll

Last night was the last game for my eight-year-old
son's soccer team. It was the final quarter. The score was
two to one, my son's team in the lead. Parents encircled
the field, offering encouragement. With less than ten seconds remaining, the ball rolled in front of my son's teammate, one Mikey O'Donnel. With shouts of "Kick it!"
echoing across the field, Mikey reared back and gave it
everything he had. All round me the crowd erupted.
O'Donnel had scored!

Then there was silence. Mikey had scored all right, but
in the wrong goal, ending the game in a tie. For a moment
there was total hush. You see, Mikey has Down's syn-
drome and for him there is no such thing as a wrong goal.
All goals were celebrated by a joyous hug from Mikey. He
had even been known to hug the opposing players when
they scored.

The silence was finally broken when Mikey, his face filled with joy, grabbed my son, hugged him and yelled, "I scored! I scored. Everybody won! Everybody won!" For a moment I held my breath, not sure how my son would react. I need not have worried. I watched, through tears, as my son threw up his hand in the classic high-five salute and started chanting, "Way to go Mikey! Way to go Mikey!" Within moments both teams surrounded Mikey, joining in the chant and congratulating him on his goal. Later that night, when my daughter asked who had won, I smiled as I replied, "It was a tie. Everybody won."

Kim Kane

One Rose

Motherhood took me by surprise. One day I was a single woman living at the beach with a ten-year career as a flight attendant, and the next, a wife and mother of four. And it happened almost that quickly.

I met and married my husband within months of meeting him. I had gone to visit my grandmother in the hospital and was introduced to her surgeon, my soon-to-be spouse. I had learned a year before meeting him that I was not able to have children on my own. So, upon learning that he had two sons that he was moving in with us, life seemed like an episode from *Ozzie and Harriet* (updated to include my keeping a solid career). His sons were nine and ten when their mother put them on a airplane from the East Coast and "shipped" them to the West Coast, having very limited contact with them for the next eight years. My husband left their mother when they were only two and three years old, so we were all literally strangers under one roof. Ironically, no sooner had I married my husband, then I became pregnant with our own child. The day after his sons moved in with us, our son was born (a month early). Three children within two days! Two years later, I gave birth to our second son.

I remember times when I would be so overwhelmed that I could only tell myself over and over, "One day they will thank you." I don't remember a lot of those tumultuous years. There was a lot of chauffeuring to and from Little League games, a lot of getting up at three in the morning to get to ice hockey practice by five, banquets, PTA meetings, and "short order" cooking. I remember witnessing the growing pains of two young men going through adolescence. Their father was often away, their biological mother completely out of the picture, their two half-brothers often felt like an annoyance to them, and their stepmother never seemed able to meet their needs. Yet, I knew in my heart that one day they would look back and realize that I did love them as my own and that I did my best.

When my oldest stepson graduated from high school, their biological mother decided to finally pay a visit. The graduation ceremony was held outside at dusk, and my husband and his "ex" stood together and watched with pride as "their" son received his diploma. My other stepson stayed by their side. I stood off a slight distance away with our two sons. There was a strange twist to this graduation ceremony. The principal of the high school delivered a speech that included a theme of "giving a rose to the person who has meant the most to you in your life." I found that odd, but each graduating student held in their hands one red rose. Upon receiving their diplomas, each student walked up to the person and handed them their rose. To this day I will never forget the feeling of holding that rose in my hands.

Jolie "Jes" Shafer-Kenney

Can I Come with You?

"Why are you going out again? Can't I come with you? I don't want you to go. I want you to stay home with me."

Words of love from my ten-year-old.

My older children used to say the same things, used to cry when they were babies, when I would leave them for an evening; used to beg, when they grew older, to tag along wherever I'd go.

"We'll be good. We won't make any noise. We promise."

Sometimes their demands would annoy me. Why couldn't they stay home with someone else for a while? The things I had to do weren't fun things. Alone I could finish more quickly and get home sooner, and then play with them.

I tried reasoning, explaining. "But we want to be with you," they insisted.

So they came. Everywhere. To the grocery store, the bank, the library, the movies. Anywhere I went, there they were, right by my side.

Most times I didn't mind, but there were days I ached for moments alone. Driving in the car, I would turn on the radio and a song would come on, one that I loved and I'd turn up the volume and a little voice would interrupt.

"What does 'Go Children Slow' mean, Mommy?" "What town are we in?" "Did I tell you what happened yesterday?" And the song would be long over by the time the story was told.

In restaurants, I'd be listening to a friend, hoping my son and daughter would talk to each other, which they did. They always tried to be polite. But there were important questions, legitimate interruptions. "Mommy, do they put celery in the egg salad in this place?" "Can I have a vanilla milk shake?" "Will you go to the bathroom with me?" And I'd wish for a time when I could finish a sentence, have a complete thought, eat one entire meal without interruption.

It was my attention they wanted. My opinion and presence they craved. I was the audience they played to day after day. I became accustomed to their stories, their interruptions. Their fresh observations enriched me. "Why is that man called a waiter, Mom, when we're the ones doing the waiting?" "How come that sign says, 'dressing room' when everyone goes in to undress?"

As they grew older, their questions became less entertaining and more annoying. The early teenage years were accompanied by a litany of demands and complaints. "How come everyone else can go out on a school night and I can't?" "No one else has to be home by eleven o'clock. Don't you trust me?"

Then, most of all, I wished they would be quiet, find something else to do, someone else to listen to them. Why did even the simplest things have to turn into confrontations? Couldn't they ever just leave me alone?

Now, too often, they do.

"How was your day?" I'll ask my seventeen-year-old son, when he comes home from work. "Where did you go? What did you do?"

"We hung doors somewhere. It was no big deal, Mom. It was just work."

Just work. This isn't fair. I want detail. I want texture. I want to know what he does twelve hours a day. I want to hear about his friends, listen to his stories.

"How was your trip, Mom? What did you see? Did you have fun?" he used to ask only a few years ago. "What did you do at night? Did you go out? Did you miss us?" The endless questions always answered, always explained.

"Are you going out again tonight?" I find myself saying.

"Can't you stay home sometime. You'll be leaving for college in three weeks and I already miss you now."

Why didn't someone tell me this was going to happen? Everything is reversed. Now I'm the one tagging along, saying, "I miss you." "When are you coming home?" Marking it on the calendar when he has a day off.

Mornings when I drive my daughter to work, if a song she likes comes on the radio, she turns up the volume and I know better than to talk. She loses herself in the music. She doesn't want to hear what I have to say. And I understand.

But underneath the understanding, there's this feeling, this growing awakening: This is how she felt, how my son felt years ago. Afraid that something—some song, some play, some activity, some person—would come along and take me away from them. She shouldn't like that song more than she likes me, a child thinks. She shouldn't be able to have fun without me. So the child complains and the child imposes. Here I am. Look at me.

Here I am. Look at me, this adult wants to say. But of course I don't. I simply understand a little better when my ten-year-old sulks when I am someplace she can't be. Finally, after all these years, I am beginning to understand why children cry when they are left behind.

Beverly Beckham

A Daughter's First Dance

She was just a little girl when her four big brothers began going to dances. She helped polish their shoes, find matching socks for them and went with her mom to pick up corsages at the florist and suits at the cleaners. She'd stand in a corner giggling as they posed with their dates for photos and she always felt so special when they'd tell her to join in the picture too. At the breakfast table the next morning she'd sit wide eyed as she listened to their stories from the night before.

"Don't worry, Amy," they'd say. "Someday you'll go to a dance, too. And then it'll be our turn to watch you and the poor guy who's gotta pass our inspection."

Of course, someday was never going to come, for she was just a little girl with ponytails and a teddy bear.

And then incredibly, someday came, but the four brothers were gone. She called the oldest in Connecticut to tell him she was going to her first dance.

"Tell me about the guy," he said.

She called her second brother at Northern Illinois University.

"Tell me about the guy," he replied.

She called her third brother at Eastern Illinois University

and her fourth brother at Notre Dame. They both responded, "Tell me about the guy."

Her wrinkled, rapidly aging parents logged 2,158 miles looking for *the* perfect dress, while their telephone compiled 964 minutes as she and her friends made plans, canceled them, made new ones and changed them yet again.

At last the big night arrived and so did the brothers. Dan came home to chauffeur the group. Mike arrived to tease her, and Bill drove in because he realized how much she wanted him there. Jack couldn't fly in, but the bouquet of flowers he sent hugged her heart in a way she would always remember.

Suddenly the door bell rang and the weeks of anticipation were over. This was it! He was here! He was everything a first date should be—good-looking, kind and easy to talk to. Best of all, he attended her brothers' high-school alma mater.

Once again, as in years gone by, the front room was filled with beautiful young people as photos were taken and flowers exchanged. Then, in a flurry of butterflies and laughter, they were gone.

When the house was quiet her parents walked past her bedroom. Amidst the wet towels, make up, nail polish, and assorted clutter, he sat—the teddy bear—a reminder that even though a young woman left for her first dance, a little girl would still return home at the end of the night.

Alice Collins

Love Notes

Talking to children is simple. It's getting them to listen that is the real challenge. As my children approached school age, I noticed they had already perfected the skill of looking attentive while tuning me out. They nodded automatically while they gazed into space and pretended they were listening. I knew I was going to have to come up with an alternate means of communication if we were going to survive the years ahead.

While contemplating the situation, I discovered that as soon as they learned to read, they couldn't resist reading a note. If it looked like it was written to a sibling or my husband, so much the better. I also noticed that notes written in small print or buried under a stack of mail caught their attention quicker than ones posted on the refrigerator.

I began to experiment with little notes such as "Please put your shoes away" and "Do not eat the cake." At first, this was successful. They felt grown-up receiving their own "letters," and I saw instant results. Unfortunately, as they grew older, they caught on. I could leave a gigantic note on a bedroom door and be told, "Gee, Mom, what note?" This is where ingenuity took over. I stopped leaving notes.

Instead, I changed my identity and became The Maid, The Management, a Demolition Crew or anyone else appropriate to the note I was leaving. If a bedroom became too messy, a large CONDEMNED sign and a locked door brought almost immediate results. The Demolition Crew left notice that they were coming in to clear things out if improvements weren't made soon. The Management posted notices that threatened to take away bathroom privileges if the sinks didn't get cleaned, or The Ants left a note if cookie crumbs were found on a bedroom floor.

Not all the notes were negative. Once The Maid left a note in the bathroom to let the children know they had been doing a good job. "Aren't you brushing your teeth anymore? There hasn't been toothpaste on the ceiling, mirror or light fixtures lately! Keep up the good work." Another one said, "Your bed has been made for two weeks straight. Have you been sleeping elsewhere?"

The notes caught on, and the members of our household never took a trip without notes tucked into their suitcases. Children going off to camp, Dad on a business trip—everyone received notes. One time my husband was cheered up in a lonely hotel room when he found the scribbled, misspelled message "I mess you" neatly tucked into a sock.

I received my share of love notes, too. The children would remind me to pick up a band uniform at the cleaners or request that I buy hair spray. Sometimes there were silly notes that stated, "Homemade cookies make children feel loved."

There were also the simple notes that touched my heart, like the one on an extremely difficult morning when my second-grader and I had gotten off on the wrong foot. She stomped off to school in a huff, and I was left feeling like the world's worst mother as I went out to do my grocery shopping. I dragged myself up and down the aisles, shopping list in hand. Glancing down at my list, I discovered in between my entries a tiny "I sorry" written in her childish handwriting. I blinked fast and swallowed the lump in my throat before I continued my shopping with a new spring in my step.

I also left notes at special times. When one of the children was facing a difficult problem, an encouraging word could be found tucked into a lunch sack, jacket pocket or even a shoe. I tried to remember important test days, choir tryouts or other traumatic events and offer a written word of encouragement. Abundant praise might be found under a pillow or wrapped around a toothbrush after a special accomplishment.

The notes were usually accepted without any verbal response. Every once in a while, I would hear a "Cute, Mom, cute," after a note was found. However, the notes always seemed to produce action and results.

Looking back, I realize our notes were a successful way for all of us to express ourselves. It saved me from having to nag about chores, brought comfort during difficult times and made praise seem more meaningful when it was put in writing. Most important, I retained my sense of humor as I tried to think of original ways to approach problems. In recent years, the notes I found were a bit different from the original, scrawled, misspelled messages. There was one pinned to a wedding dress that was left to be taken to the cleaners that said, "Mom and Dad, thanks for the wonderful wedding. It was a dream come true."

The next week, I found one after my youngest child returned to college. As I dug into her hamper to do the remaining laundry she had left behind, I found a crumpled piece of paper. It said, "Way to go, Mom . . . love you a bunch."

As the years passed and my daughters all married and left home, I thought our note-writing days were over. However, I still find unexpected notes left in strange places long after they have returned home from visits at my house. And I'm not beyond leaving notes at their houses, too!

June Cerza Kolf

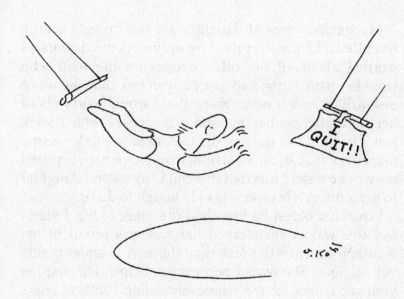

Rite of Passage

My sixteen-year-old daughter got her driver's license recently and I was surprised by my reaction. Of course, I worried about all the other drivers on the road who wouldn't have much patience or even care that she was a new driver. And it was a given that I would worry about her inexperience, her measured responses which were just a fraction too slow as she took time to think about a maneuver that must be instinctive. No, what surprised me was how sad I was that this child, my second daughter to get a driver's license was old enough to do so.

When my oldest had reached this stage of life, I didn't feel this way. I encouraged her and was proud of her accomplishment—the fact that she was confident, sure yet cautious. She would become my helper, ferrying her younger sisters for me when scheduling conflicts arose. But, my oldest was always like that—the one I depended on, the most responsible. She thrived on that image of herself and I was glad.

But, my second daughter, like her two younger sisters, was and I guess still is (at least in my mind) "one of the little ones" even though she, her older sister and I can wear each other's clothes and shoes. This rite of passage, getting a driver's license, is quite literally a right of passage—their right to leave the nest that I have created for them. They are on the road to leaving me. And even though this is, of course, what I want for them, it made me sad.

When these first two were little, about six and three, we had a swingset in the back yard. It was the kind with ladders on either side and bars across the top. A child could climb the ladder then hand over hand to from bar to bar until she reached the other side, about eight feet away. My six-year-old had no problem doing this; if she couldn't make it all the way across, she simply dropped to the ground, a distance of only about three feet. But, I didn't want my three year old to do this maneuver because, smaller and less experienced than her older sister, if she fell, the drop was far enough that she could get hurt.

One afternoon, I left them playing on the swings and went inside for something. I glanced out the kitchen window to see my three year old climbing the ladder, preparing to imitate her big sister who was happily swinging across the top of the swingset. For some reason, I did not rush outside to stand beneath my little girl as she attempted this feat. Something made me stand where I was, perfectly still, and watch.

With her big sister calling encouragement, my daughter began her trek. First one hand grasped the bar, then the other hand grabbed the next one and so forth. I could hear my older daughter telling her, "You can do it! Don't look down. Just look straight ahead! You can do it! Good girl!"

And she did it.

I ran outside, cheering and clapping, letting them both know how proud I was of each of them—the teacher and the student. The look on their faces made me glad I had stayed in the kitchen.

My daughter's achievement that day was a separation—but only a small one. I could champion them wholeheartedly then because what happened was only a childhood milestone. They could go through many such experiences and even though they learned something new each time, acquired some new degree of independence, they would still emerge on the other side of that experience as children. They would still be within my purview.

But that driver's license could take them someplace else, someplace without me. I suppose that place is adulthood.

I hadn't been sad when my oldest daughter reached that stage and I understood why. She had always exhibited the tendency to be grown-up, mature, yet she still needed me. Our bond was always clear, secure, strong even with the element of her character.

But, with number two, her new-found independence pushed her out of the grouping of "the little ones" that she had shared with her two younger sisters and into the smaller circle that included her older sister and me.

She's a harbinger, this child of mine, of what will surely be in the coming years. And I know that even though she's reached this stage, she's still a work in progress. She still needs me, her father, and her big sister to encourage her, love her and champion her. So will the younger ones when their turns come.

I have my apprehensions. But they are more for myself than for her. As I climb into the passenger seat, I glance over at my sixteen year old. And there she is, my daughter, looking straight ahead, focused as she should be, on the road in front of her.

Marsha Arons

Wishes for My Daughter

My daughter turns eighteen today. For her birthday I am giving her a set of Agatha Christie novels, a Billie Holiday T-shirt and a CD by an alternative rock group whose name I could hardly bring myself to say at the music store. But like the fairies who gathered around Sleeping Beauty's bassinet, what I wish for her cannot be bought. As she crosses the threshold into womanhood, I wish that:

- She discovers a calling she is so passionate about that it is impossible to tell where work leaves off and life begins.
- Good fortune and reasonable caution collaborate to keep her safe in a violent world.
- Just once she falls in love so hard with the wrong person that the ride is worth the fall.
- She continues to be lifelong friends with her little brothers. (Who else could commiserate with her so well about what they all call "Mom's ways?")
- She never has to wear hose and heels for work, only for dancing.
- She tries anything legal that interests her.

- She enjoys good health (accompanied someday with a recognition of the need for outerwear in winter, which other parents tell me will kick in when she is about twenty-one).
- She spends her life in the company of great dogs, good books and loyal friends.
- She finds a community of faith in which she feels at home.
- She continues to make music all of her life, even if—maybe especially if—it's just for fun.
- She finds a wonderful husband with a great sense of humor who adores women, especially her (but not for at least a decade).
- She discovers it is more important to be purposeful than happy, and more important to be happy than rich.
- She experiences sex as both profound and hilarious.
- She has at least one child, so that she can forgive her parents. (Okay, okay, only if she really wants one).
- The breast cancer epidemic is under control by the time she reaches the age of significant risk.
- In these coming years she is able to separate from her father and me without pain and guilt (well, not too much guilt).
- She continues to regard food as one of the great pleasures of life, and never gets crazed about dieting.
- She has many wonderful adventures involving passports and cross-country train trips, but that she does not terrify me with the dangerous parts until much later, over a glass of wine that she's buying.
- She always knows she can count on her parents' unconditional love, even when we drive her head-banging crazy.

Rebecca Christian

The Handwriting on the Wall

A weary mother returned from the store,
Lugging groceries through the kitchen door.
Awaiting her arrival was her eight-year-old son,
Anxious to relate what his younger brother had done.

"While I was out playing and Dad was on a call,
T. J. took his crayons and wrote on the wall!
It's on the new paper you just hung in the den.
I told him you'd be mad at having to do it again."

She let out a moan and furrowed her brow.
"Where is your little brother right now?"
She emptied her arms and with a purposeful stride,
She marched to his closet where he had gone to hide.

She called his full name as she entered his room.
He trembled with fear—he knew that meant doom!
For the next ten minutes, she ranted and raved
About the expensive wallpaper and how she had saved.

Lamenting all the work it would take to repair,
She condemned his actions and total lack of care.
The more she scolded, the madder she got,
Then stomped from his room, totally distraught!

She headed for the den to confirm her fears.
When she saw the wall, her eyes flooded with tears.
The message she read pierced her soul with a dart.
It said, "I love Mommy," surrounded by a heart.

Well, the wallpaper remained, just as she found it,
With an empty picture frame hung to surround it.
A reminder to her, and indeed to all,
Take time to read *the handwriting on the wall!*

Valerie Cox

Leftover Halloween Candy

People crave laughter as if it were an essential amino acid.

Patch Adams

I polished off the last piece of Halloween candy today. Don't ask me why I have the need to tell you this, but there it is. For trick-or-treaters, my husband and I stocked fifty Hershey bars, fifty Nestlé snacks and fifty Baby Ruths.

We had a total of three beggars. They were on the honor system. We held the basket out and let them choose. The little five-year-old was adorable. She delicately reached in and extracted a single candy bar. The kid behind her, who looked about eight, took three without batting an eye. And the oldest one, who probably had a mustache under his mask and drove the car, reached in with both pig hands and dragged out five or ten pieces. It was like one of those giant claws in a machine where you're trying to snare the diamond ring.

I had every intention of putting the leftover candy in the freezer, but my husband said, "Why? You'll just break a tooth or buy a chain saw." He thinks he's funny.

I buy candy only once a year. I know how I am. If it is around, I will not rest until every piece is gone.

I did not eat the Halloween candy indiscriminately. I used it as rewards.

I rewarded myself for remembering to take the chicken innards out of the freezer and deposit them in the trash can the night before garbage day. I got a candy for every right answer I got on *Jeopardy!* I got a treat for ironing the back of my husband's shirt and another for eating a two-day leftover.

One night just before dinner, my son dropped by in time to see me pop a Baby Ruth in my mouth.

"I thought you always told us candy would ruin our dinner."

"This is different. It's a reward."

"For what?" he asked.

"For having the strength to stop at one candy bar while I'm cooking."

"Come to think of it," he said, "all that Halloween candy we got that you stored in the freezer, we never saw again."

"I told you the ants got it."

"How could ants live in the freezer?"

"They dressed warm."

"I think you polished it off a piece at a time."

When he left, I was stressed from all the questions. A Hershey bar seemed to soothe me somehow.

Erma Bombeck

3

ON DEATH AND DYING

Unable are the Loved to die
for Love is immortality.

Emily Dickinson

Gramma's Blanket from Heaven

I couldn't have been more than seven years old the night I climbed out of bed and tiptoed downstairs to look for my grandmother. Gramma liked to sit up watching *Marcus Welby, M.D.*, and sometimes I'd sneak down in my pajamas, stand quietly behind her chair where she couldn't see me and watch the show with her. Only tonight, Gramma wasn't watching TV. Nor was she in her room when I returned upstairs to look for her.

"Gramma?" I called, my young heart pounding with alarm. I couldn't ever remember wanting my grandmother when she wasn't right there to answer the call. Then I remembered Gramma had gone on an overnight trip with some friends. That made me feel better, but there were still tears in my eyes.

I dashed back to my room and burrowed beneath the afghan Gramma had crocheted, as snug and warm as one of her hugs. *Gramma will be home tomorrow*, I comforted myself. *She wouldn't ever go away and not come back.*

Since before I was born, Gramma Rosie had lived with our family: my mom and dad and my older brother, Greg. We lived in Holland, Michigan, and when I was in the fifth grade, we bought a big new house. My mom had to go to work to help with the mortgage.

Lots of my friends went home to empty houses after school because both their parents worked. But I was one of the lucky ones. My mom's mom was always at the back door waiting for me with a glass of milk and a thick slice of buttery banana bread piping hot from the oven.

Sitting at the kitchen table, I'd tell Gramma all about my day. Then we'd play a few hands of rummy. Gramma always let me win—at least until I got good enough to put up a real challenge on my own.

Like most kids, I'd have my bad days at school or get into an occasional tussle with one of my friends. Or else maybe my parents might tell me we simply couldn't afford that new bicycle I wanted more than anything. It didn't matter what the reason; if I was upset, I could always count on Gramma to wrap her arms around me in a hug. Gramma was a big woman, too, and when she hugged you, you really knew you'd been hugged. It was great. I don't remember ever once being in Gramma's arms when I didn't honestly believe her when she told me everything was going to be just fine.

Then, one day when I was seventeen, everything wasn't fine anymore. Gramma had suffered a heart attack, and the doctors said she might never get well enough to come home.

How many nights had I fallen asleep to the muffled sounds of Gramma praying in her bedroom next door and mentioning me to God by name? Well, that night I talked to God myself. I told him how much I loved my grandmother and begged him not to take her away from me. "Couldn't you wait until I don't need her anymore?" I asked with youthful selfishness, as though there'd ever come a day when I would have stopped needing my grandmother.

Gramma died a few weeks later. I cried myself to sleep that night and the next, and for many more after that. One morning, I carefully folded the afghan my grandmother had crocheted and carried it to my mom. "I can't bear feeling so close to Gramma without being able to talk to her and get a hug," I sobbed. My mother packed the blanket away for safekeeping, and to this day it remains one of my most cherished possessions.

I missed Gramma terribly. I missed her joyous laughter, her quiet words of wisdom. She wasn't there to help me celebrate my high school graduation, or the day eight years ago when I married Carla. But then something happened that let me know Gramma had never really left me, that she was watching over me still.

A few weeks after Carla and I moved to Paris, Arkansas, we learned that Carla was pregnant. It turned out to be a difficult pregnancy with serious complications. We spent so much time in the hospital that I lost my job mere weeks before Carla's due date.

Near the end, Carla developed toxemia, and the day our son was born the doctors wouldn't allow me in the delivery room because they were afraid that neither Carla nor the baby was going to survive. I paced the waiting room, praying as the baby's vital signs plummeted and Carla's blood pressure rocketed sky high. My mom and dad were on their way south from Michigan, but they weren't there yet. I'd never felt so helpless and alone.

Then, suddenly, I felt Gramma's arms embracing me in one of her hugs. "Everything's going to be just fine," I could almost hear her saying. Then as quickly as Gramma had come, she was gone again.

Meanwhile, in the next room, the doctors completed the emergency C-section. The instant our son was born, his heartbeat grew strong and steady. Within minutes Carla's blood pressure began to drop, and she, too, was soon out of danger.

"Thank you, Gramma," I whispered as I stood staring through the nursery window at our beautiful new baby, whom we named Christian. "I only wish you could be here to give my son half of the love and wisdom you passed on to me."

One afternoon, two weeks later, Carla and I were home playing with Christian when someone knocked at our door. It was a deliveryman with a package—a gift for Christian. The box was addressed to "a very special grandbaby." Inside, there lay a beautiful hand-crocheted baby blanket and a pair of booties.

My eyes filled with tears as I read the card. "I knew I wouldn't be here for the grand day of your birth. I made arrangements by proxy to make this blanket for you. The booties I made before I left on my journey." The note was signed "Great-Gramma."

Gramma's eyesight was so weak near the end that she'd had to ask my Aunt Jeanette to help out with the blanket. But she'd struggled to finish the booties herself, and she did it all during those few brief weeks before she died.

Bill Holton
Excerpted from Woman's World

Homer and the Racing Car

A clown is like aspirin, only he works twice as fast.

Groucho Marx

During a visit to Stanford Children's Hospital in Palo Alto, California, I performed a thirty-minute show for the children in a large recreational room. After the show, I walked around visiting children who were not able to leave their rooms to attend the show. Completing this portion of my appearance, I was preparing to leave when a young woman walked up to me and asked if it would be at all possible to have me visit the intensive care ward to visit her six-year-old son. He just loved clowns, but he was dying of cancer—with but a few days to live.

As I walked up to the entrance to the intensive care ward, I was asked to place a protective mask on my face. This of course bothered me because it covered up most of my makeup and would not allow me to use the facial expressions that show a clown's character. However, I understood and permitted the hospital staff to place the mask on my face. I then proceeded to walk into the intensive care room, along with the now masked mother, to visit the child.

When I walked into the room seven other people stood around the boy. I later found out that one was a doctor, another was a private nurse, two older people were the grandparents, an older boy was a brother, an older girl was a sister and the last gentleman was the father—all wearing masks and filled with deep sadness. The six-year-old boy was lying in bed with tubes hooked up to both arms and into his nose. He was making a soft groaning sound with his eyes closed.

I looked around the room and made eye contact with each and every person in the room and noticed that one gentleman was wearing an identification tag indicating he was a doctor. I looked at him and he nodded his head indicating that I could walk up to the bed and talk to Jimmy. At his bedside, in a quiet voice, I called out his name several times. He moved his head from side to side but would not open his eyes and continued making the very low groaning sound. I then took him by his right hand and said, "Hello, Jimmy. My name is Homer the Clown, and I came here to see you because I heard you really liked clowns." His eyes opened immediately and he lay there for a few seconds in total amazement looking at me and not making a sound. I continued talking to him, telling him that I had heard he was in this room and I just had to stop by to say hello.

At that point, he started to smile and very quietly said, "Hi, Homer. I remember you." The second he spoke those words, there was a gasp from several of the people in the room and when I turned to look at them, I noticed tears filling their eyes. I turned back to Jimmy and he quietly continued telling me that he had attended a show in which I was the performer and wondered if I remembered him. I, of course, informed him that I did remember him and that I was very pleased that we had a chance to meet again. This made him extremely happy, and he looked at his parents and said, "Dad, Mom, Homer remembers me." It was at that point that I had to really get hold of my emotions because I could not allow myself to let Jimmy see the tremendous sadness I felt as a lump rose in my throat.

I quickly reached into a bag that I had with me and presented him with a small gift. All my gifts were wrapped up so children in the hospital would have the fun of unwrapping them. Then I realized that it would be impossible for him to open it with all the tubes that were hooked up to his hands and arms. So I slowly took his right hand in mine and pretended that I was helping him open the present. During the entire time we unwrapped the present, I continued talking to Jimmy, telling him what a great job he was doing unwrapping the little package. He was all smiles. The present was a racing car, and he was full of joy when he saw it. I asked him if he would allow me to come over to his home when he got out, and we could play with it together. His response was, "You bet!"

At that point I felt it was time to leave, even though I had only been there about ten minutes. I had accomplished my mission, and I did not want to overstay my visit. I gave Jimmy a light hug and told him I would be back to see him in a few days. He said that would be okay, and he would be waiting for me. I then shook the hand of everyone in the room and received hugs from the grandparents and also from the two older children.

The parents followed me outside and then the most emotional part of the visit transpired. We all cried and hugged each other and very few words were spoken. There did not need to be as we all knew what had happened. However, it was during those happy but difficult moments in the hallway that I found out Jimmy had not spoken for the past three days, and when he said, "Hi,

Homer," everyone in the room gasped with amazement. I thanked the parents for asking me to share these moments with them, shed a few more tears and prepared to return to my home. Fortunately Dee, my wife, had assisted me with the evening's program, or I would have had to drive home myself.

The next morning, when I awoke from a seemingly sleepless night, I felt tired but extremely blessed that I had been able to give Jimmy a little happiness. Later that day, I received a phone call from Jimmy's father informing me that they couldn't thank me enough for what I had done the evening before, because Jimmy had died that very next morning—still holding the small racing car in his hands. He also informed me that the family had decided that Jimmy was going to be buried with the racing car in his hands.

As a clown, I believe I am here not to understand why a young boy dies, but to make a smile appear on a face. I am here to try to make youngsters like this have a little less pain. We laugh, we cry, we share and we also make promises like the one I made with Jimmy. One day Jimmy and I will meet again, and we will play together with that toy racing car that we once shared.

Don Burda
Submitted by Joel Goodman

My Mother's Eyes

I remember a period in my childhood when I was absolutely terrified that my mother was going to die. It was the worst thing I could imagine. I worried about it every day.

She seemed to be in good health, but I worried anyway.

My father was a very difficult alcoholic, and the thought of living alone with him was horrifying.

By the time I was fifteen or sixteen, I had grown more independent and the fear subsided. I was confident that I could take care of myself, and could find another place to live, away from my father. So I no longer worried.

And then, when I was eighteen, my mother died. She was only fifty-four. But ironically, her death taught me that sometimes the thing we fear most can turn out to be a blessing.

She had developed a fast-growing, malignant brain tumor that would take her life less than three months after we got the diagnosis. My father had searched frantically for the finest internists, surgeons and oncologists in the world. His wife, he said, would have nothing less than the best medical care money could buy.

But the verdict was unanimous—there was nothing to be done.

There were experimental tests and new chemotherapy treatments, but no one thought they would help. And they didn't. What the doctors did try only made her more sick.

Six weeks before she died, her medical team announced that there was nothing further to do. Our family doctor suggested that she be moved to a nursing home. But she didn't want to go to a nursing home. She wanted to be in her own home.

We agreed, and eventually we brought her home. It was frightening, because we had no idea what would happen to her and how it would affect us. And we didn't have the communication tools we now have to deal with dying and grief.

So we had to rely on our intuition. And we had to trust in the universe. During those weeks, I experienced a peace deep inside me, something beyond my intellect. When I stood back from my fear, my mother's dying began to feel like a natural process.

Years later, I heard someone say, "Dying is absolutely safe." And that is what I instinctively felt during those weeks with my mother. Her body was changing and falling away. I don't know why, but somehow I felt that she was safe.

She ultimately lost the ability to speak. So the house became very quiet as the rest of us spoke in soft, hushed tones. It almost took on the atmosphere of a temple or shrine.

She and her hospital bed and medications had moved into the guest room. There were nurses on duty around the clock. I sometimes avoided going in to see her because I didn't know what to say. The trivial, contrived small talk we often fall into at such times now seemed profane. I gagged on the very thought of meaningless chatter in the face of the most awesome event I had ever witnessed.

One afternoon, I walked in and sat on the edge of her bed. My mother was an elegant, glamorous woman. She seemed so peaceful. . . .

She lay silent and looked at me. I looked at her. I took her hand in mine. She had no energy left, but I felt her squeeze my hand so subtly, so tenderly. I looked deep into her crystal blue eyes.

I kept looking, and as I looked, her eyes got deeper and deeper and deeper. Our eyes locked, and for the next thirty minutes we never diverted our gaze away from each other. We just sat there gazing. And I looked back and back and back, deeper and deeper into her soul.

It was like riding through a tunnel to the core of her soul. And suddenly, there, deep within the withered bulk of a body was the being I knew as my mother. Her love, her care, her nurturing and her compassion all shone through, more radiant than I had ever seen them before. All the barriers between us melted away in the brilliance of the light within her. I sensed that as her body withered, her soul had gained strength.

She squeezed my hand again. And as she did, she gently nodded her head two or three times. In that moment, though not a word had passed between us, I knew that we had said everything that needed to be said. It was okay. She was okay. We loved each other deeply. We honored each other completely. We were grateful for the love we had shared all these years. She would go on, and I would go on, and the place we had touched together would never disappear for either of us. Because somehow, there in her room that day, she and I had shared a glimpse of eternity.

I felt tears, but they were tears of awe more than sadness. And I knew that because I had been willing to go past my horror and fear, to look past her physical deformities and look deeply into her soul, that I had seen her more clearly and contacted her more intimately than ever before.

A few days later, she died. It was a beautiful, peaceful Sunday afternoon. A glorious sunset washed the house in brilliant golden hues, and a warm, gentle breeze soothed and caressed us. A profound aura of peace filled our home. My father, my two sisters and I all held hands around my mother's bed and kissed her good-bye. Then we put our arms around each other and, probably for the first time ever, shared a family embrace. We put our heads together and all softly cried.

After a while, we silently moved outdoors. The sun had nearly set, but not quite. And as I looked at it, something occurred to me that I had never noticed before. The sun is most radiant when it's setting. And though it disappears from view, it never dies.

I felt the same about my mother. Like the sun, she had faded from view. But I knew she'd always be with me, even in the darkest of hours.

I looked at my family and marveled at the sense of closeness and intimacy we all felt, at how this moment of wonder and sadness had melted away the walls of separation families often hide behind. For in that moment, the resentments, petty anger and judgments dissolved into the familial love we all shared. We were one consciousness, one heart. My mother, in giving up her own life, had brought the rest of the family together in a closeness and bond that we share to this day. Simultaneously, we felt profound sadness and profound joy.

John E. Welshons

My Dad

In every person's life there needs to be a counselor or a caring, nurturing, encouraging friend. They give people guidance. They give people hope. They help them accept themselves for who they are. They help them set goals. They help them find their purpose. It is truly the work of angels.

Tom Krause

The earliest memory I have of my father is one of me as a young boy grabbing his hand and him guiding me along as we walked together. I'll always remember that. As I grew older I remember my dad and I listening to the high school basketball games together on our transistor radio. I would write the names of the players on a piece of paper and keep track of each players points as the game went on. I never could stay awake for the whole game because I was still young and I always fell asleep before the game was over. When I would wake up in the morning I would be in my bed and the score sheet would be lying next to me. The score sheet would be filled out with the final score on it completed by my father before he carried me to bed. I'll always remember that.

I remember the times when my father would bring his bread truck by the house early in the morning on those cold days when I was home from school over Christmas break. I used to ride on the floor of that bread truck as he delivered the bread to the stores. The smell and the warmth from the bread made my mouth water and kept me warm both at the same time. I'll always remember that.

In high school I became very interested in athletics. My father would attend all my games. My senior year our football team qualified to play in the state championship game. It was the first time in the history of our school. The night before the game my father came to me and sadly told me that he would not be able to attend the game. He had to deliver the bread to the stores and the game was a three hour drive from his route. He said he would listen to the game on the transistor radio. I said that I understood. The next day as game time approached I thought about my dad. As I lined up for the opening kick-off I happened to look across the field into the parking lot. There I saw his bread truck pulling into the stadium. He made the game and we won that state championship. I'll always remember that.

Years later I had become a teacher and coach. Early one morning my wife and I were awakened by the sound of the telephone ringing at 5:30 A.M. As I struggled to answer the phone I'll never forget the sound of the sheriff's voice on the other end telling me dad had just been killed in an automobile accident on his way to work. Cattle from a nearby farm had broken through their fence and wandered onto the highway. Being a dark, rainy morning my father had not seen them as he came over a ridge. The impact spun the car sideways in the highway before a semi-trailer collided with it. I was devastated. I could hear my heart beat in my ears. I hung up the phone and walked back into the bedroom and sat on the edge of the bed. My wife kept asking me who was on the phone but I couldn't speak. The hardest thing I've ever done in my life was say the words, "my dad is gone." I'll never forget that.

After that things didn't really matter to me. I went about my life but I really didn't care. It was as if someone had taken my heart from my body and I was just a robot. I went to work. I still taught school but I was just going through the motions.

One day I was on the playground at school supervising a first grade recess when something happened that I couldn't foresee. A little boy walked up to me and grabbed my hand. His hand held mine the same way I used to hold my father's when I was his age by the last two fingers.

In that instant my father came back to me. In that instant I found my purpose again. You see even though my father was gone he had left something with me. He left me his smile. He left me his compassion. He left me his touch. My purpose was to use those gifts as he did. From that day forward I started. I'll always remember that!

Tom Krause

Whistling Pete

Freedom is not free.

Martin Luther King Jr.

The American flag, fireworks, friends, picnics, chicken, hot dogs, baked beans, parades, bands and celebrations are all part of the Fourth of July. That early summer holiday, we pause to honor a time in our history with cheers, bangs, pops and whistles. This day was given to us by the blood and foresight of generations past, and it is full of promises that we must keep for the future. A happy day, at least for most of us.

"Hi," was my greeting to one of our midafternoon customers at the fireworks booth. "Are you looking for any particular display of fireworks?"

"Yes," came the reply of the fortyish-year-old man who stood on the other side of the wooden booth. "I need a firecracker."

This was my third year selling fireworks for the Chaparral High School Band Booster Club, and I took pride in my knowledge of these "treats" for the eyes and ears. Thanks to my son, I know what every one of these does or at least what it was designed to do.

"Would you like to see one of our packaged displays or the ones here on the counter that can be bought separately?"

"Just one," returned the gentleman as he avoided eye contact.

"Well, let me see. We have some small fountains and some large ones. Perhaps you'd like a smoke ball or a whistler."

"Just one firecracker," persisted the man. "I want it to pop is all."

"How old is the child?" I responded as if he'd told me it was for a child, but I didn't know that. Not for sure.

"It doesn't matter," returned a voice that now became more determined with a man's resolve to find just the right firecracker.

It was clear to me that this child was special. That the Fourth of July was special. But I found it hard to believe that just one firecracker could remedy whatever it was that came between this father and child.

I smiled. "Well, here's just the thing," I said as I held up a party popper. "This makes one pop and sprinkles a little confetti."

"That won't do. It can't make a mess."

"Is this for the evening? Maybe a little fountain that sprinkles would be the best choice."

"No. Just a pop or a whistle."

The man allowed his voice to shake for the first time as he brushed the back of his hand up the side of his whiskered face and across his left eye. "I . . . I want this for my son's grave and I don't want it to make a mess in the mausoleum."

If one heart could touch another, this gentle, sad man had truly touched mine. He was right, the age didn't matter; neither did all the parades, fireworks, hot dogs or celebrations. All of the Fourths of July that had ever been or ever would be didn't matter to him or to his son. All that mattered was this man's need to give someone he'd loved and lost a shared moment of declaration.

"This is what you want." I gulped as I held up a Whistling Pete. "It whistles quite loudly, but it's what I'd get."

"Thanks," said the unnamed man as he edged a smile at me through watery eyes. "I'll take it."

I could have just given the Whistling Pete to this lonely man, but knew that it was a gift from a father to his son. His need prevailed over my selfish desire.

"They're fifty cents."

Two quarters dropped into the palm of my hand.

The man in a chambray shirt turned his back as he approached his sun-bleached burgundy Oldsmobile. He turned his head toward me and smiled gently as he clutched one Whistling Pete up by his face. He opened the car door and was gone.

If God was anywhere on July 4, 1995, he surely had one hand on the shoulder of this father as he knelt at the crypt of his son. Before the tears and silence that so gently fell in that mausoleum, one Whistling Pete sounded loudly and boldly on that day in July, and I know that it was heard in heaven.

Kathie Harrington

Legacy of Love

A package came in the mail today. I knew before opening it that it was from Gram.

Two months before, I traveled to England to say good-
bye to Gramps. He died in his sleep and the world had
lost a wonderful man. I lost my best friend.

Gram and I spent two weeks together. Unfortunately,
she was only a shadow of what she'd once been. The
spark had left her eyes and the spring in her step was
gone. I never saw her cry.

I wanted to take her home with me, but she refused.
Gramps' presence was in the house and she wanted to
stay there.

The day before I was to leave, Gram asked if I'd like
something of his to take home with me. She led me into
their bedroom and began to sort through his watches,
rings and cuff links. Recalling how he disliked dressing up
and "putting on airs," I asked for something special to
him—his gardening sweater.

Gram laughed, saying that she had tried for years to get
him to throw the old thing out. Feeling sad that she
didn't understand, I accepted a pair of cuff links.

That night, a sound woke me. I padded to the den and

there was Gram, sitting in his chair. She was crying softly. As I made my way back to my room, I realized something. She was wearing his gardening sweater.

I left with a heavy heart the next morning. As time passed, in her letters and phone calls, she sounded more like her old self. She was continuing on.

Then the phone call came form her dear friend. She told me Gram had died in her sleep the night before. As a final request, she asked that I not come out for her funeral. There was no one there for me to see. I respected her wishes with a heavy heart. Before hanging up, her friend said she would be sending a parcel by Gram's instructions.

I glanced down at the package on my table through tear-filled eyes, and slowly began to tear at the wrappings, sobbing. Inside were tiny boxes containing my grandparents' jewelry, which I will pass on to my own children someday. More importantly, I will tell them about two wonderful people I was blessed enough to have for my grandparents.

As I picked up the box, I noticed a thick layer of tissue covering its bottom. I reached in to remove it, and there, folded neatly, was Gramps' love-worn gardening sweater.

I took it out and slipped it on. Faintly, beneath the scent of laundry soap, sunshine, vegetable gardens, and a hint of pipe tobacco, linger the memories of Gramps. Smiling, I recall how he used to hide behind the shed to smoke that pipe, not wanting Gram to know.

I will go on to build my own family and memories that come with it. But these two dear people will never be forgotten.

Hope Saxton

The Wave Game

Giving is so often thought of in terms of the gifts we give, but our greatest giving is of our time, and kindness, and even comfort for those who need it. We look on these little things as unimportant—until we need them.

Joyce Hiffler

My mother died suddenly almost three years ago. She passed away less than two weeks before my wedding day. I was devastated. My wedding day was the best day of my life. She should have been there. I missed her terribly, and I still do. Even to this day, I do not spend many moments without thinking of her. Almost everything I do reminds me of her in some way.

Just this afternoon, I was driving home from running some errands and was behind an Explorer-type vehicle filled with what appeared to be a family of three young boys and their parents on an outing.

This brought back memories of trips my family used to take with my mother behind the wheel of the station wagon. We would all be loaded up with snacks and all sorts of neat stuff. "Are we there yet?" You know how that goes. These were some of the best times growing up. The road games we'd play were so much fun.

All three of the youngsters in the truck ahead of me today were facing my car, just staring. I thought about how my brothers, sister and I used to try to get people to wave from any of the other cars around us. Most of the time the people in the other cars were too busy driving to wave back. We got mostly frowns and brief nods from them. When someone waved, we would shriek with laughter and wave frantically back.

I suddenly got an urge to simply wave at the children in front of me. They simultaneously smiled and waved back. This made me smile. They would turn to their parents momentarily as if to tell them of our communication. We continued waving to each other. This moment was priceless. I couldn't help but giggle.

We kept this up for a few more minutes, and then I felt the need to pass this family and head on my way. I was sort of saddened that I might not be able to continue to cheer those boys—as well as have them cheer me.

I passed the truck, smiled and waved good-bye.

This was not to be the last that I would see of this family. We eventually ended up getting off at the same exit from the highway. The father waved at me to pull over. Instinctively, I got nervous. My mother had always taught me to be cautious about strangers. There are all sorts of crazy people out there these days. However, I knew we were close to the tollbooths. I felt safe in stopping.

The father got out of the truck and walked over to my car. I rolled down my window to see a wide-smiling face. "My name is Bill," he said. "I'm on a trip across the country with my sister and my three sons. My wife recently passed away, and my boys are quite uneasy about the trip. I want to thank you for what you did."

I told him I wasn't quite sure what he was thanking me for.

"My boys had been miserable this entire trip until you waved at them. You should know that you made a difference in their lives even if it is just for a brief moment. I want to thank you for being so kind."

I smiled and thanked him back. "I lost my mother three years ago," I said. "You and your boys brought back fond memories for me. Thank you for reminding me of great times our family spent while I was growing up. You and your boys have made my day a little brighter also. Please thank your sons for me as well."

I wished him well and said good-bye. I drove alongside his truck, as he returned to it. I gave one final wave at the boys as I passed. All three smiled and waved back.

Those boys will probably forget all of this in a few days, but I will never forget it. People seem to forget how one simple act of kindness can change someone forever. A wave and a thank-you, that is all it was. The thank-you I received as well as the smiles and waves I shared with those boys were more precious than you can imagine.

In the beginning, right after my mother died, I thought I would never get through the amazing grief I felt. I cried every time I thought of her. Now most times when I think of her, I smile.

This man was thanking me for making his sons smile. I hope he realizes that I was just as grateful for my smiles. I will never be too busy driving to wave.

Misty L. Kerl

Season of Miracles

As they listened to a recording of "The Star-Spangled Banner," twelve young ballplayers anxiously awaited the opening game of junior baseball in North Charleston, South Carolina. Feelings ran high among the seven- and eight-year-olds, members of the Steve Evans Reds.

One of the Reds, Jason Ellis "E. J." Fludd, eight, hovered near third-base coach Sandra Evans. "Aunt Sandy," E. J. asked searchingly, "is Coach Stevie up there watching us?"

Sandy, thirty-two, answered softly. "Yes, E. J. I think Steve's spirit is right here with us."

"Play ball!" the umpire shouted. Sandy, tears welling, watched her team dash onto the field. *This season is for you, Steve,* she thought, as her mind drifted back to a year earlier.

"Sandy, we have a dinner guest," Steve Evans called out as he strolled in the front door. Just home from baseball practice, Steve had with him a shy, black youngster the players all called E. J.

Steve always had a soft spot for kids. An easygoing thirty-four-year-old with reddish hair and a lanky frame, he had volunteered to coach the team. In the early spring of 1991, he'd rush home from his job as an insulation installer to get to the practice field.

Patient and encouraging, Steve proved an ideal coach for the restless, diverse group of youngsters—some white, some black, others Asian. "Several come from troubled backgrounds," he told Sandy. "I'm coaching to help them feel better about themselves."

One boy, E. J., laughed harder—and played harder—than all the others. He lived with his mother, who worked long hours as a cook at the Charleston Air Force Base. Having little contact with his father, E. J. was lonely much of the time. After every practice, he would give Steve a bear hug and say, "Thanks, Coach Stevie."

At dinner that first evening, E. J. won over the entire family. Soon he was coming regularly for dinner, often staying overnight. Sandy became "Aunt Sandy." Steve would include E. J. in family softball games with his son Timmy, twelve, daughter Stephanie, ten, and four nephews—Thomas, Steven and David Evans, and James Garvin. The four nephews played with E. J. on the team.

The only bad news that year was at the ballpark—where Steve's team lost game after game. E. J. would slump in dejection at every defeat, or when he made an error.

During one losing game, Steve put an arm around the boy. "Hold your head up, E. J.," he said. "You don't have anything to be ashamed of."

Steve then pulled out an Atlanta Braves baseball card. "See this?" he asked. "One day your picture will be on one of these."

E. J.'s eyes lit up. "You mean I could play for the Braves someday?"

"Sure, as long as you keep working hard and don't give up. You shouldn't ever give up on anything."

Then, on June 17, 1991, an uncle of Steve's told Sandy there had been an explosion at a chemical plant, where Steve was working that day. After a dozen fruitless phone calls to the area hospitals, Sandy heard the crushing news from Steve's employer. Steve had been killed when a chemical reactor exploded. Sandy slumped to the floor, all feeling draining out of her.

Sandy was seventeen, just out of high school, when she married Steve in 1976. They'd both grown up in modest neighborhoods. Once, while they were dating, the washing machine owned by Sandy's family broke down, and there was no money to buy a new one. Steve found a beat-up washer, fixed it, then gave it to Sandy's family. The thoughtfulness left Sandy stunned.

After Steve and Sandy were married, money remained tight—but they still had fun. Steve loved driving Sandy and the children to Florida's Disney World, or spending a day "tubing" on nearby lakes and rivers.

Now Sandy sat in the funeral home, numb with grief. Looking up, she saw Steve's team, in their uniforms, file slowly in. A few minutes later, Sandy noticed E. J., tears pouring down his cheeks, as he sat with his mother.

"He hasn't stopped crying since Steve died," E. J.'s mother said. Sandy opened her arms wide, and E. J. climbed into her lap. As he wept, Sandy held his trembling body close, trying to give him the comfort she couldn't give herself.

After Steve's funeral, the team played its remaining games in a daze. They lost them all.

In the following months, Sandy's sister, Louann Ackerman, grew increasingly worried. Sandy was sinking deeper and deeper into her private grief. When her sister stopped eating and lost forty pounds, Louann felt panic. "This may be her way of ending it all," she said to her husband, Ira.

Then early in 1992, Louann had an idea. "In Steve's memory," she told Sandy, "I want to sponsor this year's team for you."

"Funny," Sandy said. "I'd been thinking I might sponsor

the team myself as a way to honor Steve. He loved those kids." Sandy and Louann renamed the team the Steve Evans Reds, for Steve's red hair. When Sandy told E. J., he said, "I promise you Aunt Sandy, we're gonna win all our games for Coach Stevie." Steve's friend, Ron Gadsden, agreed to become coach and continue as manager.

On a warm March afternoon, the Reds gathered for their first practice. Forming the nucleus of the team were E. J., Sandy's four nephews and Ron Gadsden's son, Ryan. Because some of the previous season's players were over the age limit, new ones were added. Younger and smaller than the ones they replaced, some of the new boys had no idea how to catch or hit. *This is going to be a rough season,* Louann thought.

Coach Gadsden drilled the new kids on how to hold a bat and swing. E. J. coached them on the man that the team was named for. "Coach Stevie took a lot of time with us," E. J. explained, his voice cracking. "He was always nice, and he made us laugh." Then E. J. told the team, "We've got to win this year for Coach Stevie." Slowly, the message sank in, as the Reds approached their opening day on April 11.

In the first inning of the season's first game, the Charleston Apartments Giants took a quick two-run lead before the Reds came to bat. E. J. hit a home run to lead a four-run counter-attack. By the bottom half of the final inning, the score was tied 8-8. Then Thomas Evans hit a home run. To everyone's surprise, the Reds had won.

When the Reds won again, Louann noticed changes in her sister. During the games Sandy, leaden and unemotional after Steve's death, started clapping and shouting. By the time the Reds won their third game, she had begun eating again.

"With this team," Sandy told Louann, "I feel that Steve's not gone completely. There's a piece of him still here with all of us."

The team was also changing. The youngsters began saying, "We can't be beat!" Sandy, worried that E. J. and her nephews were feeling too much pressure to win for Steve, called them aside. "Remember," she said, "it's just a game."

"You don't understand, Aunt Sandy," E. J. said earnestly. "We *have* to win for Coach Stevie!"

Sandy turned away, fighting back tears. *If we ever lose,* she thought, *these kids'll be shattered.*

As the season entered May, the Reds kept on rolling. They took one game 16-7 and another 17-6.

Sandy drew strength from E. J. *Just look at this little boy,* she thought. *He's hurting so much, yet he's still so loving and joyful.* Slowly, Sandy began looking forward to the games and practices with a gladness she once feared she'd never feel again. Now when a game ended, she took the team for pizzas. She even found herself laughing out loud.

"It's a miracle we're winning," Louann told her husband after another Reds victory. "But the real miracle is seeing E. J. help Sandy to heal. I'm getting my sister back."

Near the end of the season, the undefeated Reds stood at the top of the league. To win the championship they had to beat the Giants—the team the Reds had defeated by only one run on opening day. That game stood as the Giants' only loss.

The day of the final game, May 23, the temperature soared into the nineties. The Giants took an early lead in the first inning with four runs. The Reds fought back, and by the end of the second inning, the two teams were tied 4-4. Then the Giants went on a hitting spree and moved ahead 10-4. This was the first time all season that the Reds had been so far behind. "Come on, we can still win," E. J. shouted to his teammates.

However, the tension became too much for Thomas Evans, and he suddenly burst into tears. Sandy raced out and pulled him close. "It's okay," she whispered.

"We're gonna lose, Aunt Sandy!" Thomas said.

"Don't worry about losing," she assured him. "We've done our best, so it's all right."

Although the Reds reduced the Giants' lead, they couldn't catch up. The Giants went ahead 12-9 with one inning to go.

The Reds trotted off the field for their last time at bat. Suddenly, Thomas Evans knelt near the pitcher's mound, drawing in the red dirt with his finger, then walked silently toward the dugout. On the mound he'd written his uncle's name.

"I wanted Uncle Steve to know we were thinking about him," Thomas told Sandy. Word of what the boy had done spread quickly through the Reds' dugout. Moments later, however, reality set in. The Reds had two runners on base—but there were now two outs. The dugout went silent.

The Reds' last hope was David Evans, the smallest player on the team. As he walked toward the plate, Louann prayed silently. *Dear Lord, please, help these kids. And Sandy.*

David, not much taller than his bat, made up for his small size with a scrappy attitude. On the first pitch, he swung awkwardly and missed. Then he fouled off another pitch. *It's finally over*, Sandy thought sadly to herself.

With the next pitch, David made contact, but the ball headed in the worst possible direction—straight toward first base and the best player on the Giants' team. Coach Gadsden, figuring the game was over, began walking toward the Reds' dugout.

The Giants' first baseman reached down to scoop up the ball—but it squirted past him.

David raced to second base as one run scored. This cut the Giants' lead to two, and there were runners on second and third. Thomas Evans, next at bat, sent the ball flying for a clean hit. Sandy waved two runners home. With the game now tied, the Reds and their fans traded high-fives.

The next batter, Ryan Gadsden, got another hit, and by the time E. J. got to the plate, there were three runners on base. On the second pitch, E. J. connected perfectly, and the ball sailed deep into right-center field—a grand slam.

His teammates mobbed him. Sandy jumped up and down in the coach's box.

The Reds now led for the first time in the game, and more hits followed. When the third out finally came, the Reds had pushed across eleven runs in all. "I've seen it, but I can't believe it," Louann yelled when Sandy returned to the dugout.

Disheartened and exhausted, the Giants went down without scoring. The Reds had won the league championship, 20–12. That night, E. J. went to sleep clutching his player trophy for the championship.

Eight days later, Sandy stood at Steve's graveside with E. J. and her four nephews. The date—May 31—would have been Steve's twenty-sixth birthday.

Sandy knelt and, on her husband's grave, placed a photograph of the Reds holding their team trophy. The picture was signed by all the players and coaches. "The team won the championship for you, Steve," Sandy said softly. "And we know you helped them do it."

She held a small figurine dressed in a baseball uniform with "Number 1 Coach" written on it. She placed the figurine on the grave. *I'll always remember you, Coach Stevie,* E. J. thought.

Then they all joined hands and prayed. A few moments later, they walked silently away.

After their undefeated regular season, the Steve Evans Reds entered the town's annual junior baseball tournament. "We'll win the tournament for Coach Stevie, too," E. J. told Sandy. And so they did. They won the final championship game 19–3, ending their 1992 season with a perfect 16–0 record.

John Pekkanen

The Gift of Joy

Humor is not a trick, nor jokes. Humor is a presence in the world—like grace—and shines on everybody.

Garrison Keillor

Chuck was thirteen when he came home from the hospital not because he was getting better, but because he wanted to be with the people he knew and loved when he died. A nurse was on duty to help with medications, and I came by the house to visit with him and his family several times a week. On most of my visits, Chuck was unconscious or groggy from the heavy intravenous doses of morphine he was given for pain control. But the last time I saw him alive, he was awake and remarkably lucid.

"I got something for you," Chuck said to me. He reached under his pillow and withdrew a rolled-up, somewhat crumpled sheaf of papers. "I want you to give this to my mom and dad after I die. You'll know when it's right, I guess. Will you?"

"What is it?" I asked.

"It's a list of all the fun we had, all the times we laughed."

I almost gasped in amazement. With all the fear and anger and disappointment he had every right to be feeling, here he was trying to look out for his parents.

"Like what?" I asked feebly, trying to regain my composure.

Chuck grinned and launched into a story I wouldn't have thought he had the strength to tell.

"Like the time Mom and Dad and Chrissie and Linda and me were dressed up as those guys in the Fruit of the Loom underwear ad, and Dad's driving us to the costume party. Dad was a bunch of grapes and I was an apple, and the others were different things like bananas and stuff. And Dad gets pulled over for speeding. When the policewoman came up to the car she looked in and just started laughin' really hard. I mean she could hardly stand up, ya know? And we all started laughing, and the cop said, 'Where you all headed—a salad bar?' Dad said he was sorry to be speeding, but his kids were getting so ripe that they were starting to draw flies. The cop laughed till she had to take off her dark glasses and wipe tears from her eyes, and then she said, 'Well, get out of here, but go slow. I don't want to find you squashed all over the highway.'"

Chuck laughed, and so did I. Later that night I looked over the pages to see a list that included Disneyland, horseback riding, camping, the speeding-fruit story and others, some of which made me laugh out loud. *What an incredible gift,* I thought. The list ended with a note from Chuck to his parents.

"I know you're real upset right now that I'm going away, but I don't want you to forget this stuff. I don't want you to just remember me being skinny and sick. Think about these things, too, because this is what I remember most."

C. W. Metcalf
Submitted by Shelley Jackson and Joel Goodman

Al

His room is rectangular with two sets of windows looking out on the street six floors below. There are two beds: One is Al's, the other his roommate's. Family pictures sit on a wooden night table that separates the beds. Over his bed are tacked greeting cards from his children and grandchildren. A yellow rosary stands guard as it hangs from the bedpost. He cannot clearly see any of what surrounds him.

Al is my father-in-law. He sits quietly in his soft contour chair at the foot of his bed. His eyes, once sharp and focused, are now clouded with cataracts. He stares down at his hands coupled in his lap. The same hands that turned the pages of dozens of books; built bookcases and shelves to hold them; animated his many conversations and arguments; the same hands that gave his daughter in marriage—now reach out in front of him as I approach. The arms seem to be clearing imaginary cobwebs as his eyes try to see who it is visiting with him. We shake hands, and I realize he knows who I am. His mouth begins to take the shape of a crescent moon lying on its back as he smiles and says simply, "Mike." He always recognizes me. He seldom knows his own family.

I pull up a chair next to him and place my arm over his shoulders. As is my custom when we visit, I begin our conversation. There are so many memories that are stored up in my brain. I leaf through them and bring one out to him. I recall our first meeting. I was dating his daughter for two weeks when she thought it was time I met her father. I tell him how apprehensive I felt wondering if he would accept me. A faint smile begins to form, but just as his cheeks begin to allow his mouth to expand into a smile, he stops. I realize this partial description of his past may not be enough to strike the responsive chord of memory. I tell him how, as we approached each other, I quickly brushed the palm of my sweaty hand across the front of my jacket extending it with all the confidence of a mouse cornered by a hungry lion. Now I notice the smile return.

He is a die-hard New York Yankees fan. I throw out a few names from the early teams like Ruth, Gehrig, Crosetti, and I watch his reaction. I realize I have unlocked another memory, which has been hidden in a file drawer in his brain. I always pictured his brain containing long hallways in which there were dozens of five-drawer file cabinets, crammed full. He smiles, reaches out his hand and places it on my arm. He remembers Crosetti on third, Ruth on first. "The one-two punch," he calls them. We cannot linger long on one subject; it is too much for him.

I talk to him about the bungling son-in-law he inherited when it came to being mechanically minded. I look to see if he remembers the time that I wanted to impress his daughter by putting up wall paneling. He was present in the living room as I began. It seemed easy; the book said it was. He likes this story. Al becomes a bit more animated. His arms lift from the arms of his chair and his hands draw an imaginary square on the space in front of him. He chides me about the number of nails I bent attempting to hammer the paneling to the wall. "You couldn't hit the broad side of a barn with a bass fiddle, I used to tell you, Michael, remember?" Yes I do. I had already ruined half a box of nails and a sheet of paneling. It would have caused more loss to my confidence had he not stepped in and removed the bass fiddle from my hands. "You Irish still haven't learned a thing yet," I remember him saying.

He immigrated from Italy with his family. He fought the battles of the streets as a youngster, learned the language and lived the poverty that so many early immigrants lived. He had an appetite for learning. At times during our weekly conversations, he will ask me, "What did you steal with your eyes today?" His eyes stole all the time. He would watch a skilled craftsman at work and learn how a particular job was done; then store it away in one of the file cabinets in his brain. When it was needed, all he had to do was reach in, pull it out and proceed with the task at hand. I tell him how I still have problems with some household plumbing or electricity, and I can tell that he would be anxious to help, if only he could remember. He gestures with his outstretched arms repeating the paneling episode and we both have a smile about it. Sometimes he cannot remember this. It's happening more now.

The books Al read over the years could fill a small room in a local library. His enthusiasm for what he read would spill over to all of us. He would paint pictures in our minds of the stories. I remember Irving Stone's *The Agony and the Ecstasy*, the story of Michelangelo. I had to read that book, after just listening to Al's descriptions. I talk to him now particularly about that story. I know he remembers because his eyes rise up and search the ceiling in his room. Have his eyes painted a scene there?

He asks me if I am married and how many children I have. I tell him that his daughter and I have just celebrated our twenty-fifth wedding anniversary and have five beautiful children. "The Irish couldn't possibly have beautiful children," he says, smiling at his own joke. I point to the picture on his night table and recite their names to him. He does not remember. I tell him how they used to bounce on his knee and play hide-and-seek with him in his apartment. I describe how they would hide in one of the closets waiting for their grandfather to find them. Opening the door, he would fumble around the hats and scarves on the top of the closet calling out their names as if they were hidden there. He would hear their tiny giggles and would only look harder and harder without seeing them. Then suddenly he would reach in between the coats and suits and grab hold of them. He tries to remember, and I know he wants to. "Did I do that every time they saw me?" he says. "Yes," I tell him, "and they loved it."

I cherish these memories. Al's room is his world now. I simply visit it. Hopefully, I can keep his world revolving for a long time to come.

Michael Haverty

The Gift

The parish priest was picking me up to take me to the funeral parlor. I was relieved I didn't have to walk because it was a bitter cold March day. The wind was as cold as I felt inside. My seventeen-year-old godson, Michael, was being buried the following morning. I had been sent to take care of Michael two years before. I was a health aide thinking that, at sixty-three, I should retire. But my supervisor asked me to take this case, a fifteen-year-old boy with muscular dystrophy. The hours were midnight until eight in the morning—hours I normally didn't care for. But Michael's home was within walking distance, so I took the job.

I met Michael's mom when I entered her modest home. I had taken care of many clients throughout the years, but nothing prepared me for Michael. A mere seventy pounds, large brown eyes, silken brown hair and a smile that would brighten any room. He required total care. Michael had one useless arm, which was positioned against his chest while his legs were permanently drawn up. He could not change positions by himself. His favorite expression was "No problem." I learned about Alf, the TV personality who used that expression, and replicas of Alf hung all over Michael's room.

During the long nights, Michael taught me to play Nintendo games. My guys fell between the buildings while Michael's men leapt over any obstacle. I was delighted one night to have my guys doing really well. Michael had a twinkle in his eyes when I discovered he had switched controls. We laughed a lot.

Every morning when I left Michael, I left part of myself with him. I spent my days just waiting to go back to him. It was a few weeks before his mother agreed to let me come in the daytime occasionally. I encouraged her to go out and have a little free time. She accepted. I discovered that Michael was an avid fan of our hometown football team, the Buffalo Bills. He was so excited when we watched them on TV that I soon got caught up in 'Bills fever,' too. I called their office and in just a few days, one of the players paid Michael a visit. They had a wonderful afternoon, taking pictures that we later had made into a poster.

It was about that time Michael saw Mrs. Barbara Bush on TV. He said, "She looks like a kind grandma." I wrote to Mrs. Bush. Later, when the letter with the return address of the White House arrived, Michael's eyes were larger than ever. I hadn't told him that I had written for fear she might not respond. Her answer was a warm, caring, encouraging letter. We framed it. Many times Michael told me how lucky he was to have his mom, friends and me. I was the lucky one.

It was agreed that Michael could spend a few days at my home. I wanted him to be in my large dining room, so he could see out the picture window. I called a second-hand dealer to take my dining room furniture. My pharmacist loaned me a hospital bed and the MD Association gave us a wheelchair, which could be adjusted so Michael could lie down. He couldn't sit up. Our parish priest had baptized Michael a few months before. He gave me the honor of being his godmother. I picked Michael up in the wheelchair and pushed him the half block to the church. I placed him near the altar. Father said, "We've been praying for Michael and here he is." Michael said he didn't know people clapped in church. The applause was deafening. On the way home, he told me he could happily die that day. He didn't die, but gained four pounds during his stay. Michael loved everyone, never complained and smiled always. He told me how he always wanted to be a football player or a policeman. His one regret was that his mom wouldn't have grandchildren. He was an only child, and his mother's two brothers died from MD.

Michael's seventeenth birthday was festive. Friends and relatives and I hired a man to entertain dressed in a gorilla costume. There was much laughter, many gifts and Michael's smile. Michael asked if for his eighteenth birthday we could have a belly dancer. Michael died two weeks before his eighteenth birthday.

His father and I entered the crowded funeral parlor. I heard him talking about having angels in the family. I knew we did. Michael's mom handed me an envelope. She said he had asked her to write it for him the night before he died. He told me of his love and how lucky he was. Also to always keep smiling. He said that the first star I saw every night would be him smiling at me. It's been nine years and no matter what the weather, I step outside and that star is as bright and beautiful as the boy who gave it to me.

Mildred Shreve

Mr. Michael Ted's Big Production

Michael Ted Williams passed away last week. He was ninety-four. He was tall and skinny and had been a part of the landscape in Sawyerton Springs for as long as anyone could remember. When I was a kid, we often stopped by Mr. Michael Ted's house after school. He was old then, but you'd never have known it. Always laughing, he lived alone in a big two-story house—just he and his cats.

Mr. Michael Ted had over ten thousand cats—or at least it seemed that way. There were cats inside the house, outside the house, around the house and on the house.

There was only one place in his house where the cats were not allowed. It was an area that the whole town knew about because most of us had been through it. We younger people thought it was neat, but its very existence caused most of the adults in town to think Mr. Michael Ted Williams was rather a nut. I am referring to the Elvis Room.

Mr. Michael Ted *loved* Elvis Presley. It seemed rather strange to us that an older person would be so crazy about an entertainer like Elvis, but he was. "Bing Crosby and them guys ain't got a clue," he'd say. "Elvis does it all. He can sing, he can act and he loved his mother."

The Elvis Room was at the end of the hall on the second

floor. It was a shrine. Hundreds of pictures were stacked on shelves anchored by Elvis decanters or other figurines. Movie posters were on the walls—*Fun in Acapulco, Viva Las Vegas, GI Blues* and *Girls, Girls, Girls.*

By the door, a filing cabinet held all Elvis's single records, which were still in their original jackets. One hundred twenty-nine ticket stubs were neatly displayed on a table in the corner. Each stub was a reminder of a particular concert attended by Mr. Michael Ted.

"That there's the scarf Elvis wore in Louisville," he would say as he showed someone through the room. "Real sweat on it, too. See that stain? Here's a popcorn bag from Tallahassee. Somebody threw it on stage. Elvis kicked it off, and I caught it. I was right there—right in the first row."

Every now and then, one of the kids in town said something mean about Elvis just to get a rise out of Mr. Michael Ted. It always worked. Once, Jeff Deas made a comment about prescription medicine.

Elvis had migraines, Jeff was told, and suffered from several old karate injuries. And unless Jeff wanted to know firsthand how a karate injury felt, he was to keep his opinions about pharmaceuticals to himself!

When Elvis died in 1977, Mr. Michael Ted left his cats with his nephew Billy Pat and headed to Memphis. We saw him drive out of town; he passed the school with tears rolling down his face. For three days, he stood outside the gates of Graceland, paying his respects with thousands of others.

He met a lady about his age, Patsy Jones, from DeKalb, Mississippi. She had met Elvis once at a train station. Having missed her connection that night, she hadn't had any money to eat supper. Patsy showed Mr. Michael Ted the five-dollar bill Elvis had given her for food, and as he held the bill admiringly, he asked why she hadn't spent it. She had been too excited to eat, she told him, and besides, she added, it was the nicest thing anyone had ever done for her.

When he got back to town, there wasn't a trace of sadness in Mr. Michael Ted Williams. "Elvis was way too young to go," he explained, "but the young fellow had a good life. He helped people ease their loneliness, and I, for one, will always be grateful. We still got his music . . . so we still got him."

From that point until his own passing last week, Mr. Michael Ted actually increased his obsession with Elvis, but in a happy way. He traveled hundreds of miles to talk to someone who knew the singer. He bought and traded more memorabilia, and he even held an Elvis dance every spring for the high school. Nothing but Elvis songs were played for the kids, who were all dressed like Elvis and Priscilla. Priscilla was, according to Mr. Michael Ted, the only woman Elvis ever really loved.

About a year ago, Mr. Michael Ted started giving away his cats. "I ain't real young anymore, y'know, and these fur balls need to be kicked around by somebody," he said. Almost every person in town took a cat or two. We knew that he was preparing for the end. What we didn't know, however, was how prepared he actually was!

"I'll be stopping by the bank on the way in to work," Billy Pat said to his wife, Ginny, at breakfast Wednesday morning. "Everything is already set, I think, but the will said that the funeral instructions were in a safety deposit box." As the closest blood relation to the deceased, Billy Pat Williams had been named executor of the estate.

It was all very simple, actually. The house and lot were to become the property of the Methodist church, where Mr. Michael Ted had attended. The contents of the house were to be divided between friends and family, except for the Elvis memorabilia. It was all to be packed and shipped to DeKalb, Mississippi, in care of a Patsy Jones.

Billy Pat arrived at the bank, followed a teller into the

vault, unlocked box number 30024, and inside found an envelope marked "INSTRUCTIONS." Billy Pat thanked the teller, left the bank and drove directly to the only funeral home in Sawyerton Springs, Max's Mortuary.

Max Reed, the mortician, met Billy Pat in the foyer, took the unopened envelope and assured him that all would be taken care of. "I'll call you after lunch with the final details," Max said, "but let's go ahead and set the service for Friday at 2 P.M."

Ten minutes later, as Billy Pat walked into his office, his secretary held the phone out toward him and said, "Mr. Reed is on the phone. It must be important because he insisted on holding, and he has been holding for seven or eight minutes!"

Billy Pat wrinkled his eyebrows in a confused manner and took the phone. "Yeah, Max, this is Billy Pat," he said.

"Billy Pat, did you read the instructions your uncle left?" Max asked.

"No," Billy Pat replied. "I never even opened the envelope."

Max continued. "Did he, by chance, ever give you any idea of his plans?"

"No, I don't think so."

"Did Mr. Michael Ted's will say anything about the funeral?"

"Just that his instructions were to be followed," Billy Pat said. "What's this all about, anyway?"

"It's about the biggest send-off this town has ever had. Or is likely to ever have. For God's sake, get down here— you're not going to believe this!" Max said.

On Friday afternoon at two o'clock, the Beauman's Pond United Methodist Church was filled to overflowing. In fact, I believe it is safe to say that the entire town was there—every man, woman and child.

Near the casket were rows and rows of flowers.

Gorgeous sprays of carnations and roses surrounded say-
ings like "GONE, BUT NOT FORGOTTEN" and "IN OUR
HEARTS FOREVER." Near the steps of the church's pulpit was the arrangement from Miss Luna Myers and Miss
Edna Thigpen. It was a plastic telephone encircled by
purple gladioli and white mums. Above the phone were
the words "JESUS CALLED . . . MICHAEL TED
ANSWERED."

Max Reed stood to the side. He was horrified. He knew
what was about to come, and although it seemed to him
almost indecent, he had done exactly as the man requested.

Pastor Ward sat in his chair in the pulpit. Crossing and
uncrossing his legs constantly, he kept wiping his face
with a handkerchief. Maybe it was the music. "Love Me
Tender" was playing in the background. New things
always made Pastor Ward nervous, and today he was
about to perform his first Elvis funeral.

Max nodded at Terri Henley as she approached the pulpit to sing a song. *This is nuts,* she thought. *A song like this
at a funeral?*

Terri sang "Hounddog," "Heartbreak Hotel" and "Teddy
Bear." Several people snickered when she finished her last
song and said, "Thank you. Thank you very much."

Then it was Pastor Ward's turn. "Brothers and sisters,"
he began, "we are gathered here to mourn the loss of a
friend. He was a very unusual man." Pastor Ward said
later that that was the only occasion in his ministry when
the whole congregation "amened" a single statement. As
he finished his prepared words about how wonderful a
person the deceased had been, Pastor Ward paused to say
a silent prayer of his own. "Dear God," he muttered, "get
me through this next part."

Reading from a sheet of paper Max had given to him
earlier, Pastor Ward said, "And now, ladies and gentlemen
. . . the moment you've all been waiting for, from

Sawyerton Springs, Alabama, Michael Ted Williams."

Max Reed pushed the button on a tape player and started toward the coffin. As the music from *2001: A Space Odyssey* filled the sanctuary, Max slowly lifted the casket lid. As the lid opened, the mourners (if indeed they could have been called that) stood up to get a look. At the loudest part of the song, when the casket was fully open, people broke into applause.

There, amid the flashbulbs popping, was Mr. Michael Ted Williams. His hair had been dyed jet-black. He was wearing fake sideburns and a gold tux.

He looked good. In fact, that's exactly what everyone said—"Doesn't he look good?" He didn't look natural, but a few people said so anyway. Everyone did agree, however, that he looked exactly as he had intended. He looked like a ninety-four-year-old Elvis!

It is an understatement to say that no one will ever forget Mr. Michael Ted. He was a great old guy who provided us with laughter even after his passing. One can imagine him chuckling as he wrote down the instructions for his own funeral—the most amazing production any of us had ever seen. There was one more time during the service in which the congregation applauded. It was out of respect and admiration for the old man. Applause is intended as acknowledgment for a job well done, whether that job is a show or life itself. So the congregation stood as one, clapping and cheering, as the casket was carried out of the church.

Pastor Ward looked at the people and with a big smile said, "Ladies and gentlemen, you can all go home. Mr. Michael Ted has left the building!"

Andy Andrews

$\overline{4}$

ON TEACHING AND LEARNING

We are all teachers, or should be. Anyone who relays experience to another person is a teacher. Not to transmit your experience is to betray it.

Elie Wiesel

Wrestling

Her chocolate curls obeyed the rhythm of her dancing feet, as she twisted and bounded on limber toes beside me all the way to my classroom. Once inside, I pulled out the materials I would need to evaluate the learning problems of this spunky little first grader. She sat there, skinny legs swinging wildly under her chair to the cadence of some jump-rope chant she was humming under her breath. Her bottom lip reached up to recover a small crumbly remnant of lunch as she grabbed the pencil I placed in front of her. Big eyes, eager to please and full of mischief, smiled at me as I began to recite the spelling words.

"Big. The big dog jumped over the wagon. Big." I watched as she struggled with her pencil grip and scratched out a "d" for a "b" and a "6" for a "g". "That un's wrong too, huh?" I watched the light in her smiling eyes fade word by word to dreary surrender. She scowled at her little hands, as though she was scolding them for their misbehavior. I winced, suddenly very doubtful for my purpose and decency. Time paused for a moment as we sat there in silence, pondering our predicament. Then, very unexpectedly, those little feet that had hung there so lonely for a dance recovered their rhythm. She banished the pencil from her hand and produced a grin so intense with mischief and sport that it startled me.

"Ya wanna wrestle?" she invited. My bewildered gaze was met with a challenging grin. Slow to catch on, I repeated her query, "What? Do I want to wrestle?" She was not about to leave me with such a humble impression of her talents. Her invitation announced what she was good at—wrestling.

After some negotiating she settled on four matches of arm wrestling, one for each remaining spelling word. And when we were finished she skipped out of my classroom boasting a winning record. Her gentle yet pointed appraisal of my testing etiquette left me contrite yet resolved to level out the playing field. I instituted some new rules. Rule one: It is illegal to use learning difficulties as an excuse to sneak up on young learners and rob them of giggles and dancing feet. Rule two: If I ever forget rule one, I must spend an entire recess in the middle of a dodgeball circle, surrounded by sixth-graders.

Renee Adolph

The Cage

It's what you learn after you know it all that counts.

A. C. Carlson

I remember hearing their voices all the way down the hallway—passionate and loud, threatening and unforgiving. Barely twenty-two, fresh out of college and headstrong (though some might say inexperienced, opinionated and stubborn), I was prepared to face the challenge before me. I was escorted by a security guard, armed only with a walkie-talkie and a sincere smile. It was a smile of sympathy.

I had received the call the night before. The Portsmouth City Schools needed a long-term substitute immediately. The class, a "bridge" class, consisted of students with dis - cipline problems. The term "bridge" was a euphemism for students too young to drop out of school and too old to keep back. It was a school built in the early 1940s for a sub - urban community that eventually became urban. The regular teacher had a nervous breakdown in February. It was not March, and I was the sixteenth teacher. After the first thirteen teachers quit in eight school days, school security and an assistant principal took over the job of baby-sitting. I didn't know it then, but other teachers in the school had christened the classroom "The Cage," a place where wild animals lived, and no one stayed long enough to be eaten alive.

Room 211 was a classroom situated at the far end of the enormous school, next to the stairwell. I thanked the security guard and entered. Twenty-eight pairs of eyes surveyed me. Some of the eyes were hazel green, but mostly they were dark, the color of burnt cinders in a fireplace. They were the eyes of adults in the faces of children. Not children really. Some were twelve, most were thirteen, but there were some fourteen- and fifteen-year-olds in this sixth-grade classroom.

I stood by the door. Two panes of glass were broken, and the metal vent at the bottom of the door was missing. This allowed students to crawl through it even when it was closed. The bulletin boards were bare, save for some old, faded crepe paper in the corners. Some of the students watched me, watching them. Others ignored me completely and carried on as if I did not exist. The noise continued. I watched them, and then I looked at my watch: 8:19 it read. I didn't say a word. I looked at my watch again. I learned a few names and noticed on which desk they placed their belongings. Finally, in what I call my teacher voice, I said, "For as long as you keep me waiting, I'll keep you waiting after school." And then I looked at my watch again. Some rolled their eyes at me. Others continued to ignore me. None really settled down. The security guard walked past the classroom. "Do you need any help?" he asked me. I said, "No," though my stomach was in knots, and I wanted to run home. And he left, but I don't think he went very far.

After looking at my watch for the last time, I said, "So far you've kept me waiting for six minutes, therefore, you will wait after school for six minutes. Quentin, I want you to sit in the second row, first seat. Abdul, first row, third seat. The rest of you have exactly thirty seconds to settle down. Upon which I will introduce myself and will memorize your names by 8:45. We will begin with spelling. And on Friday, I will give you a test."

By the time I had finished and heard the usual "How'd she know your name?" or "She think she gonna be our teacher now?" and other, more colorful parts of speech, I had their attention. The stage was mine. I pulled out a large neon yellow poster board and a roll of gray duct tape. With exaggerated effort, I taped the poster to the chalkboard. In big, black letters, the poster read, "MS. CLANCY'S RULES: GOD HAD TEN COMMANDMENTS, I HAVE TWELVE." And slightly smaller but equally important were two columns of six rules. I then turned to the class and began: "My name is Ms. Clancy. I'm twenty-two, and I just moved here to Virginia. I'm from New York. I'm going to be here until June. And now I'm giving you two choices: (1) you do as you're told and you follow my rules; or (2) you don't do as you're told and you don't follow the rules. Either choice, however, will not get rid of me. If you choose option number two, I can assure you a miserable existence. Because anything you think you can do to me will not work. And anything you can do has already been tried, or I've tried it myself less than two years ago. Now, I will take attendance."

At 2:36 that afternoon, I dismissed the class. By 2:37, I sat at the desk and cried. I had before me students who did not know what a noun was, couldn't name the vice president of the United States and could read only at a third-grade level. I didn't even get to math, science or social studies because I had to break up two fights and send another four students to the office. No one had left lesson plans, and half the class didn't have books.

I gathered myself together and was about to go to the main office and tell them to get another substitute for tomorrow when I picked up an essay by a student named Tameisha. I had given them an essay (translation: busy work) while I tried to figure out what I was going to do after lunch. The title of the essay was "The Most Important Person in My Life." Tameisha wrote about her aunt. When Tameisha was six, her mother died of a brain aneurysm in the family's kitchen, forcing Tameisha, her older sister and two younger sisters to live with their aunt and her four children. Tameisha's father was in prison, and she didn't remember meeting him. Tameisha's essay, while not grammatically the greatest, spoke volumes about perseverance and self-sacrifice. She wrote about how hard her aunt worked. She talked about how she struggled to feed and clothe eight kids. She said that her aunt could have let Tameisha and her sisters become wards of the state, but, instead, she insisted that some things were more important than nice clothes and fancy meals.

I felt guilty. I looked down at my college ring. To me, it represented the culmination of sixteen years of education. It represented hard work and sacrifices to pay my own way through college. But then, we always had plenty of food and nice clothes in our home.

I tried to rationalize my decision to not come back. After all, I was educated in private, Catholic schools; I was white and came from a "regular" nuclear family in suburban Long Island. My father went to work, and my mother stayed home to care for my two brothers and me. What could I teach them? I questioned the importance of adverbial clauses in a world where metal detectors at the school's entrance were a reality. I questioned my ability to teach American history when many of these children wouldn't leave the streets of their city, let alone leave the state. Two girls in the class were pregnant. I don't have the slightest clue as to what they were going through. But I read again about Tameisha's aunt. I went up to the blackboard and wrote the next day's date. I also wrote five spelling words and, in big block letters, "AS SOON AS YOU WALK IN, WRITE THE WORDS 5X'S EACH, GET A DICTIONARY, WRITE THE DEFINITIONS, THEN PUT EACH WORD IN A SENTENCE. AND, OH YEAH—GOOD MORNING CLASS." I left my poster taped to the board.

I finished out the school year at Hunt-Mapp Middle School. We played grammatical bingo using prizes bought at the dollar store. We diagrammed sentences from rap songs. We had the strangest-looking bulletin boards in the school. We had extra help sessions after school. I learned all the street names in the projects by driving home anyone who got a ninety percent or better on a test. With a full carload, I was rarely home before 3:30.

I don't know if I made an impact on any one student's life. I don't know if it's possible to even make an impression in three months. But I do know that I learned more in those three months than I ever could have sitting in a classroom studying the problems of the inner city for twenty years. I can't say that there was a happy ending. For every one day I came home late because I drove a car full of students home, there were three days I came home frustrated and angry. But at the same time, for every one student who made me angry, there was another who earned my respect.

Regina Clancy-Hiney

Don't Touch Me

As the passing bell rang, I hurried out of my office to take my duty at the doors of the cafeteria. Being a teacher in a large, urban high school certainly has some drawbacks: having to supervise a loud, crowded mass of starving teenagers is one of them. After twenty years, I have a sixth sense when it comes to trouble developing in school. And somehow, I knew this was going to be one of those days.

It happened twenty minutes into the period. The noise level rose. Students pushed their chairs back and got to their feet. Some jumped up on the tables to get a better view of a fight that had broken out in the back of the room.

Being short, slight, and somewhat intelligent, I knew better than to try to break up a teenage brawl. So, I did the next best thing. I attempted to get the onlookers back to their seats and out of the way. In doing this, I approached two students from behind. Gently laying a hand on each of their shoulders, I began asking them to take their seats. I had uttered only a few words when one of the boys swung around, grabbed my wrist and pushed my arm away from his body. His eyes were burning, and his grip tightened as he lashed out with clenched teeth, "Don't touch me!"

There was that all too familiar phrase, coming once again from an angry, frightened youth. Teachers expect it, but I never let it stop me. I firmly believe children need to be touched. Of course, one risks physical injury—as I was finding out.

It felt as though the circulation of blood was being cut off in my arm. It made me angry, even though I thought I understood his hostile behavior. Now it was my turn to grit my teeth. In a very controlled but firm voice, and with strong, demanding eye contact, I said softly, "You may touch me—but not hard!"

He kept his grip. We stood frozen, our eyes locked together in what seemed a piercing challenge of defiance. Then a strange look came over his face. His hand flew open, releasing my wrist. In that same moment he stepped back; but his arm was extended, his fingers wide apart, as if to stop me from entering his space.

"I'm sorry," he said. "But I told you not to touch me. Don't ever touch me!"

"Okay, that's fine," I said, in a condescending voice. "Just take your seat, please."

I left school that day, still thinking about the incident and remembering the stunned and puzzled look on the young man's face when he dropped my wrist. Could it be that for one brief instant he knew that I understood his anger? And in giving him permission to touch me, had he felt my compassion? Probably just wishful thinking. But I thought about him a lot during the next two days. I wondered if maybe he came from an abusive home where a touch most often meant pain. There was such a vulner- able look in his eyes when he stepped back. I kept seeing that look in my mind. And though I didn't know his name, I remembered him in my prayers each night.

The end of the week was approaching, and I entered

school feeling good. I was early, and there were only two or three people in the hallway. Suddenly I realized that my young man was walking just ahead of me.

What an opportunity, I thought. *God is giving me a chance to know this child and perhaps to see my prayers answered.* "Please, God," I prayed quickly. "Help me!"

Now I was in step by his side. "Hey!" I said with a grin, as we continued down the hall. "What's all this silliness about not wanting anyone to touch you?"

"I don't let nobody touch me!" he snarled.

"Nobody?" I asked. "How about your mama? Don't you ever give her a hug?"

He stopped short, pivoting to face me head on. Again I saw that fiery look in his eyes. "I hate my mother! I never let her touch me!" he bellowed.

I cringed inside, knowing my initial fears of abuse were probably on target. But there was no time to belabor the issue. I quickly responded, teasingly, "Well, there. You see? You need us teachers to touch you once in awhile— to let you know we care about you. Everybody needs to be touched sometimes." I tilted my head and lifted my shoulders. "Right?" I asked, still in a teasing voice.

The corners of his mouth turned up and he lowered his head to hide the hint of a smile. As I turned the corner, I looked back over my shoulder and flashed him one last grin with a wink. He had not moved. His eyes were still on me. But now his smile was full, and his face was lit up. I entered my office, closed the door, clenched my fists and screeched, "Yes!"

At 11:30 that morning, I made my way down to the cafeteria. I took my usual position at the door and proceeded to check the student's ID cards as they entered. I smiled, made small talk, checked faces with pictures. It was business as usual until I glanced down and saw the picture of what was becoming a very familiar face. By the time I looked up, he was nearly through the doorway. But as he took his last step through, facing straight ahead as though he did not see me, his hand caught mine. And for one brief moment I felt a squeeze. Then he was gone. I put my arm out to hold back the next student, so that I could step through the doorway myself and acknowledge his gesture. He had moved quickly and was several feet away. Still not knowing his name, I stood looking after him, wishing I could call out. Then abruptly he stopped walking, turned toward me and smiled. Our eyes met, and I felt a warm, wonderful spirit of understanding pass between us.

I know that I will never have to feel his rage again. And perhaps, if my prayers for him are answered completely, no one will have to hear him repeat those cold, angry, lonely words—"Don't touch me!"

Kay L. Pliszka

Two Little Boys Named Chris

When my firstborn child, Christian (Chris), was a little over three years old, he was diagnosed with cancer. After two to three years of treatment and several surgeries, it became apparent that his learning abilities had degenerated. With the help of Cancer Institute personnel, we were able to get Chris into a special-education class in a local school.

His teacher soon realized there was a problem in identifying two little boys in the class named Chris. Every time she called the name Chris, both boys answered. So she decided to ask each one what his mother called him at home. The other little boy answered, "Chris," and my son answered, "Sweetheart."

Delores Lacy

Big Heart

I'm a flight attendant for a major airline. One afternoon while running through LAX to my plane, I tore one of my nylon stockings. It was a really bad tear, and I wasn't carrying another pair with me. Fortunately, there was a convenience store in the terminal that was close to my gate where I knew I could buy a new pair. However, to my surprise, as I waited in line at the sales register, I discovered that I had *no money* in my purse.

I thought to myself that maybe the store manager would sell me a pair of four-dollar nylons and let me pay her back the next time I saw her. I've been inside her store a lot, and she always smiles and is friendly to me, even though we've never been introduced. When it was my turn to pay, I showed her my leg and explained that I had no money on me. And that I was desperate. She laughed and simply said, "Take them."

Well, for whatever reason, two months passed, and I still had not paid the manager back the money I owed her.

Then one day at work before my flight departed, I was busy doing my usual preflight preparations when a passenger asked me for a newspaper. There was no paper on the plane to give him. He then asked me if I wouldn't mind going into the terminal to buy him one. I said, "Sure," and he handed me a quarter.

I deplaned and walked to the same convenience store. Before I entered the store, I noticed the manager was there. I was too embarrassed to go inside because I had never paid her back, and I wasn't carrying my wallet.

So, I decided that I would just stand outside the store and flag down the first person I saw and ask him or her to buy me a paper.

A giant of a man with a friendly face approached. Before he could walk past me, I stopped him and asked if he would buy me a newspaper. He smiled and said that he would do so gladly but wanted to know why I couldn't do it myself. I told him that I was too embarrassed to tell anyone the reason. He was rather jovial and kept saying, "Aw, come on, tell me. Surely it isn't that bad." I liked him. There was something very sweet and gentle about him. I needed a newspaper, so I gave in and told him.

Suddenly he said, "Hold on," and in one fell swoop whisked me up into his arms and carried me into the store, right over to the counter where the manager was. I was laughing the whole way. With his free hand he reached into his pocket and pulled out a five-dollar bill and said, "I'd like to pay for the nylons this person owes you for and for a newspaper."

I later learned that the big, gentle man was Rosie Grier, the former L.A. Ram and Hall of Fame football player.

Heather Bull

A Touch of Lemon

When I met Mr. Jim Lemon I was a seventeen-year-old freshman at Houston's Jackson Junior High and the chances of my finishing high school were slim. I was a troubled teenager with an attitude, living in a neighborhood that fostered troubled teenagers.

Mr. Lemon taught American history and it was clear from the first day that his classroom was not going to be disrupted. It was apparent very quickly that Mr. Lemon was quite different from the other teachers I had known. Not only was he a disciplinarian, he was a great teacher. He would never settle for my usual standard of classroom work. Mr. Lemon pushed and prodded and never tolerated the mediocrity that had become my standard.

On the occasion of our first semester report cards, Mr. Lemon called me aside and asked how it was possible that I was a B student in his class and a D and F student in the rest of my classes. I was ready for that question. I passionately told him about my divorced parents, the local gangs, the drugs, the fights, the police—all of the evils I had been subjected to. It was then that Mr. Lemon patiently explained that the only person responsible for my situation was me. And the only person with the potential to change my situation was me, and that when I personally accepted that responsibility I could make a significant change in my life. He convinced me that I was failing not because I was a failure, but because I was not accepting the responsibility for my results in those other classes.

Mr. Lemon was the first teacher I had who made me believe in myself. He inspired me to become a better student and he changed my life.

Ten years later I was preparing to graduate from Chaminade University in Honolulu when I spoke to him again. It had taken weeks of telephone calls to find him but I knew what I had to say. When I finally did get him on the telephone I explained what his classroom toughness had meant to me, how I finally graduated from high school, and how I was a staff sergeant in the Army, married with a daughter.

Most of all I wanted him to know that I was about to graduate magna cum laude after going to school for four hours a night, four nights a week for three years. I wanted him to know that I could never have done it if he had not been a part of my life.

Finally, I told him that I had been saving money that I could invite he and his wife to come to Hawaii at my expense to be a part of my graduation.

I'll never forget his response. He said, "Who is this again?" I was just one of hundreds of students whose life he changed and he had no idea of his impact.

Mr. Lemon never came to my graduation, but his absence taught me another valuable lesson.

Mr. Lemon's final lesson for me was that we will probably never know or understand the impact we have on other people's lives. He taught me that we all have the opportunity to effect people's lives for the better . . . or for the worse.

Rick Phillips

The Dustpan Carrier

"It is always the English teacher who holds the dustpan."

The last time I saw Mrs. Jones was in 1991. I had graduated from college and, proud of my accomplishments, came back to Douglas Anderson School of the Arts to find and thank the woman, the teacher, who changed my life.

I spoke to her classes that afternoon about the importance of self-esteem and setting high goals for oneself. I heard myself speaking, but I was somewhere else in that classroom, five years back, sitting at the corner desk with my fingers twisting and twisting that long black hair I once had.

In December 1986, my father, a rabbi and teacher himself, had brought me to Douglas Anderson School of the Arts, in desperation. I sat in the hallway while he went into the principal's office and spoke to her. I only heard a few of those words, in between the clutter of strange faces in the hall and the pit-pat of ballet-slippered feet on the white tile, but I knew why I was there and why they chose to whisper. In a nearby practice room, I heard the rhythmic clicking of a metronome, followed by a hesitant piano scale.

"I don't know where else to put her." My father's voice broke, and then I heard a muffle of a deep, authoritative female voice.

"Rabbi, I understand your position, but we only hold auditions in the summer." For the first time in my life, I heard my father weep. I pressed my head tight against the green door, felt the cold on my cheek, and closed my eyes, tried counting to ten the way my therapist had taught me only a week before, breathing in on every number, then out, slowly.

My father's voice interrupted at seven. "She was raped by a group of boys at her school a month ago. She can't go back there."

I auditioned for The School of the Arts that day, sitting at the piano in the stuffy little practice room I had heard someone struggling in earlier. I lay my hands heavily on the yellow-stained keys and with my heart, with tears, with pain, I played Rachmaninoff, Beethoven, and finally, my father's favorite Chopin *Nocturne*. The teacher nodded, the principal put her hand up to her mouth and shook her head, and my father's face melted into quiet relief. It wasn't until Friday, however, that I met her, Mrs. Jones, when I was transferred into her creative writing class at 11:00 A.M. In my memories of her, she is always the same. She wore brown sandals, a blue flower-printed skirt, and a wrinkled white blouse with its frilly collar bent. She held a constant confused expression and played with a charm on her necklace, sometimes the wisp of hair that often fell over her eye. As she walked closer to my desk in the corner, I noticed she was pigeon-toed. She didn't bend over me the way the other teachers had, but rather, knelt at my desk, and smiled at me, eye-level.

"We'll be working in our journals today," Mrs. Jones said softly. She smelled like soap and mothballs and lilacs. "Do you have a notebook you can use as your journal?"

I could feel the inquisitive eyes in the classroom on "the new girl." A pretty blonde-haired girl in the front of the room mumbled loudly to her neighbor about my "special audition."

"Get to work, please," Mrs. Jones told the class. Please, I thought. I believe it was the first time I had ever heard a teacher say "please" to a student!

I pulled a green notebook out of my book bag and Mrs. Jones lay her cool, dry hand on mine. "I'm so happy to have you in my class," she whispered.

That journal, I believe now, saved me from insanity. I wrote everything that day and from that day forward; I turned myself inside out and dumped it into my green notebook the way I'd seen my mother plop her matzo balls into her chicken soup. I wrote about "them." I wrote their names down and crossed them out, then wrote them again and again, until it didn't hurt so much to hear them in my head. I wrote the word "rape" in red because it felt hot and burned and it was sore and I knew that even if I ignored it, it would not go away.

Mrs. Jones didn't judge my words the way the district attorney had. She didn't probe and pry and prick me like the psychologists or the nurse examiner at the hospital. She didn't insult and blame and scream like my mother initially had—or weep like my father—Mrs. Jones became much more than my English teacher. She was a partner in my internal battle, guiding me with her red-penned words on the many pages of my always-read, always-understood, journal.

In 1991 I went back. I walked through the bustling hall-way (I had arrived just as the bell rang), and was surprised at how young the students looked. Had I been so young just five years ago? No, I believe I was much, much older. By coincidence, Mrs. Jones was just leaving her classroom as I approached. She carried a crumpling cardboard box full of journals. At first, she just smiled, had that confused, but friendly look of unfamiliarity. And then it hit her. "Tali, is it really you?"

I've been told that it is the English teacher, always the English teacher, who is directly faced with the at-risk students. The faithful dustpan carrier who picks up the pieces when they fall. Perhaps this is because writing so often mirrors our innermost fears and dark secrets, places where a science or math teacher have no grounds to step.

I chose to teach English because I had no choice.

I will never forget what Mrs. Jones did for me. It's been almost ten years since high school. I have my own group of students now and I, too, carry around a worn cardboard box full of journals. And a dustpan.

Tali Whiteley

The Influence of the Insignificant

Once there was a dear lady named Hazel who loved to sing simple, common gospel songs. She decided to try out for the church choir. She told the choir director that she couldn't read music, so he said, "We'll let you sing, but just stay on tune." But she couldn't stay on tune, so she had to drop out of the choir. Nothing really seemed to have any meaning in Hazel's life. Her mother had recently died. When Hazel was young, she had spent most of her time caring for her mother, instead of dating and enjoying her adolescence. Consequently, she had never married.

At the age of sixty, she felt as though she had failed in her attempt to find happiness in life. Alone, with no spouse or children, she couldn't even fulfill her life goal of singing. Distressed and worried, as you can well imagine, she lived in a tiny one-bedroom apartment three or four flights above the street level in a big city. With her mother gone, she lived alone in an old, run-down, apartment building where only old people on Social Security usually lived.

One day, as Hazel was on her way out, she saw a young hippie-looking guy moving into one of the small tenements. He had a full beard and long hair. When she returned, all of her friends were talking about the new tenant. "We're in real trouble now," said one lady. "Once these tough-looking characters move in, they always take over!" And all the old folks living in the apartment building started taking extra precautions, just in case the stranger was a thief. Many even put extra locks on their windows and doors. Nobody trusted him.

This went on for several weeks. Then one night Hazel came in later than usual. She entered the lobby very quietly, so she wouldn't disturb any of the other tenants. After climbing two flights of stairs, she saw a suspicious-looking man in the hallway. Instead of screaming or running back down the stairs, she began to sing! In her own off-key way, she sang the first words that came to her. "When you walk through a storm hold your head up high and don't be afraid of the dark." That's the only song she could remember and she wasn't even sure if the words were right. She sang on: ". . . Hold your head up high and you'll never walk alone. Walk on, walk on, with hope in your heart and you'll never walk alone." By this time she had reached her apartment. So she quickly opened the door and locked it securely, listening at the door for some kind of sound. She heard nothing, so she went to bed, grateful that she had made it safely to her place.

The next morning she saw a torn, crumpled piece of paper under her door. It was from the rough-looking young man that everyone feared. This is what it said: "I don't know who you are, but thank you for singing to me last night. I was ready to cash in—to commit suicide—but then you started to sing: 'When you walk through a storm hold your head up high and you'll never walk alone.' I want you to know that you saved my life. I'm going to another city where I know I can find the job I need. Thank you. Good-bye."

Robert H. Schuller

A Neighbor I'll Never Forget

Perhaps I was nine, no more than ten, years old when an elderly couple moved to my neighborhood. They were serene and conformed to their Italian ancestry in their dress, and in the decoration of their home. The wife's appearance scared me—her jet-black eyes were as cold as stones in an icy brook and she wore long, dark dresses with a stiff white lace collar. Her glossy, black patent leather shoes were bound by a thin strap, and buttoned with a large pearl. Her hair reminded me of a bird's nest.

In the early 1930s, many people associated Italians with dangerous gangsters. The woman was lonely, probably because no one in the neighborhood made her feel welcome. She loved birds and, searching for acceptance wherever she could, fed them every day. Walking slowly, she tossed seeds in every corner of the large yard. Her menacing eyes remained downcast as she talked softly to her feathered friends. Unlike the birds, I was petrified of her.

In stark contrast, her husband was outgoing and friendly. Whenever he saw me he raised his arm high and waved wildly. His lips would part in a wide smile showing huge white teeth. His full flowing white hair reminded me of a classical music composer. I had never heard the word *obese* but he surely was just that. His face made me think of Santa Claus, and, after some months, he became a mythical figure in my life.

I probably would have paid little attention to Mr. Conti had it not been for his 1928 Buick. One morning, acting on a spontaneous impulse, when he backed his beautiful car out into the sunshine, I raced across the street to close the heavy wooden doors on his garage. I wished to be as close to that automobile as possible! Because of his enormous body he appreciated sitting in his car as the friendly neighborhood boy performed a thoughtful service.

"Hey sonny, what's your name?"

"Jack," I answered.

"Well, Jackie, thank you, here's some gum."

His fat liver-spotted hand held a five-stick pack of chewing gum. His gift was quite valuable in 1932! After that day, whenever I saw his car approaching, I rushed to open the doors and, in return, he provided me with a steady supply of gum.

Our relationship stayed at that level for months. Some time later, tragedy paid a visit to the aged couple. Mrs. Conti became ill. The birds went hungry. They chirped and called for their friend, whom they would never see again.

One day I saw crepe hanging on the front door. A stillness had settled over the large house. Long black cars arrived, stopping only to pick up and return Mr. Conti. Meanwhile, the Buick sat in the damp darkness of the garage. Still too young to know what I could do to help, I waited.

Time floated by. Finally the garage doors swung open and Mr. Conti waved to me. A wide black band circled the sleeve of his coat. I didn't move. He called, "Come on over, Jackie, I have some gum for you." Feeling uncomfortable I sheepishly crossed the yellow brick street. I knew that there had been a sadness in my friend's life, which I was at a loss to grasp.

"Jackie, I'm going to the cemetery to take care of the flowers on my wife's grave. If you want to go for the ride, ask your mother if it's okay." Taking only a moment to consider, my mother gave the necessary permission.

I waited as the large green car backed out of the garage, then I closed the doors. I climbed into the automobile that I had been worshiping for so long. I stroked the velvet seats, so soft to the touch. The shiny wooden steering wheel looked so smooth I wished to hold it. The engine purred as we drove down the street. Mr. Conti was sad, but I could not have been happier.

We parked the car on the narrow road in the cemetery, then walked to the mound of fresh dirt covered with wilting and dead flowers. I thought perhaps he was being careful not to disturb his wife, he worked so quietly. Nearly missing his request as he grunted and huffed leaning over his task, I asked him to repeat his words. "Sonny, will you get the watering can in the car and fill it at the pump? I want to water this plant so it will live." He didn't say, "so it won't die." The most precious gift he gave me was a positive attitude toward life.

Taking the large iron handle in my hand I pumped up and down, and cool, fresh water splashed into and around the sprinkling can. It was heavy and it bumped against my leg as I lugged it back to the grave. Satisfied that all was in order, Mr. Conti blessed himself and said a soft good-bye, then put his hand on my shoulder, guiding me to the waiting car.

"Jackie, now we both need to have some fun. Let's stop at the Drive-O-Links down the road and hit some golf balls, okay?" My eyes lit up as I shouted, "Yes!" The tires on the big car crunched as they rolled across the gravel at our destination. He purchased a bucket filled with golf balls and picked out two clubs. He then stood on the square wooden box. A giant could not have looked larger. His club swung in a mighty circle, hitting the little white sphere past the 200-yard sign and the 250-yard sign. It finally fell onto the smooth grass at the 300-yard sign. "Okay, Jackie, now it's your turn."

My attempt to send the ball more than a few yards was futile. Patiently, he showed me the correct stance and how to hold the club. A golfer I would never be, but I was having the time of my life. The trip to the cemetery followed by a stop at the Drive-O-Links became a weekly occurrence. I looked forward to the exciting ritual, counting the days until the next Sunday.

Mr. Conti owned several quarries. He had contracts with the state, and when roads were tarred and pebbled, it often was with stones from one of his locations. During the summer I was a constant passenger on his business trips. He taught me much about taking pride in myself.

I saw him embrace a man who had recently lost a child. I looked on as he put twenty dollars into the hand of a handsome young man whose marriage was only days old. He told one of the old workers to stay with his dying wife, assuring the man that he would be paid. A child played in front of a wooden shack that was a worker's home and Mr. Conti laboriously leaned his heavy body over to pat the child on the head, digging into his pocket for a pack of gum. Nearly everyone felt a fondness toward him.

I was still young when I learned to grieve the loss of a loved one. Mr. Conti died suddenly while having a glass of wine with a few friends. My spirit was broken. Sadly, I missed his funeral since no one cared to take me. His house became dreary and bleak. The birds had long gone to a happier place. My final good-bye to my mentor came the day someone opened the garage, then backed the big Buick out into the daylight. Through tear-filled eyes I watched as it disappeared. The automobile was gone but the portrait of a gentle, caring, smiling man, who had taught me much about living a life for others, remains in my memory forever.

Jack Alexander

5

OVERCOMING OBSTACLES

Nothing is impossible to a willing heart.

John Heywood

Everyday Heroes

I don't remember having a hero as a child, although there have been individuals throughout my life that I greatly respected. I found my hero much later in life, and he wasn't at all like I imagined a hero should be. He wasn't rich and famous. He wasn't a star athlete or a movie star. He was just a guy I'd taken for granted all of my life. This is a story about my hero, who also happens to be my big brother.

My brother, Tony, met his wife, Sheila, while he was in medical school. I remember attending his graduation and meeting her for the first time. Sheila was from England, and she was full of life. She had a smile that brightened any room and she loved to laugh. Sheila was a nurse, and at that time, nurses were in high demand. She had been recruited by U.S. hospitals, was given a work visa and settled in the Dallas area. Sheila met my brother at Parkland Hospital, where she was employed as a nurse and he was a medical student.

Tony had always been too consumed with his schoolwork to become involved with anyone on a regular basis. Somehow, though, I knew that this was more than a casual romance. I caught a glimpse of them sitting quietly in the auditorium, holding hands, deep in conversation. After graduation, Tony accepted a residency in Louisville, Kentucky. Sheila moved with him. While living in Kentucky, Sheila went on "holiday" to Canada. When she attempted to return to Kentucky, she was refused entry into the United States because her working visa had expired. She was deported to England, and it took a month or so to clear up the mess. Tony, meanwhile, was going nuts without her. The minute Sheila returned to Louisville, they were married. The following year, they flew to England, where along with our parents, relatives and a few friends, they were remarried in a traditional ceremony, top hats and all. So their life together began.

The first few years of their life together went fairly smooth, other than a few moves—Kentucky to New Mexico, New Mexico to Texas and then back to New Mexico. During that time, their two boys, Cameron and Sheldon, were born, three years apart. My brother had accepted a position with the University of New Mexico Medical School, and Sheila was working as a nurse in the intensive care unit of the same hospital. In 1989, they bought a beautiful new home in Corrales, New Mexico, complete with a corral and pasture, and with a beautiful view of the mountains. Sheila had always had a passion for horses, and their new home offered her the opportunity to pursue her hobby on a daily basis.

New Mexico can be a really nice place to be in the spring. On April 22, 1989, it looked to be one of those beautiful spring days, a great day to spend outdoors. Tony decided to take the boys on a fishing expedition. Sheila had a new horse to train. No one knows for certain what happened on that day, but from what information could be pieced together, Sheila was riding in the pasture when her horse fell. Sheila fell forward, facedown into the grass and mud, and the horse landed on top of her, pressing her face into the mud and cutting off her air supply. Across the pasture, their neighbor, who was also a physician, was outside working, when he saw Sheila lying in the pasture. When he reached her, she was unconscious and not breathing. The neighbor began emergency treatment and called the air rescue unit. Sheila was transported to the hospital where she and my brother both worked. Tony saw the air rescue helicopter from their fishing spot, not suspecting it could be Sheila. Tony and the boys returned late in the day to the news of the accident.

I was preparing to go on a picnic when my mom called and told me. All of my family headed to Albuquerque to be with my brother. Sheila had a fractured skull, was breathing with the help of a respirator and was comatose. We did not know how long she would remain unconscious or, for that matter, if she would ever wake up. We did not know how much damage had been done to her brain as a result of the trauma. I remember not knowing what to say to my brother as I watched him by her side, holding her hand and talking softly to her. I watched as the nurses Sheila had worked with the day before cared for her in her unconscious state. I thought about how quickly things can change in life and how different my brother's life might be if she did not recover. Months after the accident, Tony told me that one night he prayed and asked God to take her quickly if she wouldn't be able to live without the artificial support she was receiving. He said he felt a strange calmness after that, and that he just knew everything was going to be okay. Sheila's eyes opened two weeks after the accident. Once again, they began a life together.

The damage from the accident was evident. Sheila had no memory. She could not walk, talk, bathe or feed herself. She needed help with every basic function. The doctors believed that Sheila would eventually regain some of her motor skills, and perhaps some of her memory, but it was going to be a long and difficult journey. Tony began a daily ritual of reviewing pictures and names with her, working a full day and then returning after work for a couple of hours. Once home with his boys, he fixed meals, read stories and tucked them into bed at night. Although he was exhausted, he never complained. This ritual continued even after Sheila was transferred to a rehabilitation hospital, where she remained for several months. When Sheila was finally able to come home, she could not walk, her speech was barely audible, she could not write and she had no memory. She did not remember their meeting or courtship, nor did she remember their wedding or the birth of their children. For the longest time, she thought that Tony was an auto mechanic. Still, Tony bathed her, styled her hair, lavished her with gifts and attention. Progress was very slow. As time went on, we began to relish even the smallest accomplishment—new memory, remembering family names, cutting her own food, brushing her own hair, walking a few steps with a harness.

Even though Sheila was making progress toward self-sufficiency, most of her daily care was left up to Tony. This dependency must have been hard on Sheila, and she seemed very depressed. I worried that their marriage would not survive. The love, laughter and life they once shared no longer existed. Every day was a struggle.

Then it happened. The moment that my brother became my hero. I was visiting for the weekend. Sheila sat in her wheelchair. Tony was running around like a madman, cleaning and cooking; the kids were watching television; the stereo was playing—typical Saturday morning chaos. All of a sudden, Tony turned up the music really loud. He began to snap his fingers and dance all by himself. All of us were looking at him, when the kids giggled and began to dance along. The kids and Tony were laughing and dancing and having a grand time. Tony looked over at Sheila and noticed tears streaming down her face. Sheila loved to dance, and it was as though at that moment, she remembered their life before. Without saying a word, Tony walked over to her and picked her up from her wheelchair. Holding her tightly, he rested her feet on his shoes and began to dance with her around the room. Time seemed to stand still, and everyone was silent as we watched them dance about. Then, the kids began to smile and giggle, and as everyone joined in enthusiastically, Sheila smiled and started to laugh. It had been a long time since we had seen her smile; it seemed like forever since we had heard her laugh. I looked at my brother as he stared at his wife, and not only could I see the love for her in his eyes, I swear I could feel it from across the room. At that moment, I found my hero.

It has been almost ten years since that awful day in April. Tony, Sheila and their boys still live in their home in Corrales. Tony continues to practice medicine. The boys are now thirteen and eleven, and active in sports and school. Sheila has continued to make progress and is now self-sufficient. Sheila walks with the help of a cane, drives, takes care of their home and once again passed her board exams for nursing. Although she has never regained all of the memories of her past, she is now able to remember much more than ever before. They continue to struggle with the challenges that face those individuals in recovery from a serious accident, but their commitment to one another remains intact. As I have watched them struggle with each of their challenges, I have often been reminded of that simple moment that had such an impact on my life. I now realize that simple moments and actions are what can make a difference in someone's life. Eleven years ago, I didn't have a hero, but I found one in an ordinary guy that I am also proud to call my brother.

Shawn Blessing

Weep with Those Who Weep

In helping others, we shall help ourselves, for whatever good we give out completes the circle and comes back to us.

Flora Edwards

The first time we met Ginny, we were sitting around a conference table. She arrived late and waddled into the room, followed by her husband, Bob. I say she "waddled" because Ginny was in the sixth month of her pregnancy, and it was the only way she could enter a room. Bob sat down to join us, and Ginny attempted to sit down gently and gracefully. Instead, she had to move the chair away from the table and then did not have any lap in which to fold her hands.

We had never seen a pregnant woman at our bereavement support group before. I watched the faces of our elderly widows soften as they smiled at Ginny and Bob and tried to make them feel welcome. Our group had been meeting for several months, and I was the facilitator for the group. In addition to me, the group consisted of eight widows, all senior citizens. As Ginny told us about their loss at the first meeting, tears ran down the cheeks of everyone in the room. She and Bob sat with their hands clenched together as they related the details of the day their daughter died.

Ginny told us it had seemed like any normal day. She and little Shawna had gone shopping and stopped for a hamburger on the way home. Shawna was a perfectly healthy, normal two-year-old who got a bit cranky as nap time approached. After Ginny unloaded the packages from the car, she settled Shawna down for her nap. Ginny gave Shawna an extra hug when she felt Shawna's chubby arms clamp around her neck.

A few minutes later Ginny heard Shawna cry out. It was a sound unlike any she had ever heard before, and goosebumps appeared on Ginny's arms as she told us about it. Ginny is a registered nurse, so she went into action immediately to check for blockage in the throat and then took resuscitation measures. When Shawna was again breathing on her own, Ginny called the paramedics.

The medical reports showed that Shawna stopped breathing repeatedly in the next few hours, but she was resuscitated each time. At last, she seemed to be out of danger and was placed in a special unit in the hospital. A few minutes later, she stopped breathing again and could not be revived. The entire episode took about four hours.

Bob was out of town at the time. Ginny was not able to contact him during the emergency because he was on a plane returning home. Later that night, Ginny went to the airport by herself to meet Bob and break the news to him. Neither of them could describe their agony. They said no words were available to adequately express the devastation they felt that night.

It was interesting to observe the changes that took place in our group in the following weeks. The widows no longer focused on their personal grief. Instead they were all reaching out to Ginny and Bob. One woman began to knit a pair of booties for the new baby, and another embroidered bibs. We began to have nutritious snacks instead of the usual brownies and cookies the women had been bringing.

One evening, Ginny mentioned it was almost time to have the new baby. She confessed she was filled with fear about having to return to the hospital where Shawna had died. She had even considered having the baby at home, but her doctor had discouraged it. Bob just shook his head sympathetically.

I noticed other group members exchanging words and I felt a special electricity in the room. When our meeting ended, nobody got up to leave except Ginny and Bob. They were barely out the door when conversations began to buzz all around me.

"What can we do to help?"

"Ginny must get over this fear so that she can enjoy the birth of her new baby."

"Let's take Ginny over to the hospital in advance and help her get over her terror."

"Can we pray for Ginny and Bob?"

We most certainly could, and that's just what we did, right then.

The following week I spoke with several psychologists and physicians. They all agreed that going to the hospital in advance would do no harm. I called the hospital, explained the situation and was granted free access to all areas.

I called on three of our widows who had shown special concern. If Ginny agreed, we would meet at the hospital, return to the rooms where Shawna had been, and then go up to the maternity ward and look in the nursery window.

I phoned Ginny and told her about our idea. There was a long silence. Then I heard her sniffle, and she answered me in a very small, choked voice.

"You couldn't have made that offer at a better time. Today would have been Shawna's third birthday. I've been praying all day long about the new baby and asking God to help me look forward to his or her arrival."

When we met the following day, Ginny was extremely nervous. We walked up the stairs into the lobby and had to stop before we got much farther. Ginny said her heart was racing, and she felt as if the walls were closing in on her. We left the building and bribed her with an ice cream cone if she would come back a second time. I have never known a pregnant woman to turn down an ice cream cone, and Ginny was no exception. The cone became our standard bribe each week.

We met once a week for our hospital walks. Ginny was courageous. At times she clutched my hand, and I would see the perspiration bead on her upper lip. But after the first trip, she never made us turn back. I know it was more than the ice cream cone that kept her going!

Eventually we came to the day when she didn't grasp my hand quite so hard, and then one week she even smiled. That day, we let her have a double dip of chocolate mint, her favorite.

The following week Bob came to the meeting alone, proudly carrying a bouquet of white roses tied with blue ribbon and a large color photo of his new son. He told us Ginny had gone confidently into the hospital the night the baby was born. He felt a miracle had taken place, and so did we. I was the only one who realized two miracles had taken place.

Our group continued to meet for a few weeks after that, but I knew it was needless. Our widows' wounds had been gradually healing as they reached out to Ginny, bringing about healing in their own lives, too.

June Cerza Kolf

[EDITORS' NOTE: *The names in this story were changed for confidentiality.*]

Sandy, I Can't

No matter how little money or how few possessions you own, having a dog makes you rich.

Louis Sabin

As long as Jeremy could remember, he had wanted a dog. For his eleventh birthday, his parents gave him a large box that wiggled and yapped.

"A dog! I know it's a dog!"

Jeremy hurriedly opened the loosely wrapped container and out tumbled a wagging, licking cocker spaniel whose tail was flipping from side to side so quickly that its whole rump seemed to jump from the floor.

"Is it a boy or a girl?" Jeremy asked, as the puppy tried to climb into his lap, lick his face and chew the box all at the same time.

"It's a girl."

"She's beautiful! Her color reminds me of the sand on a beach. I'm going to call her Sandy."

One of their very favorite times together was when Jeremy would ride his bike in the park with Sandy running alongside. She would stop, sniff, toss her floppy ears

and then zoom ahead of Jeremy. She would then wait for
him to catch up and then zoom off again. She just thought
this was the greatest game. When Jeremy stopped and got
off his bike, she would then run up to him, barking happily and then sit looking at him with her tongue hanging
out. Sandy always looked so silly Jeremy would have to
laugh. She then would tumble into his lap proudly as if
she had just told a very funny joke.

A year went by. That summer, at the end of a busy day
swimming at the beach, Jeremy complained to his mother
that he had a headache and stiff neck. The next morning,
Jeremy was worse. He could not get out of bed. When the
doctor was called, the stiffness had gotten so bad he could
hardly move.

"I'm afraid Jeremy has polio," the doctor said.

Jeremy spent three months in the hospital. When he
finally came home, he had a brace on one of his legs and
needed crutches to walk. Sandy was so happy to see him,
she refused to leave his side.

"Every time Sandy saw someone ride by on a bike, she
would bark and run back and forth in the yard, then she
would whine and whine," his father told Jeremy.

"Well, I can never ride a bike now," Jeremy half
whispered.

The next morning, Jeremy limped out to the garage
with his crutches to look at his Schwinn-Flyer, all red and
chrome and shiny. Sandy immediately began to jump and
yap and wag her tail.

"No, I can't Sandy. I can't," Jeremy cried. Sandy just
whined. She did not understand.

Every day after that, Sandy would run out to the garage
and back to Jeremy, barking and wagging her tail.

Sandy did not understand the word "can't."

Finally, Jeremy said, "Okay, okay, Sandy, but my leg is
so weak."

As Jeremy climbed on the bike, Sandy barked happily, ran furiously around the bicycle and wagged her tail like a fan. Jeremy started to ride, then suddenly fell! He started to cry, and immediately Sandy ran up to him where he lay sprawled on the ground and started to lick his face. His crying turned to laughing because Sandy's tongue tickled him.

"Okay, I'll try again!" The second time, he fell again but not as hard. The third and fourth time, he fell and started to laugh.

"Sandy, now I'm getting mad!"

Finally, after a number of tries, he did not fall.

Sandy sat on the ground and if she could talk, she would probably have said, "I knew you could do it."

It was a slow process but after three months Jeremy was slowly riding his bicycle again. After another four months he was walking with a cane and no brace on his leg.

Sandy never knew that she was one of the main reasons that today Jeremy is a normal grown-up who does not even limp. She was only a dog and did not understand.

Or did she?

Lawrence A. Kross

Perfectly Normal

The year was 1963.

That's when I was born ... to "perfectly normal" parents at a "perfectly normal" Cleveland hospital.

I would like to say that I was a "perfectly normal," healthy baby, ready to take on the world. But instead, I was born with multiple deformities. My eyes were almost on the sides of my head, and I only had holes where my nose was supposed to be. I had a club foot and was missing all but one toe, if it could be called that. Also, three of my fingers were missing on my right hand. A cleft palate had an opening in my top lip and extended all the way to the right eye. Unfortunately, even one leg was shorter than the other.

The hospital staff, I was told, thought I had too many problems to survive. The doctors, in fact, refused to show me to my parents and, incredulously, even gave my parents forms to sign to "give me up for science."

I can only thank God that my parents had other plans for my life. I belonged to them and to God. They intended to love and accept me just as I was, despite acknowledging that it would be a long, hard road ahead.

At the age of seven months, I began to undergo a very

long series of operations. However, the first seven were deemed failures. The surgeons, it seemed were trying to do too much at once. I, on the other hand, was like a puzzle that needed to be "put together" one piece at a time.

While successive surgeries were a little more successful, my appearance was still far from normal. In fact, very few people knew that I had already had sixteen operations by the time I was ready for third grade.

When I began kindergarten, I was placed in a special-education classroom because my appearance and imperfect speech were not accepted. Aside from being labeled a "special-ed" kid, I endured constant ridicule from other students who called me "stupid," "ugly" and "retarded" because of my looks. I also walked with a limp and had to wear special shoes and braces on my legs. I spent almost every school holiday in the hospital having operations and also missed a lot of school. I wondered if I would ever get out of special classes. My desire to become a "normal" child prompted my parents to pursue tests that would place me back in regular education classrooms. My parents and I worked very hard that summer to get ready for the big test. Finally, I was tested.

I'll never forget the day I waited outside the principal's office while my parents received my test results. The brown door between them and me seemed to loom bigger and bigger as time went by. Time passed in slow motion. I longed to put my ear to the door to hear what was being said.

After an hour passed, my mother finally emerged with a tear streaming down her cheek. I thought, *Oh, no, another year in special-ed.* But much to my relief, the principal put his hand on my shoulder and said, "Welcome to 3B, young man!" My mom gave me a big hug.

Another milestone in fourth grade was the "miracle" that my parents and I had longed for. I was selected to undergo a very experimental surgery that would resculpt my entire face with bone grafts. The surgery was life-threatening and lasted ten hours. I survived this operation, my eighteenth, which really changed my life. At last, my nose had a shape, my lip was "fixed" and my eyes were very close to being in their normal position.

While I now faced a new chapter in my life from a physical perspective, I hadn't seen the end of my trials.

Within the next few years, my mother developed cancer and died, but not before instilling in me a sense of worth and the determination never to give up.

When other kids called me names, she had prompted, "Don't let those names bother you. Feel sorry for those kids who were not brought up right."

In addition, my parents taught me to be thankful for my blessings, pointing out that other people might have even greater challenges.

Their words eventually impacted my life when I did see people with greater challenges—in hospitals and whenever I did volunteer work with children who were mentally challenged.

As a teenager, I came to realize that my purpose in life was to help others become successful with whatever gifts they were blessed with, despite the things that society might point out as handicaps or shortcomings. In fact, my father advised, "Mike, you would make a great special-ed teacher." I knew what it was like to be a special-ed child.

However, I simply wasn't ready to make teaching my career choice at that point. Instead, I earned a degree in business and went on to become a very successful salesman, spending seven years in retail management. Then, I went on to become a very successful bank employee, spending five years as a loan officer. Still, something in my life was missing.

Despite the fact that I had met and married a special-ed teacher, it took me twelve years to realize that was my calling also and that my dad had been right.

Continuing my college education, pursuing a master's degree in education, I now teach in the same school district as my wife.

My classroom is a kaleidoscope of children with special needs—emotional, physical and mental. My newest career choice is my most challenging yet. I love to see my students' smiling faces when they learn something new, when a few words are spoken and when an award is won in the Special Olympics.

I've now gone through twenty-nine surgeries. While many have brought a lot of pain to my life, the fact that I have survived them all only seems to reiterate to me that God has a purpose for my life, as well as for every other life. I see my purpose being fulfilled one child at a time.

I may not have been a "perfectly normal" healthy baby, but I am ready to take on the world—thanks to God and to people like my mom. The motto she gave me will always be the motto I use in my own classroom: Never give up.

Michael Biasini

The Pony

The doctor tried to break the news as gently as possible.
"You know how when you're little and you ask for a pony, you pray and hope for it, and you never get it? Well, this is that same type of situation. Sometimes you don't get the pony."

He was trying to tell Chris Wood's parents that the situation was hopeless, even beyond their prayers.

Chris was twenty-one and stationed in the Navy in San Diego that June of 1989. After an afternoon of drinking at a Padres game, he fell out of a pickup truck on the way home when the driver switched lanes.

After he landed on the four-lane highway, a car hit him. He bounced into another lane and was hit by another car. Luckily, the next vehicle to come along was an ambulance. Chris had a broken pelvis, jaw, elbow and knee, massive head injuries, and tire marks across his back.

For the next three months, the doctors' pronouncements on Chris's prognosis were all negative.

He will not live. . . . He will be a vegetable. . . . He will never walk. . . . He will never have a meaningful life.

His family back in Akron started prayer chains. One night, his sister was awakened, she says by God, who whispered to her these words: "He will live, and not die, and proclaim the mercies of God."

From then on, that was the family's mantra.

It got Chris through thirty-two surgeries, a three-month coma and years of treatment at the Veterans Hospital in Cleveland, where he still goes for rehabilitation.

Chris, now twenty-nine, has the same bright blue eyes and sandy hair as before, but everything else has changed.

His speech is slurred, as if he's been drinking. The breathing tube damaged his vocal cords, the head injuries slowed his thinking and his face is a bit crooked from his jaw healing incorrectly.

A purple zipper-shaped scar runs up his left arm, which dangles at his side. He must concentrate to open his hand.

Chris is a walking hardware store. There's a screw in his elbow, a brace on his leg, a hinge in his knee and a plate in his head.

His brain no longer works the same. He used to excel at math, but now he struggles with the basics. When he enrolled at Kent State University six years ago, he got Ds and Fs even in the simplest classes. One of his rehab workers urged him to drop out.

He gave it some thought. His mind told him he was wasting his time. But instead of listening, he turned to his favorite scripture passage, Prov. 23:7: "For as he thinketh in his heart, so is he."

"In English, it means what you believe is what you're going to be. If you think you are second and a failure, or number one and front of the line, that's what you will be," he said.

He credits his mother for his successes. Linda coached him along, using the Bible as her playbook. Chris now has three jobs: He interns at Edwin Shaw Hospital, working with head injury patients; he does computer design work for Living Water Fellowship Church in Akron; and he is an usher for the Akron Aeros.

It took three tries to pass his driver's test, but he finally got his license.

It took six years of therapy, but last month he put away his wheelchair. Today he is able to use a walker.

He still struggles to come up with the right words when he talks. He pauses, squints hard, trying to force his brain to remember how to work.

Two weeks ago, Chris Wood gave a commencement address at his graduation without saying a word.

He walked across a stage at Kent State University and picked up his diploma—he earned a bachelor of arts in psychology—to a standing ovation.

He wasn't the smartest one there.

He wasn't the most talented one there.

But he was there.

His mother never lived to see it. She died right before June of a heart attack.

But she lived long enough to know the doctor who said it was hopeless even to pray was wrong.

That doctor got a postcard from Chris's dad, Daniel, letting him know how it all turned out.

It simply said, "We got the pony."

Regina Brett

Consider This

The person interested in success has to learn to view failure as a healthy, inevitable part of the process of getting to the top.

Dr. Joyce Brothers

Consider this:

The movie *Star Wars* was rejected by every movie studio in Hollywood before 20th Century-Fox finally produced it. It went on to be one of the largest-grossing movies in film history.

E.T., Forrest Gump, Home Alone, Speed and *Pulp Fiction* were all rejected by major studios before they finally found a studio willing to produce them.

An executive at MGM penned this memo after a screening of *The Wizard of Oz:* "The rainbow song's no good. Take it out."

Another MGM executive sent this memo advising against investing in *Gone With the Wind:* "Forget it. No Civil War picture ever made a nickel."

As a child, Sylvester Stallone was frequently beaten by

his father and told he had no brains. He grew up a loner and emotionally anguished. He was in and out of various schools. An advisor at Drexel University told him that, based on aptitude testing, he should pursue a career as an elevator repair person.

In 1887, the *Musical Courier* wrote: "Brahms evidently lacks the breadth and power of invention eminently necessary for the production of truly great symphonic work."

In 1932, during a Minneapolis bank robbery, a man was murdered. A small-time thief by the name of Leonard Hankins was arrested, convicted of the crime and sentenced to prison. Later through the testimony of others, it became clear that Hankins was innocent. Jack Mackay, an Associated Press correspondent in St. Paul, worked on the case, trying to get him free, for nineteen years. Mackay wrote about the case again and again, drawing attention to the injustice of Hankins's imprisonment. He was Hankins's only advocate. Finally, in 1951, Governor C. Elmore Anderson convened the state pardon board in a special session. They ordered Hankins freed from prison and agreed that he had never committed the crime. The power of persistence!

> *You will never stub your toe standing still. The faster you go, the more chance there is of stubbing your toe, but the more chance you have of getting somewhere.*
>
> Charles F. Kettering

IBM founder Tom Watson, believing in a new product and its development, supported one of his vice presidents in promoting the product. It was quite a risky venture and ended up in financial disaster to the tune of $10 million. The vice president came to him in shame and offered his resignation. Watson was reported to have said, "You must be kidding. We've just spent $10 million educating you."

Success is 99 percent failure.

Soichiro Honda
Founder, Honda Motor Company

Einstein was criticized for not wearing socks or cutting his hair. One observer noted, "He could be mentally retarded."

For those of you who have been using age as an excuse, consider this:

Grandma Moses didn't begin painting until she was seventy-six years old.

Ruth Gordon won her first Oscar for *Rosemary's Baby* when she was seventy-two years old.

Golda Meir was elected prime minister of Israel at the age of seventy-one.

And finally, if you think your vote is not important, consider this:

In 1645, one vote gave Oliver Cromwell control of England.

In 1649, one vote caused Charles I, King of England to be executed.

In 1868, one vote saved President Andrew Johnson from impeachment.

In 1875, one vote changed France from a monarchy to a republic.

In 1876, one vote gave Rutherford B. Hayes the presidency of the United States.

In 1923, one vote gave Adolph Hitler leadership in the Nazi party.

In 1941, one vote saved the Selective Service—just weeks before the bombing of Pearl Harbor.

Jack Canfield and Mark Victor Hansen

Casting a New Mold for Heroes

Football wasn't easy for Jamie, but he refused to be pampered by his teammates. He became annoyed, at practice, if his teammates didn't hit him as hard as they did everyone else. So he egged them on: "Come on, you wuss, can't you hit any harder than that?" So Jamie's teammates complied with his challenge to their macho nature and drilled him to the turf. No problem. Jamie just got back up and baited his teammates into blasting him again. Jamie wanted to experience the full impact of football and felt that he had earned his right to do just that, cerebral palsy or not.

The first time I set eyes on Jamie, he reminded me of the poster boy for the March of Dimes. He was a cute, frail-looking middle school sixth-grader, with dishwater-blond hair and glasses. He also had his own wheelchair.

Jamie had just gotten back from the Shriner's Children's Hospital, where he was operated on to eliminate hip muscle restrictions and buckling knees, while correcting his toes-out and knees-in style of walking—a condition that encouraged years of teasing and multitudes of discomfort. The operation was the latest in a series of operations designed to help him function properly, operations that manipulated his tender and helpless young body via hip muscle cuttings, heel cord cuttings, stapling and realignment of leg bones.

Sometime during Jamie's career as a sixth-grader, he graduated from his wheelchair to restrictive walking casts and crutches. It was then that I witnessed the casting of a new mold for heroes, a mold that was producing a boy with a willful intent to beat the malady of mediocrity.

Jamie had no intention of depending upon others, which, in Jamie's awkward and unsteady state, would get him into troublesome predicaments. He often fell crashing to the floor, his books, crutches and body flying in all directions. Those of us who witnessed his dilemma wanted to go to his aid, but there was always something about his composure that refused coddling of any kind. He simply untwisted his contorted frame into a suitable position, gathered his books, struggled up into the security of his crutches and started over, his mission accomplished.

Sometime before Jamie started seventh grade, he ditched his supportive crutches and restrictive casts and took on the normal world with an intense determination. It would be his to conquer with or without his support, and if he sensed that his new condition would, in any way, present difficult obstacles in his path toward wholeness, he wasn't letting on.

Yet, whether Jamie wanted to recognize these new challenges at the surface of his conscious thinking or not, they were there. Jamie now walked (shuffled) with his hips forward while his head, chest and legs tagged slightly behind. His gait was unsteady, much like that of a newborn calf, yet his head, while lagging slightly behind, was always held high. An accidental bump, though, in the crowded hallways between classes, would once again send Jamie sprawling to the floor with his materials flying in all directions. The incident always left Jamie's surroundings in a state of melodramatic hush, a condition Jamie chose to ignore or maybe not even notice. After all, the incident was just another dot on the paper for Jamie in a lifetime of falls, teasings, frustrations and bruises. Why should he react anyway? Was it that out of the ordinary just to fall down? So Jamie would collect his books off the floor, struggle to his feet and continue on as though the only moment in time would be the one he experienced next.

Jamie continued his choreographed shuffle-and-stumble routine throughout the eighth grade with some variation, since he was slightly bigger and slightly stronger. In the meantime, gigantic growth was occurring within him. He was transforming from a boy to a man, and the inward strength and spirit of a giant were urging him to conquer anything in his path. These urgings came to the surface by the ninth grade.

Alex Karras once said that toughness comes from the soul and spirit, and not from muscles and an immature mind. As a freshman, Jamie made a prophet out of Karras. He tried out for football.

The coaches, understandably cautious, asked Jamie if he would consider becoming a manager. They were concerned about his physical well-being out on the gridiron. Yet his dream was to become a football player, not a manager. Jamie, not about to succumb to overprotectiveness, joined the team.

As a player, Jamie was the smallest, slowest and most susceptible to getting hurt. Yet he was also the most courageous. His lack of physical talent may have frustrated him, but he never let that hold him back or get him down. He refused to give up his soul to self-pity. When the rest of the team finished a fifteen-yard windsprint and waited for Jamie, who was only halfway, he just kept on shuffling with his head back and his head up. He may have sensed that he was being watched by the other team members, who waited for him to finish, but what he couldn't be aware of was the sense of awe his teammates felt for the courage and determination that he projected.

Jamie committed himself to freshman football. He always stayed after practice to improve his game, and he was always the first to raise his hand when coaches asked for volunteers during practice. But he was used sparingly during games. He was no doubt disappointed at being relegated to the sidelines, yet it gave him an opportunity to utilize his role as inspirational sideline leader. When he wasn't begging the coaches to let him in the game, he was a cheerleader. He awkwardly threw his arms into the air in jubilance when his team made a good play. Oftentimes this jubilant display left him sprawled face down on the sideline grass. If this was embarrassing to anyone else, it wasn't to Jamie. He merely picked himself up and continued cheering.

On occasion, freshmen football games include a "fifth" quarter intended to give the reserves some well-earned playing time. During the fifth quarter of one game, Jamie got in on defense. On one particular play, Jamie got knocked down as soon as the play started. Jamie got up as quickly as his body allowed him to and faced the flow of the play. The ballcarrier was headed right for him. Jamie braced himself, lowered his shoulder, reached his arms around the ball carrier and dragged him to the turf. His teammates on the sidelines cheered, and his teammates on the field gave him high-fives. At that moment, Jamie got to be the ballplayer he had always hoped to be; he became part of the heat of the moment and heard the cheers for his accomplishment. It was only a tackle, yet he felt the thrill of scoring the winning touchdown or of intercepting the key pass that saved the game. Every knock to the turf during that entire season was now more worthwhile than he had already perceived it.

Jerry Harpt

Angels All Around

Dorothy Wright's husband, Forrest, shook her hard, "Wake up, Dorothy! Get up! There's smoke everywhere!"

Dorothy coughed, opened her eyes to a gray haze in their bedroom, bolted upright and screamed, "Get the kids!" She grabbed the phone to call 911 but before she could tell them where they lived the line went dead.

Oh Lord, help us, Dorothy prayed as she and Forrest ran in opposite directions to wake their children, Forrest Junior, sixteen; Danielle, fifteen; Leonard, thirteen; Dominique, twelve; Joe, eleven; Anthony, ten; Marcus, eight; Vinny, seven; Curtis, five; Nicholas, three; and Ja-Monney, three. (Ja-Monney is her nephew that they've raised since his birth.)

Scared and confused, the children rubbed their eyes and stumbled down the stairs and out the front door. Dorothy counted heads.

"Someone's missing!" she screamed. "Who? Curtis! Forrest, Curtis is missing!"

Forrest, ran back into the house and up the steps as smoke poured out the front door. Five-year-old Curtis, who'd been hiding under his bed, struggled into the smoky hallway when he heard his Daddy's voice. He couldn't see Forrest in the thick smoke but he ran right into his Daddy's arms. Forrest grabbed him and tore back down the stairs. Halfway down Forrest fell, sprained his ankle and stumbled outdoors.

Dorothy dashed to the neighbor's house. The woman who lived there had been studying all night and had just gone to bed when Dorothy banged on the door. The neighbor finally saw the orange glow through the Wright family's windows and called 911. Within minutes the fire trucks arrived. By now the flames had spread between the walls of the old wood frame house and moved to the second floor.

Neighbors took the children into their homes. But Dorothy couldn't move. As firefighters slammed their axes into the roof, she stood there and watched her dream evaporate. Everything inside that house went up in flames. Furniture, clothing, housewares, linens, photo albums, cash, jewelry, the only picture she had of her mother who died when Dorothy was a teenager. Everything was gone.

Our dream, Dorothy thought, *How can it end like this?* She and Forrest had wanted so much more for their eleven children than was offered in the inner-city. They'd just moved to the suburb of New Milford, outside Hackensack, New Jersey four years earlier. They didn't want the kids growing up around drugs, alcohol abuse, fighting and gangs. They didn't want the sub-standard education or the run-down neighborhoods.

What a blessing when they found the big frame house and met Diana, their landlord. They convinced her that they were hard workers and that their children were polite, good kids and that they'd take care of her home. The rent was reasonable and the Wright family moved in.

Now as Dorothy stood there four years later watching their dream evaporate into smoke, all she could think about was two things: *Thank You, God, my family is safe!* And then, *Where will we ever find another house for our big family?*

After visiting the hospital to make sure the kids were okay and to get a cast on Forrest's sprained ankle, Dorothy went directly to Social Services in her blue pajamas and sneakers a neighbor had given her. As she stood in line people looked at her like, *What's your problem, lady?*

Dorothy didn't care what she looked like. She was a woman on a mission. The only thing the emergency assistance program could do was to put them into a family shelter back in the inner city. Thirteen people crowded into four tiny rooms.

"It was awful," Dorothy told a friend, "So much goes on in a shelter like that. People moving in and out every day. Drugs. Yelling. Women getting beat up by boyfriends. No play area. Nothing for the children to do."

That's when the guardian angels started to arrive. Dorothy's friend Lisa, who owns Alfredo's restaurant brought food for the family every night for dinner for four months. Pizza, spaghetti, garlic bread, fresh salads, lasagna, eggplant parmesan . . . all the foods kids love. Their neighbors from the old neighborhood, Jerry and Cynthia, brought a TV to the shelter. Strangers brought brand new clothes. The kids' teachers brought school supplies, coloring books, crayons. Other teachers from New Milford high school, middle school and grammar school had fund-raisers for the family.

The whole town adopted the Wright family and the gifts continued all summer. But Dorothy continued to worry about how they'd ever get out of the shelter and back into the wonderful neighborhood they'd worked so hard to get into four years earlier. How would they ever find another house big enough for their family that they could afford?

One day, one of Vinny's classmates came to visit. When little Michael Kontomanolis and Vinny saw each other they just hugged and started crying. Michael said, "Mommy, can Vinny come live with us? We have to help him. He's my friend."

Michael's parents, Pauline and Nicholas were so touched by the boys' deep friendship that often that summer they took the Wright children back to their home in their old neighborhood on the weekends. Dorothy was relieved that her kids could get out of the shelter for awhile, but she said to Pauline and Nick, "You only have two kids. How can you stand so many at once?" Nick would laugh and say, "We love it! It's like a big party when they come over."

Then the biggest surprise of all. One day Pauline said, "Dorothy, Nick and I have decided to buy a house in our neighborhood and rent it to you for four years. Then you can buy it from us. We want you to have your own home. We want you to come back to the neighborhood where you belong."

Dorothy and Forrest couldn't believe it. Why would this couple who hardly knew them before the fire do such a thing for them? Pauline just smiled and said, "We connect through our hearts, Dorothy." Together Dorothy and Pauline found a two-story Cape Cod with six bedrooms, a huge living room, big dining room and finished basement. The thirteen members of the Wright family moved in in October, just five months after the fire. On moving day the family opened the doors to discover huge "Welcome home!" banners taped everywhere. The neighbors had supplied the house with everything from toothpaste and toilet paper to laundry soap and paper towels; even make-up for the girls.

One couple, Agnes and Ralph, bought eight expensive twin beds and pillows for all the children. Others brought quilts, sheets, and bedspreads for everyone.

Since then, "Aunt Pauline and Uncle Nikkolas" as the

children call them, have become like brother and sister to Dorothy and Forrest. They cook out together, share things, spend time together.

Every day as Dorothy watches her children come home from volleyball or basketball practice or a yearbook meeting, she thanks God that they have their dream back. Danielle wants to speak eight languages and go to Harvard to be a lawyer. One of the boys wants to be a fighter pilot. Three of them want to be doctors. Dominique wants to be a nurse. Leonard wants to be a technician for NASA.

Dorothy Wright says it best, "With as many guardian angels as this family has, and with the love we have for each other, the dreams of the entire Wright family will continue for generations."

Patricia Lorenz
Excerpted from Woman's World

The Bicycle

When I was nine I needed to earn some money, so I asked Mr. Miceli, the Herald-American's man in my Albany Park neighborhood, about an after-school paper route. He was old, about thirty, but he spoke to me as though I was a grown-up, and I liked that. After awhile he said that if I would show him my bicycle, he'd give me a route. My dad was then working four jobs: He built neon signs in a sheet metal shop during the day, delivered flowers until eight o'clock in the evening, drove a cab till midnight, and on weekends sold insurance door-to-door. He bought me a used bike, but right after that he was hospitalized with double pneumonia and couldn't teach me how to ride. But Mr. Miceli hadn't asked to see me ride, merely to see the bike. I walked it down to his garage, showed it to him, and I had a job.

At first, I filled my delivery sack with rolled papers, slung it over the handlebars, and walked my bike down the sidewalks. But pushing a bike with a load of papers was very awkward; after a few days I borrowed Mom's two-wheeled shopping cart: a folding, steel-mesh device.

Delivering papers from a bike is tricky. You get one chance to throw each paper, and if it misses a porch or stoop, too bad. Delivering from Mom's cart, I left it at the sidewalk and carried each paper to its proper destination. If there was a second- or third-floor porch, and I missed the first throw, I retrieved the paper and threw again. Sundays, when the paper was big and heavy and I couldn't throw it above the first floor anyway, I carried all of them up the stairs. If it was raining, I put my papers inside the screen door or, at apartment buildings, in the entrance hall. The cart was especially useful in rain or snow, because I could put Dad's old raincoat over the canvas bag to keep everything dry.

It took me longer to deliver the papers than if I was on a bike, but I didn't mind. I got to meet everyone in the neighborhood. These were solid, working-class people, many of them of Italian, German or Polish descent, and they were invariably kind to me. If I saw something interesting while walking my route, such as a dog with puppies or a rainbow of oil on wet asphalt, I could stop to watch for as long as I wanted.

When Dad returned from the hospital, he resumed his job in the sheet metal shop, but he was too tired and weak to work his other jobs and had to give them up. Now we needed every dime we could raise to pay bills, so we sold my bike. Since I still didn't know how to ride it, and I was used to Mom's cart, I didn't object too much. Mr. Miceli must have known I wasn't using a bike, but he said nothing about it to me. In fact, he rarely spoke to any of us boys, unless it was to give us hell for missing a customer or leaving a paper in a puddle.

Eight months after I began delivering papers, I had built my route from thirty-six subscribers to fifty-nine, mostly because customers sent me to their neighbors, who said they wanted to take the paper. Sometimes, people stopped me on the street to tell me to add them to my list. I earned a penny a paper, Monday through Saturday, and a nickel for each big Sunday paper. I collected every Thursday evening, and since most customers gave me a nickel or a dime extra, soon I was making almost as much in tips as I got from Mr. Miceli. That was good, because Dad still couldn't work as much as before, and I had to give most of my wages to Mom. She usually let me keep a dollar, if I agreed to share some of it with my younger brothers and my older sister.

On the Thursday evening before Christmas, 1950, I rang my first customer's doorbell. While the lights were on, nobody answered the door, so I went on to the next house. No answer, nor did anyone respond at the next family on my route, or the one after. Soon I'd knocked and rang at every subscriber's door on the first of the two blocks of my route—but not one person was home. I was very worried; I had to pay for my papers every Friday. And while it was almost Christmas, I never thought that everyone would be out shopping. So I was very happy when, going up the walkway to the Gordon's house, I heard music and voices. I rang the bell. Instantly the door was flung open, and Mr. Gordon all but dragged me inside. Jammed into his living room was almost every one of my fifty-nine subscribers! In the middle of the room was a brand new Schwinn bicycle. It was candy-apple red and it had a generator-powered headlamp and a bell. A canvas bag bulging with colorful envelopes hung from the handlebars.

"This is for you," Mrs. Gordon said. "We all chipped in." The envelopes held Christmas cards from every subscriber, along with their weekly subscription fees. Most also included a generous tip—I counted over $100 when I got home, a windfall that made me a family hero and brought our household a wonderful holiday season. I was dumbstruck. I didn't know what to say. Finally, one of the women called for quiet, then took my shoulder and gently led me to the center of the room. "You are the best paperboy we've ever had," she said. "There's never been a day when a paper was missing or late, never a day when it got wet. We've all seen you out there in the rain and snow with that little shopping cart, and so we thought you ought to have a bicycle." All I could say was, "Thank you." I said it over and over.

They must have called Mr. Miceli, because when I got to his garage the next day to pick up my papers, he was waiting outside. "Bring your bike tomorrow at ten o'clock, and I'll teach you how to ride," he said, and I did. When I had begun to feel comfortable on a bike, Mr. Miceli asked me to deliver a second route, forty-two papers. Delivering both routes from my new bike went faster than delivering one from the shopping cart. But when it rained, I got off my bike to carry every paper to a dry place. If I missed a throw to a high porch, I stopped, put down the kickstand and threw again. I knew my subscribers expected nothing less.

I joined the Army after high school and gave my Schwinn to my younger brother, Ted. Now I can't recall what became of it. But the Gordons and my other subscribers sent along with that bicycle and their cash another gift, a shining lesson about taking pride in even the humblest work, a Christmas present I try to use as often as I remember the kind Chicagoans who gave it to me.

Marvin J. Wolf

6

LIVE YOUR DREAM

*It's a funny thing about life; if you refuse
to accept anything but the best, you very
often get it.*

W. Somerset Maugham

A Glass of Lemonade

It was 1980. I was fifteen years old.

We were docked at a harbor in Chu Hai, a village just outside Saigon. The pounding of our hearts nearly drowned out the motor. There were 120 of us inside the cabin, our bodies lying on top of each other. Ten dozen people, all with one dream: freedom.

Freedom from oppression. Freedom from the communist regime. Freedom, even if it meant our lives.

Capture meant imprisonment in the brutal labor camps, never to be seen again.

I knew that fear. Last attempt out, one year earlier, they nearly got me. I hid in a rice field till dark before sneaking onto a bus back home. Even so, I only avoided detection because my clothes looked like the yellow khakis of the government soldiers.

We kept still as the boat slipped out in the middle of the night. Thailand, our destination, was just hours away, yet it was also an eternity. I thought back to when I hugged my family goodbye just a few hours earlier. They could only afford passage for me, their eldest son. Suddenly it hit me: even if I made it, I might never see them again.

The tension inside the cabin was thick, our breath

clinging to our skin. We were still under fire. Armed soldiers manned the peninsula. It would be an entire day before we were completely beyond detection.

We had enough food for two days; a satchel of rice, some milk, two steel canisters of water. We couldn't drink the ocean water because the salt would dry us out. The dirt and rust inside the canister turned the water orange. But it was all we had. I pretended it tasted like my mother's lemonade. I could not have drank it otherwise.

Once beyond detection, we could relax—at least, mentally.

The weather is very humid in Vietnam; add 120 bodies inside a cabin half that size, and you'll know how suffocating it was. Things got even worse that night: we hit a storm. Raging winds and monstrous waves terrified us for two straight days. The stench of our own waste and vomit made breathing unbearable. I climbed on deck to get some air. I felt a small object zoom past my head. Suddenly a surging wave knocked me right back into the cabin. I passed out. When I came to, the woman holding me said I was lucky. "That wave roll behind you," she said, "you land in the ocean."

I closed my eyes. When I was little, my mother reminded me every night that God never stops watching over us. Maybe that's what he was doing now. Bad as things were during the storm, they were nothing compared to what faced us were we ever caught.

The storm had barely passed when another disaster set in. The captain had lost his compass in the storm—maybe that was what nearly hit me two nights before. Not only were we hopelessly off course, we were out of power, and out of gas.

We were devastated. Our worst fears had come to pass. Only instead of a brutal death at the hands of the government, we would wither away under the merciless sun.

We drifted aimlessly for days. Sometimes we'd see a vessel on the horizon, but we could not signal for help. Our flare gun was also lost at sea. Though we were easier to spot during the day, no boat stopped to help. Maybe we were too far away. I hope that's true. I hate to think anyone could sail past a boatload of dying people and still do nothing.

Our food was gone. Our bodies were so dehydrated, our clothes stuck to our skin, for some, they stuck to the bottom of the boat. Though the ocean was filled with sharks, many of us jumped overboard—not to swim, but simply to let the waters soak through our skin.

Some women drew water from the ocean and mixed it with sugar, but we could only have a cupful because of the salt. We were all starving and thirsty, but it was hardest on the children. One nine-year-old boy drank all the water when no one was looking. He died that night; we wrapped him in a blanket and buried him at sea. We took his death hard. His father was an American soldier; he would have been treated well had he made it to the United States.

Though we were resigned to our fate, we tried comforting each other. My friend Don asked me, "If you could have just one thing before you die, what would it be?"

I didn't want much. If I couldn't have my family, perhaps a reminder would do. "A glass of lemonade," I answered. "That would be heaven."

We were sitting on deck later that night when I noticed a glorious blaze on the horizon. I poked Don in the shoulder and pointed: *"Giah KHoan! Giah KHoan!"* We spread the word, and soon the boat was brimming with hope and anticipation.

We'd spotted an oil rig.

Some men used wooden planks to steer us closer, but soon gave up because the current was too strong. By morning we had one choice left; swimming for it. Even that was a long shot. The waters were shark-infested, and the ship was several miles away.

Three men volunteered. The first man never returned; either he drowned or the sharks got him. The second man gave up after an hour because the current kept pulling him back. The third man, a fisherman, swam diagonally so that eventually the current began pushing him toward the rig. Though he had to stop several times because of leg cramps, he finally reached the oil rig twelve hours later.

They picked us up the next morning, our eighth day out of port. Our lips were parched and bleeding, our skin bruised and infected, our stomachs swollen. We couldn't eat anything solid, so they made us rice soup. I've never had a more delicious meal in my life.

We were alive. We had survived. The ship would take us to a refugee camp in Malaysia; from there, we would eventually be allowed into America. Our dream of freedom was finally at hand.

I was naturalized in 1990. I studied engineering at Rutgers University, and have owned my own business since 1991. My family is very proud of me.

Those eight days were frightening, and I wouldn't wish them on anyone. Yet the perspective that experience has given me on life itself has made it worthwhile. My path has not always been smooth; occasionally I still experience some prejudice, and, like everyone else, some days at work are very stressful. But even those kinds of pressure seem like nothing once you've come that close to death.

My mother was right. God never gives us anything we can't handle. I could lose my business tomorrow, and it wouldn't really matter. I know I'm a survivor, and that in itself makes me a success.

And every time I drink a glass of lemonade, I remember that.

Ed Robertson, Vincent Luong and Mary Gardner

From Hodgkin's to Ironman

It is by tiny steps that we ascend the stars.

Jack Leedstrom

"It's possible to eat an elephant—but not in one sitting. It can only be consumed one bite at a time."

These words, spoken by a close friend, influenced the outcome of the most difficult and grueling endeavor I ever attempted.

In early 1994, I was very ill and had lost twenty pounds.

That February, oncologist Dr. Jack Chritchley told me I was dying of cancer. Instead of being filled with panic at the diagnosis, I experienced a profound sense of peace because of my spiritual connectedness to God. However, I was terrified for my family. Thinking of having to leave them left my knees weak and my heart pounding. I broke the news to my wife, Caroline.

At supper that night, we told our two teenagers. Jodi was only fifteen, in grade ten, and her brother, Chris, was two years older and in his senior year.

They were stunned. I explained how Dr. Chritchley suspected advanced Hodgkin's disease.

That night as I was watching TV, Jodi slowly approached my rocker. I saw the hurt in her dark eyes. She asked me, "Daddy, are you going to die?" I felt as if a knife were thrust into my heart.

There was only one answer I could give her. I held her close, and, with my tears falling onto the top of her head, I gave her—and myself—the answer we had to hear.

"No, honey, I'm not going to die."

After a month of medical procedures, Dr. Chritchley's diagnosis of Hodgkin's disease was confirmed.

He sentenced me to eight months of aggressive chemotherapy, two treatments a month. Three weeks after my first poke, I began losing my hair. I watched in fascination as clumps of hair snaked down my body, swirling in large circles into the drain.

I envisioned my life being sucked away. Shortly after that, I lost my job because the sweats, mood-altering steroids and other drugs made it impossible to work.

As spring turned into summer, I gradually became weaker because of the chemotherapy. My muscles were atrophying. I could not risk any kind of scrape or cut because an infection could prove fatal to my weakened immune system. Even a cold was dangerous.

In August, Caroline and I watched the Ironman Canada Triathlon held each summer in Penticton. Eighteen hundred athletes from around the world entered the 2.4-mile swim, 112-mile bike ride and 26.2-mile marathon, which must be completed in less than seventeen hours to earn the finisher's medal.

I turned to Caroline, and with tears in my eyes, croaked, "I'm going to do that someday."

At the end of October, I completed my sixteenth poke.

With difficulty, I struggled at getting back in shape. My shoulders, hips and heels were constantly sore, an after-effect of the ravages of the chemo.

I started a new job in January 1995 and intensified my workouts. In September, Caroline and I met with Dave Bullock, a three-time Ironman competitor. We asked questions about the commitment required to complete the race and whether I could finish it.

The answer came back a resounding *"Yes!"*

There was only one fly in the ointment—I had never learned to swim. This would be high on the list of things to do.

My running began in October 1995, and in early November, I enrolled in swimming lessons.

Over the winter, I ran indoors on a treadmill and learned to swim. On Victoria Day weekend, I finished the Kelowna half-marathon in two hours and two minutes. I had never run thirteen miles nonstop before.

At times, though, I had to fight the black thoughts of uncertainty. The mental struggle was often as difficult as the physical training. I was hoping the cancer would not come back because of the stress on my body.

My blood ran cold at that horrifying thought. Ian Mandin, a close friend, was battling cancer. One evening by phone, I told him about my mental struggle, and he told me something very profound.

He said, "If you take on a challenge and it seems to overwhelm you—pretend it's an elephant."

"Pardon?" I asked incredulously.

He explained, "You can't eat an elephant in one sitting, but you can one bite at a time."

He said I had beaten cancer one "poke" at a time.

Now I would earn my Ironman medal, one stroke in the water, one pedal push and one running stride at a time.

In July, I entered the Peach Classic, an Olympic-distance triathlon consisting of a one-mile swim, twenty-five-mile bike ride and six-mile run. This would enable me to defeat the demon of deep water.

I was the last of three hundred triathletes in the water. I fought back waves of panic as I saw the beach drop away below me into the blue-green murkiness of Okanagan Lake. I screamed at myself, *You can do it. You're taking another bite out of the elephant.*

Thirty-two minutes later, I was back on the beach at the finish line. With a mile-wide grin, I pumped my arms into the air. I'd conquered the lake.

Three hours later, soaked in sweat from the midday heat, I jogged over the finish line into the arms of Caroline and Dave.

My confidence mushroomed.

At four o'clock in the morning on August 24, my alarm sounded.

It was Ironman Sunday!

The four of us gathered in the living room and had a family hug. Tears sprang to our eyes as we again thanked God for strength, and we prayed for one more day of the same—for all of us.

I arrived in darkness at registration before five o'clock, and at six-thirty, as the sun rose, I put on my wet suit and warmed up in the lake. The cannon boomed the start of another Ironman at seven sharp. *I'm swimming in the Ironman!* my mind screamed as I dove in.

One hour and forty-two minutes later, I touched sand. I got up and jogged through the finish line, up onto the lawn.

Suddenly, I stopped short.

There in front of me was Dr. Chritchley. I grabbed him in a big bear hug. He looked at me and said, "In my thirty years in oncology, I've never seen anyone who was as sick as you come back to do something as brutal as this."

Soon I was on my bike for the seven-hour ride.

By eleven o'clock, the sun was blazing in the sky, and I had passed Osoyoos and was on my way up the difficult Richter Pass. The hours melted away under the afternoon heat. Through Cawston and Keremeos, I arrived at the steep incline to Yellow Lake. Halfway up, I felt a sudden stab on the outside of my left knee.

With each downward push the pain increased. I had to pedal the last twenty-two miles using only my right leg.

At the medical tent, Dr. Chritchley and two other doctors examined the knee. Finally they wrapped it with a tensor bandage, gave me several Tylenol and said, "Go do it."

I couldn't run. I looked at my watch—5:25 P.M. I had to average four miles an hour to get back before midnight.

Several miles up the road, I came on another triathlete, Peter Diggins, an Australian, who was limping along. I introduced myself to him. Soon we were heading south on Eastside Road past orchards, a few feet away from Skaha Lake. By eight-thirty, as the sun was setting into the mountains to the west, we made it to the turnaround, about a mile and a half south of Okanagan Falls. I picked up my sweatshirt in my special-needs bag.

I tied it around my waist, knowing the cool mountain air would soon make the night chilly. I looked at Peter and said, "Well, buddy, only thirteen more miles to go—just a little jaunt in the country."

Night arrives quickly in the mountains. The walk back became a surrealistic trip. My knee was throbbing. Every step hurt. I knew blisters were forming on the bottoms of my feet.

At the seventeen-mile marker, I sat down to shake some small rocks out of my right runner. I tried to get up.

To my horror, my legs would not respond. A jolt of panic hit me. My legs had seized up. I shouted to Peter, who was now forty yards ahead of me, "Help me!" He came running back, and I told him I couldn't get up.

He held out his hand and jerked me to my feet. My legs, which moved stiffly, felt like concrete pilings. In a few minutes, the awful sensation passed. I knew I would have to walk through the pain till the end.

By eleven o'clock, we had reached the south end of Penticton. Two more miles to go.

Over the past ten miles, we had seen a dozen ambulances pass us to rescue those who were unable to finish.

It was a very sobering parade of flashing red lights. Each time, I gritted my teeth and vowed not to quit.

I looked at my watch: 11:15 P.M. One mile to go.

I began to cry. My dream was about to be realized. With three blocks to go, I put my arm around Pete's left shoulder and thanked him for helping me get through the previous twenty-six miles.

One more block to go. At the end of Main Street, the racecourse turned left to the finish line. One hundred yards away.

I could hear the voice of announcer Steve King as he brought home another exhausted triathlete.

At the corner, I saw six thousand people waiting at the finish line. The big white Ironman Canada structure housing the finish line gleamed like a brilliant star.

My emotions exploded in a fireball of hot, salty tears, which clouded my vision. I began to run.

Suddenly, I heard Steve in an excited voice, *"And now, ladies and gentlemen, here's a local man who just last year finished chemotherapy and conquered advanced Hodgkin's disease, and now he's conquered the Ironman—Mr. Wally Hild."*

His voice trailed off as a loud cheer went up from the crowd. They had surged forward, allowing me a narrow, twisting trail to the finish line. Hands went out in front of me, and I touched as many as I could.

I was sobbing, choking and unable to breathe. My windpipe was constricted with indescribable emotion. I pumped my hands high into the air as I approached the tape emblazoned with the words "Ironman Finish Line."

I looked up and saw my time: sixteen hours, thirty-four minutes and seventeen seconds. I stumbled over the finish line into the arms of my family. Moments later, the medal was around my neck. We were oblivious to the cacophony of sound and kaleidoscope of motion around us.

I was given my Ironman Finisher's T-shirt, which I triumphantly put on. We walked slowly to the massage tent, my body now racked with pain.

But I didn't care. I couldn't wipe the grin from my face.

Just before we got to the massage facility, I turned back to look at the giant structure above the finish line. Right before my eyes it vanished.

I had eaten the elephant.

Wally Hild

The First Step

To take the first step
Is a frightening thing.
To face the unknown
The uncertainty is brings.
But like the child
Who is tired of the crawl,
The first step is
The most important of all.

It expands your horizons,
You can see a new light.
The joy of discovery
Is like taking flight.
The first step you take
Will open all doors,
To see yourself as
You've seen you before.

And, like the child
Who gives it his all,
Sometimes he falters,
He will teeter and fall.
But strong arms are there

To catch him and then,
They stand him back up
To start walking again.

The longest journey,
Takes one step at a time,
But once you get going
You'll do just fine.
Take my hand, friend
I'll help you along
I'll be right beside you . . .
As two we'll be strong.

Yes, that first step's a big one,
The most important of all.
But I'll be there to catch you
Should you teeter and fall.
We'll set our sights forward
Grit our teeth and walk on . . .
When we see that road ending,
We'll break into a run.

I love you, I'll help you
All the way through.
But to take that first step,
Well . . . that's up to you.

Rabona Turner Gordon

I Promise, Mama

A promise made is a debt unpaid.

Robert W. Service

"Jean Oliver Dyer," a voice said, and Jean crossed the stage, her head held high, her gown rippling in the breeze.

Suddenly, Jean's eyes fluttered open. Groggily, she wiped the sleep away and sighed. No graduation. No diploma. *It was just a dream—a dream that won't come true,* Jean thought sadly—*and a promise I can't keep. I'm so sorry, Mama!* She cried.

Growing up in Richmond, Virginia, Jean could read by age four. Whenever she asked for help with her homework, her mom, Amanda, said, "You're so smart you can do it yourself!"

Jean was smart enough to skip a grade—and to know how hard her mom worked. Amanda, who had left school to help support her family, now washed dishes to make a living. "But someday," she'd tell Jean, "you're going to college."

The night Jean started the tenth grade, she found a new sweater and skirt on her bed. *They're lovely!* she thought,

But Mama must have spent a month of paychecks on these! Her face burned. *Mama shouldn't work so hard,* she thought. *I love school—but Mama needs me more.* Soon, she dropped out, too. Disappointed tears shone in Amanda's eyes.

But it's for the best, Jean reminded herself. She found work at fast-food eateries and laundromats. One day, a young man with a shy smile asked her out. Almost before she knew it, they were married.

Jean became a mom—six times in seven years. Between sewing and washing sticky hands, she worked as a teacher's aide. But money was tight. *I'd earn more if I had my diploma,* she thought.

So Jean went to night school. "*Mommy* has to go to school now," she'd laugh, kissing six little faces and racing off.

When Jean earned her GED at twenty-eight, her mom was ecstatic. "I knew you could do it!" she cried.

Jean enrolled in Virginia Commonwealth University for one class—and earned an A.

"That's my girl!" Amanda cried.

But as Jean began her second term, it was hard to stay focused. *Does Ervin need help with fractions?* she'd wonder. *Did Dana take her bath?*

"It's too much," Jean cried. "My children need me." She was able to find a job as a supervisor at the housing au - thority, and she encouraged her kids to study hard. "Mama," she'd boast, "all the children are on the honor roll!"

"When are *you* going to school?" Amanda would ask. *Why is that so important?* Jean fumed inside. *I'm a hard worker, a good mother—why isn't that enough?* But soon after her kids began heading to college, Jean's marriage crumbled. One day, she found herself alone, staring at a wall of job commendations. There was one vacant area— a spot for a college degree.

"Mama," she told Amanda, "I'm going back to school."

"I'm so happy!" Amanda cried.

But it was hard. Jean needed three jobs to pay her bills *and* tuition. She often fell asleep over her books. That semester, she stared in shame at a row of *F*s.

"It'll get better," Amanda encouraged. "I'll help however I can."

Amanda's persistence—*nagging*, even—perplexed Jean. *I was doing all right without a college degree,* she'd think. *So why . . . ?*

One day, she got her answer. Amanda had been offered a post on the church council—and she'd turned it down.

"Why?" Jean cried.

Amanda looked down at her feet. "There's so much paperwork to do," she blurted. "And I . . . I can't read!"

The words felt like a slap to Jean. *How could I not have known?* she wondered. She thought back to how, as a child, she'd had to read recipes aloud, how Amanda wouldn't help with her homework. *That's why it matters so much to her for me to achieve!* she realized.

"Oh, I'll teach you to read, Mama!" Jean cried.

But Jean didn't have that chance. Soon after, Amanda was diagnosed with a brain tumor.

I can't bear to lose her! Jean wept. She tiptoed into Amanda's room, where her mom reached out a hand.

"What is it, Mama?" Jean asked.

"Promise one thing," Amanda murmured. "Promise me you'll finish college."

Jean bit her lip. This had been her dream for so long. *How can I not?* "I promise, Mama," she whispered.

From then on, Jean threw herself into her studies, rushing to Amanda's side after class. "I'm here, Mama," she'd say softly.

"You should be studying!" Amanda would scold.

When Amanda slipped away, Jean felt hollow with grief. There was only one thing to do: keep her promise.

Then one day, Jean awoke with chest pains and needed surgery for a heart problem. And now, as she recovered at home, she worried she'd never make Amanda's dream come true. *I've failed you, Mama,* she wept. *I'll never graduate!*

All of a sudden, she could swear she heard a familiar voice. "Yes," it urged. "Yes, you will."

"You're right, Mama," she whispered. "You've always been right."

Soon, Jean was back on her feet—and back in school. On her lunch hour at work as an investigator for the police department, she'd read textbooks, then stay up late into the night writing papers.

And on Mother's Day 1996, as Jean slipped her graduation gown on, she felt a rush of pride. *I kept my promise, Mama,* she thought. *How I wish you could see me now!*

As she crossed the Saint Paul's College stage to accept her bachelor's degree and her grandchildren cheered, "Way to go, Granny!" Jean looked heavenward. *You do see me, Mama, don't you?* She smiled.

Today, Jean, fifty-eight, is one course away from her master's degree, and she's establishing a parenting program for low-income moms. "I want to be a source of strength for them, like my mom was for me," she says.

Each night as she studies, she gazes proudly at her diploma on the wall. But her real inspiration comes from the photo on the table—the one of Amanda smiling. *I finally did it, Mama,* Jean thinks. *For me—and for you.*

Jean Oliver Dyer
Excerpted from Woman's World

A "Real" Beautiful Person

What is the definition of beautiful? Webster's Dictionary says, "Beautiful is the assemblage of perfection through which an object is rendered pleasing to the eye."

My definition of beautiful is embodied in a young man that I was fortunate to have as a student and friend: Larry Chloupek. Larry was diagnosed with cancer of the bone when he was seven. Surgeons removed his leg, giving him a 5 percent chance of recovery. That occurred more than thirty years ago.

I remember when Larry first came into my physical education class. *How is he going to fit into my class?* I thought. I felt I had to make adjustments to accommodate him. However, Larry was never a problem; I was the problem. I was an inexperienced teacher and was worried that he would get hurt, but he never did.

Once we were playing basketball, and it seemed like every time Larry would get close to the action, the team went in the opposite direction. This happened repeatedly. I wanted so badly to tell Larry "Just stand still." It didn't appear to bother him at all. It bothered me a lot because I never saw him reaching his goal, and I badly wanted him to attain it. It is natural for me to want everyone who has a goal to reach it.

Larry also participated in The President's Physical Fitness Test. The first test involved chin-ups. He completed some—I don't know how many, but it was enough to be in the 95th percentile. This is required to earn The President's Physical Fitness Award. I did not realize the significance of that score at the time.

The next test was the standing broad jump. Larry came over to me and asked me if he could do it at home. When I asked why, Larry said he needed to take his leg off to compete effectively. He said, "Mr. Carruthers, would you be embarrassed for me to remove my leg at school?" I agreed with him, so he did the next test at home. The next day, he brought the score to school. He had jumped longer than 6 feet, which put him in the 95th percentile again. Now I knew what was on his mind. He wanted to get The President's Physical Fitness Award.

The next two tests were the 300-yard run and the shuttle, which involves changing directions and bending. These are very difficult tasks for someone with an artificial leg. Knowing what was on Larry's mind, I phoned the director of The President's Physical Fitness Program and asked if he had a scale for a person with an artificial leg. He said no, but added that we could determine our own criteria. We decided to waive the 300-yard run and the shuttle because Larry had performed at a high level in all the other activities.

The final test was the softball throw. I showed Larry the adjusted scale and he thought it was fair. On his first throw, Larry was short. I had a sick feeling in my stomach; I wanted so badly for Larry to attain his goal. He did make it on his second throw. I was so relieved and proud! He earned the award.

On another occasion, Larry was playing soccer and broke the foot off his artificial leg. One of the students carried him into the school while a teacher carried in his foot. What a bizarre-looking situation. We laugh at it now, but at the time it made a young man who just wanted to fit in feel different from everyone else.

When that year ended, the physical education department selected Larry as the Physical Education Student of the Year. Most junior high students do not acknowledge their peers' achievements, nor do they respect people who are different. However, it makes the hair on the back of my neck stand up even now to visualize Larry walking with a different gait across the gym floor to accept the award. The student body gave him a standing ovation. That was the first time I saw a student body respond in that manner.

Larry now works as an administrator for the National Cancer Institute at the National Institutes of Health. He also counsels cancer patients and amputees. Athletically, he ran a nine-minute mile, five- and ten-kilometer races, and won a gold medal in the five-kilometer race. He carried the Olympic torch in the last Olympiad and participated as a member of the Para-Olympic team in Atlanta in the sport of sitting volleyball. He also enjoys water and snow skiing and golf. Nothing holds Larry back. I was very grateful recently to have Larry visit the high school where I teach to share with our students and play some basketball. Everyone was blessed that day.

I'm sure glad I had the opportunity to teach and know Larry. Larry defines "beautiful" for me.

Dave Carruthers

This Is Not a Permanent Situation

A chilly day in 1974. Mrs. Fox teaches the fourth grade at Beardsley Elementary. The morning-bell rings. Single file, the restless children enter the stuffy classroom to the now familiar command of "take your seat." Attendance taken, flag saluted, Mrs. Fox has an announcement. "Class," she says in her ancient voice, "today we are going to change our seating assignments. I have decided to place the smartest child in the first seat of the first row. The next smartest will sit in the second seat of the first row, and so on and so on. Now remember, this is not a permanent arrangement, you can move up a seat as you improve your grades." The first child is called to her place of honor. Mrs. Fox directs the former occupant of row one to take her things and move back a seat. Quickly gathering my things, I did as I was told.

Names called, new seats taken. I continued to move back, desk by desk. Left standing, it seemed that all eyes were on me that fateful day as Mrs. Fox reached the bottom of her list. I yearned to hear my name. Surely I wouldn't be the last name called! Finally, the humiliation ended. . . . but not before Mrs. Fox announced that I was the "dumbest kid in her fourth-grade class."

It shouldn't be surprising that when I finally dropped out of high school, I was still reading at the fourth-grade level. That day, Mrs. Fox planted in me a seed of worthlessness. It would take eleven years and a personal tragedy to uproot this spirit of inadequacy and create a new life of purpose and achievement.

I believe that the most valuable result of all education is the ability to make yourself do the thing you have to do, whether you like it or not. My education began on board a helicopter. Seven months pregnant, the prognosis grim, I was airlifted to UCLA Medical Center. My life would never again be the same.

Only those familiar with the sounds and smells of a neonatal intensive care unit can fathom the sense of the surreal that one experiences in such a place. I was there, off and on, for seventeen months. My precious baby boy, Derek, was born with a life-threatening birth defect. His chances for survival slim.

The Bible says that all things work together for good for those who love the Lord. Well, I love the Lord and if there is one "good" thing that came from this experience, it was the transforming power of a mother's love that motivated me to create a new belief that I can do, be and achieve anything. And I do mean anything.

For seventeen months I cared for Derek. I found myself working side-by-side with the best pediatric surgeons in the world. These wonderful physicians became my mentors. They believed that I possessed the natural abilities necessary to become a good doctor. They taught me medical procedures and asked me to go on rounds so that I might offer encouragement to other parents. I became the subject of a documentary and was interviewed by prominent psychiatrists to discuss the coping mechanisms I utilized to survive such a horrific ordeal. Although I didn't realize it at the time, the hospital experience was to be the easy part of this journey.

Thank God that the seed of hope was buried deep in my pain. When Derek died before his second birthday, I would suffer such severe grief that I truly felt that my heart was physically damaged. It is said that time heals all wounds. This I know to be untrue, that a piece of this mother's heart is missing, at the cusp of the wound, a festering hurt.

For over a year, God comforted my soul and brought healing to my broken heart. As he worked on my spirit, I worked on my body. I found that the intense physical exercise not only strengthened my muscles, it also strengthened my mind. With renewed energy and clarity of thought, I made a decision to return to school.

I can't even remember his name today. He was my guidance counselor at the adult school. Although his name has slipped my mind, his words will never be forgotten. "You want to be a public speaker? Who would listen to you? What have you got to say? And look at your test scores. My God, you're at the fourth-grade reading level. It will take you years to finish high school let alone college." I can't recall my exact words, but they went something like this: "You don't know me so will you please SHUT UP!" You know, there was a lot of truth in what my counselor said that day—it did take seven years to complete my undergraduate and masters degree in psychology.

Today I share hope and encouragement to anyone who will listen. I challenge people to find the gift in the pain. There is good in every bad experience, we just have to believe that it is there, and that if we search for it, we will find it.

Krista Buckner

The Confidence Course

*Effort is a commitment to seeing a task through
to the end, not just until you get tired of it.*

Howard Cate

At ten minutes to seven on a dark, cool evening in
Mexico City in 1968, John Stephen Arkwari of Tanzania
painfully hobbled into the Olympic Stadium—the last to
finish the marathon.

The winner had already been crowned, and the victory
ceremony was long finished. So the stadium was almost
empty as Arkwari, alone, his leg bloody and bandaged,
struggled to circle the track to the finish line. The
respected documentary filmmaker, Bud Greenspan,
watched from a distance. Then, intrigued, Bud walked
over to Arkwari and asked why he had continued the grueling struggle to the finish line.

The young man from Tanzania answered softly, "My
country did not send me nine thousand miles to start the
race. They sent me nine thousand miles to finish the race."

Walter Anderson

Twenty Things You Should Do in This Lifetime

When I was a young boy, my grandmother always asked me the question, "What is it you want?" I'd give the age-appropriate answer whether it was "candy" at age five, "a bicycle" at age twelve, or, "not answering dumb questions" when I was fifteen. She always listened carefully, and then asked, "What is it you *really* want?" I hated when she did that because it made me think—and thinking was painful. Invariably what I really wanted was different than what I'd originally asked for. Her final question was always the same. "What price are you willing to pay, in order to get that?"

When I was sixteen, she increased the complexity of the task. She asked, "What are twenty things you should do in this lifetime?" Each year, on Thanksgiving, she made me rewrite the list adjusting it as my maturity and wisdom grew. For twenty-eight years, I gave her my list before I ate her turkey dinner. I was never able to give her the twenty-ninth list. She died two days before Thanksgiving. However, I think she would have been proud of how she'd helped me grow, from the five-year-old who just wanted candy to this end result of twenty-nine years of refinement:

1. To leave the world a bit better by my having been here.
2. To love unconditionally.
3. To dream big dreams and be willing to pay the price to make them come true.
4. To visit the Lincoln Memorial at dawn.
5. To earn the affection of children.
6. To hike and raft the Grand Canyon.
7. To find out what I'm good at, and give it back to the world.
8. To watch a sunset on a tropical isle.
9. To earn the respect of intelligent people.
10. To learn my family history and visit the homeland.
11. To drive and bike across the country.
12. To help a stranger in need.
13. To make something that is still standing when I die.
14. To play a game for more than I can afford to lose.
15. To meditate and pray daily.
16. To do something others said was impossible.
17. To walk beaches under a full moon at midnight.
18. To take a stand on something and not back down under pressure.
19. To never lose childlike enthusiasm.
20. To swim naked under waterfalls.

What's on your list?

Mike Buettell

7

A MATTER OF PERSPECTIVE

Watch, wait. Time will unfold and reveal its purpose.

Marianne Williamson

My Dream House and My Boy

There must be more to life than having everything.

Maurice Sendak

It seemed the perfect place to raise a family: a beautiful lot in Spokane, Washington, surrounded by ponderosa pines, near forests and streams. When my wife, Joy, and I found it, we knew it was the ideal site for our dream house.

The lot was expensive, far beyond what I could afford on my modest salary as a philosophy professor at Whitworth College. But I started teaching extra classes and moonlighting in real estate.

We finally bought the lot. Sometimes I'd put my infant son, Soren, in a backpack and take him for walks in our future neighborhood. "You'll love roaming these fields and streams," I'd tell him.

Then came the wonderful summer when I helped the contractor build our home. My brother-in-law, a California architect, had designed elaborate plans as a gift. I'd work sunup to sundown, rush home for dinner and often go teach a night class. Confronted with choices for materials,

I'd always answer, "Give us the best. We're going to be here for a lifetime."

I'd take one of our girls, Sydney, five, or Whitney, seven, with me whenever I had errands to run. But at the dinner table, I'd just nod as the girls tried to tell me about their day. Rarely was my mind fully with our family. Instead, I'd be worrying about the escalating costs of the house.

But we made it—a four-year goal fulfilled! I felt pride and satisfaction the day we moved in. I loved helping my children explore the neighborhood to meet new friends.

Only a week later, we had to move out.

Unable to sell our other home, we'd arranged to rent it to meet the house payments. At the last minute, the renters backed out. "We can make it somehow," I assured Joy. But she faced the truth of our overextended finances, "Forrest, we wouldn't own the house; it would own us."

Deep down, I knew she was right. The exquisite setting and distinctive architecture meant our new home would sell faster than the old. I reluctantly agreed, but disappointment led to lingering depression.

One afternoon, I drove to the new house just to think. To my surprise, I was engulfed with a sense of failure and started to cry.

That fall and winter, I kept wondering why this loss bothered me so much. My studies in religion and philosophy should have taught me what really matters—it's what I try to help my students understand. Still, my mood remained bleak.

In April, we all went on vacation to California with Joy's parents. One day we took a bus trip to the Mission of San Juan Capistrano, where swallows return each March from Argentina.

"Can I feed the pigeons?" begged Whitney, heading toward the low, stone fountain inside a flower-filled courtyard. The four adults took turns taking kids to feed

the birds, visit the souvenir shop and enjoy the mani-
cured grounds. When it was time to get back to the bus, I
looked for Joy and found her with the girls and their
grandparents.

"Where's Soren?" I asked.

"I thought he was with you."

A horrible fear hit as we realized it had been nearly
twenty minutes since anyone had seen him. Soren was a
very active twenty-two-month-old who loved to explore.
Fearless and friendly, he could be anywhere by now.

We all started running through the five acres of the mission grounds. "Have you seen a little red-haired boy this
high?" I asked everyone I saw. I ran into back gardens,
behind buildings, into shops. No Soren. I started to panic.

Suddenly I heard Joy scream "No!" Then I saw Soren,
lying on the edge of the fountain, arms outstretched. He
was blue, bloated and looked lifeless. The sight burned like
a branding iron in my mind. It was one of those moments
when you know deep inside that life will never be the same.

A woman cradled Soren's head as she gave him mouth-
to-mouth resuscitation, and a man pressed on his chest.
"Is he going to be all right?" I yelled, fearing the truth.

"We're doing the right things," the woman said. Joy col-
lapsed on the ground, saying over and over, "This can't be
happening."

Lord, don't let him die, I prayed. But I knew he couldn't be
alive, not after nearly twenty minutes underwater.

In less than a minute, paramedics arrived, connected
Soren to life-support systems and rushed him to the hospital. A trauma team pounced on him, led by a specialist
in "near drownings."

"How's he doing?" I kept asking.

"He's alive," said one of the nurses, "but barely. The
next twenty-four hours are critical. We want to helicopter
him to the Western Medical Center in Santa Ana." She

looked at me with kindness and added, "Even if he lives, you must realize there's a strong chance of significant brain damage."

Nothing could have prepared me for the sight of my young son in the intensive care unit at Western. His limp, naked body was dwarfed by the machines connected to him by countless wires. A neurosurgeon had bolted an intracranial pressure probe into his head between the skull and the brain. The bolt, screwed into the top of his head, had a wing nut on top. A glowing red light was attached to his finger. He looked like E.T.

Soren made it through the first twenty-four hours. For the next forty-eight hours, we stayed by his side while his fever skyrocketed past 105 degrees. We sang his favorite bedtime songs, hoping we could soothe his hurt even in his comatose state.

"You both need to take a break," insisted our doctor. So Joy and I went for a drive and started to talk.

"There's something besides Soren that's really bothering me," I told her. "I've heard that when couples go through a tragedy like this, it may separate them. I couldn't bear to lose you, too."

"No matter what happens," she said, "this isn't going to break us up. Our love for Soren grew out of our love for each other."

I needed to hear that, and then we started to cry, laugh and reminisce, telling each other what we loved about our mischievous son. He delighted in balls, and before he was even a year old I'd hung a miniature basketball hoop in his bedroom. "Remember how he scooted in his walker and tried to land one, squealing 'yeaaa' if he came near?" I asked.

We also discussed our fears about brain damage. "The doctor seems more hopeful now," I reminded Joy. He had told us Soren was alive only because all the right things were done immediately after he was found. Thinking earlier that we'd lost him, we felt grateful he even had a fighting chance. We'd take him any way we could get him. But we wondered what the impact would be on the family if brain damage was extensive.

"Can you believe that, for these past months, what mattered to me was losing that house?" I asked. "What good would a new house be if we came home to an empty bedroom?"

Even though Soren was still unconscious, that conversation gave us some peace. We'd also been receiving wonderful support from friends, family and strangers and felt the power of their prayers.

In the following days, four visitors dropped by to see Soren. First came Dave Cameron, who had discovered Soren underwater. A Vietnam veteran, he led tours at the mission. "I arrived early that morning. Standing near the fountain, I suddenly had this strong sense of foreboding," he said. "That's when I saw the backs of his tiny tennis shoes. Instinct and training took over from there."

Soon after came Mikiel Hertzler, the woman who applied mouth-to-mouth resuscitation until the ambulance arrived. "I've been trained in CPR," she told us. "When I first saw him, I couldn't find a pulse. But faint bubbles in the back of his throat made me think he was trying to breathe."

I shuddered. *What if someone with less medical knowledge had discovered him and given up sooner?*

Then two strapping paramedics, Brian Stephens and Thor Swanson, told us that they were usually stationed ten minutes away, but that day they were on an errand a block from the mission when they got the call.

As we remembered the doctor's words about Soren's being alive only because all the right things happened immediately, their stories touched us deeply.

On the third night, the phone woke me in the hospital

room my wife and I were using. "Come quick," shouted Joy. "Soren's waking up!" When I got there, he was slowly stirring, rubbing his eyes. In a few hours, he regained consciousness. But would he ever be the same boy who had brought such exuberance to our home?

A couple of days later, Joy was holding Soren in her lap. I had a ball in my hand. He tried to get it—and he said, "Ball." I couldn't believe it! Then he pointed to a soda. I brought it to him with a straw, and he started to blow bubbles. He laughed—a weak, feeble laugh, but it was our Soren! We laughed and cried; the doctors and nurses did, too.

Just a few weeks later, Soren was racing around our home, bouncing balls and chattering as usual. Full of rambunctious energy, he gave us all a sense of wonder at the gift of life.

Almost losing Soren helped me look closely at my role as a father. What really matters is not that I provide my children the ideal house, the perfect playroom, even woods and rivers. They need *me*.

Recently, I drove back to my dream home. Prisms of sunlight shone through its fifty-two windows and, yes, it has a beautiful site. But I wasn't troubled anymore, and I know why. As I returned home to take the kids on a promised picnic, all three ran out. Soren squealed, "Daddy, Daddy, Daddy!" And I had time to play.

Forrest Baird
As told to Linda Lawrence

The Tattooed Child

What do we live for if it is not to make life less difficult for each other?

George Eliot

It is impossible to tell what a casual observer in the waiting room at the clinic in the children's hospital might expect to see. The reason for this is that no one ever comes here just casually to observe. Here, people bring gravely ill children for treatment. But, as I found out, what I observe and what others, my small daughter included, see here are not necessarily the same things.

I had brought my six-year-old daughter, Elli, to the hospital to have a specialist check out a birthmark. It wasn't in a noticeable place, wasn't life-threatening, but the pediatrician just felt that it should be watched. So, once a year, I brought Elli here. The birthmark was one of those small imperfections that cause mothers such as I to walk out of places like the children's hospital grateful—very grateful.

On this particular visit, the doctor was running far behind schedule. Elli and I settled down with a book to wait our turn. Elli also took some markers and paper to draw on while I read to her. I looked around the room. I noticed that the walls were brightly painted—cheerful without being cloying. In some places, the pictures were of animals—true-to-life ones, not cartoons. They were all families, I saw, parents nurturing their young in various poses of play and rest. Other pictures were of sports figures, silhouettes caught in midmovement—active, vibrant, joyful.

The room itself is divided into several stations to accommodate children of all ages and interests. There is a music-listening area with headphones and a wide selection of CDs. There is an art area complete with clay, paints, markers and other art supplies. And there is a reading area. The chairs, I noticed, are big and comfortable—large enough to accommodate two adult figures cuddled close. The reason for this, I learned, is that children of all ages like to be read to. This is especially true when the child is undergoing a painful treatment. Reading gives them a respite.

I learned this from Anthony. And I learned some other things as well.

When Anthony first walked in, I instinctively moved closer to Elli. He was big—over six feet tall, very muscular and generally intimidating. His head was shaved and he wore several earrings in various places—both ears, his nose, his eyebrow. His black jacket, slung over the back of the chair, had some insignia on it, but the symbol did not mean much to me. His jeans were faded and torn. On one arm was a huge tattoo from his knuckles to his shoulders. Anthony was imprinted with a giant, coiling snake. Its fangs and tongue ended just over his ring finger. After surveying the room, he chose one of the large reading chairs close to us. He made me very uncomfortable.

But my daughter had no such inhibitions. She started a conversation with Anthony, asking him all kinds of questions: "Why do you wear earrings? Did it hurt to have your nose pierced? Why do you have the snake on your arm?" I moved to take her away, thinking that what Anthony did was his own business and that he probably did not like the intrusion of an inquisitive six-year-old.

But Anthony looked at Elli and calmly answered her: "I thought they looked good. Everybody I know did it. And yes, it did hurt to have everything pierced. I thought the snake looked tough."

Then, Elli asked Anthony the one question I did not want to know the answer to: "Why are you here?"

Anthony was not offended. He said, "The medicine they give me for my sickness hurts. Today, they are giving me something for the pain."

"Good," said Elli. "I hope it works fast." I did, too.

Then I opened *Charlotte's Web*, one of her favorite books, and began reading to her. Elli's six-year-old imagination loved talking animals, ones who were sensitive and caring. Anthony closed his eyes. I thought he was trying to sleep, so I suggested to Elli that we read elsewhere.

But then I learned why Anthony had chosen to sit near us. He said, "No, please read here—to me." I did.

The time went by, and we were so caught up in the book that I did not notice that my creative daughter had found an unusual outlet for her drawing. On the other side of her new friend, while his eyes had been closed, Elli had been drawing on his other arm with her markers. Now to my horror, I saw that this young man's left arm was completely covered with red, green and blue hearts and flowers!

"Elli!" I said loudly. "I don't think Anthony is going to like that. You'll have to wash that off for him right away!" I was more than a little afraid of what this big, tough stranger might say or do to my little girl.

But Anthony hadn't been sleeping. He opened his eyes.

"It's okay. I don't mind. Please could you read more? It . . . helps me."

And then I saw what my daughter saw—Anthony wasn't any different from any of the other children in that room who were in pain, who had come for treatment, except for one thing. It wasn't his size or his dress or even his scary tattoo that made him different. No, what set him apart, I realized, was that he didn't have a mother there to read to him. And he needed one.

Elli was called in for her appointment. I stayed and read to another woman's child, one with a tattoo on one arm and a six-year-old's drawing on the other.

When it was time for us to go, Anthony smiled at us and said thank you. He seemed to feel better. I thought for a minute about what had just happened. I had approached Anthony with fear. He looked so tough, so different from me and anyone Elli and I had ever known. And maybe I also was afraid of him because I wasn't ready to let my daughter know that there are serious diseases in the world, diseases that cause pain, that may or may not be treatable. That was information I wanted to protect her from for as long as I could.

But Elli hadn't seen any of that. She had only seen another child in that hospital setting, one who, like her, enjoyed being read to. And one who liked drawings on his arm.

I guess what you see depends a lot on what it is you're looking for.

Elli smiled and said good-bye to her friend. And even though I knew perfectly well how to get to the elevator, I took my daughter's outstretched hand and let her lead the way.

Marsha Arons

Coat of Many Colors

I know of no more permanent imprint on a life than the one made by mothers.

Charles Swindoll

When one thinks of Dolly Parton they are likely to envision one of the most statuesque, opulent, prestigious entertainers in the world. While Dolly is one of country music's most successful female entertainers and probably the best known country singer, her beginnings were far from grandiose.

Born on the edge of the Smoky Mountains National Forest, in a modernday log cabin, she was the fourth of twelve children. Her father, Robert Lee, was a struggling tobacco farmer and his wife, Avie Lee, was often inca-pacitated with illness.

Their impending poverty made the Parton children the barb of their classmates' and neighbors' jokes.

When Dolly was nine years old, her fellow students at Canton's Chapel School ridiculed her patchwork coat of many colors, inspiring her most famous song. She was proud of the love and sacrifice that went into that coat and she used this experience to fuel her talents.

She is one of the most prolific singer/songwriters in American recording history, having cut approximately three hundred of her own songs.

Mama began to make me a coat. A lot of times when she made something out of patchwork, she would try to find scraps that matched as close as possible so that it wouldn't be so obvious. But she knew me and my personality, so she decided to make my coat out of the brightest, most different colors she could find. This was going to be a colorful coat with no apologies.

"It's a lot of work to tailor a coat for a child and line it all by hand, even if you cut it all out of one piece of cloth. You can imagine how much work it took to make one out of little pieces. I knew she was making it for me, so I watched her almost the entire time. She told me the story from the Bible about Joseph and the coat of many colors. Joseph's coat was given to him as a sign that he was loved and special, and I felt the same way about mine. I watched how she folded every edge of every little piece under and sewed it with close stitches so that there wouldn't be any ragged seams. When there are so many kids in a family, you can imagine how a mother's time has to be divided up among them. So to see my mother spending this much time to do something just for me was special indeed.

"As soon as it started to look anything like a coat, I would beg her to let me put it on, and I would strut in front of the fire in it like some kind of patchwork peacock. I could tell the other kids were getting jealous, probably not so much of the coat as of the attention I was getting from Mama. I started to understand how Joseph's brothers got so jealous of him that they put him down a well and sold him into slavery. Aside from Denver, I don't know if any of the other kids would have actually sold me into slavery; but I could easily be in for a few spiteful pinches or hair pullings. I didn't care. After all, it was me they were being jealous of—me and my beautiful coat. And it was beautiful.

"I remember the night Mama finished it. I wore it around the house until she made me take it off and everybody got sick of telling me (with my none-too-subtle prodding) how beautiful it was. That night, I almost never got to sleep. It was worse than Christmas Eve. I couldn't wait to wear my coat to school the next day. It wasn't really cold enough for a coat yet, but Mama let me wear it anyway. She could see it was no use trying to dissuade me, so off I went down the path, lickety-split. It's the only time in my life I have ever been anxious to get to school.

"I burst through the school doors like a multicolored whirlwind, wondering just how many people I could find to admire my coat. I was so proud of it. I wanted to be seen in it. I wanted to be noticed. 'See my new coat?' I said to one boy. 'New,' he sneered, 'it looks like a bunch of rags.' My heart sank a little, but he was just one boy. Surely the others would see how wonderful and special my coat was. My heart sank further as other children poked fun at me and my coat. Soon it turned into a whole room full of mocking faces; laughing, pointing, jeering at me . . . me and my coat. I wanted to tell them the story Mama had told about Joseph and make them understand how special, how singular, how beautiful . . . but they would not hear it.

"My heart was broken. I couldn't understand the cruelty, the ignorance that made them laugh at me that way. The teacher came in and noticed I was being picked on, so she tried to help. 'Don't you want to put your coat in the cloakroom?' she suggested, but I would not. They would not shake my pride in my coat, my love for my mother, my faith in myself. I would not have it. I would sit there and be hot and wait them out. I would wait until school was over and walk proudly from the building wearing my coat like a banner of pride. I would walk with my head high into the autumn afternoon and show my coat to God. He would know how special it was, how special I was. He did. He liked the way it complemented his ever-greens and the rich brown earth of the path. He watched carefully to catch glimpses of it from his side of the clouds as I marched proudly home. He loved the way it looked on his Dolly Parton.

"As painful as it was, that experience at school that day was a great blessing to me. It was what inspired me years later to write the song that has become my signature piece. 'Coat of Many Colors' is still my favorite song that I ever wrote or sang. It also was a big hit, and that did a lot to help me forget that early pain."

Dolly Parton

When Social Security Speaks

"I'm sorry, Ms. Senter. We cannot issue you a new driver's license without verification of your Social Security number." For the third time, I patiently try to explain that I don't have a Social Security card anymore. It was stolen at the train station along with my driver's license, wallet, credit cards, bank cards, cash and children's pictures.

Isn't it bad enough that I have to be here today, fighting traffic, facing long, irritating lines of people who would rather be anywhere but here? I take a number and wait my turn, only to be told, "The computers are down at this facility today, but you may obtain a license at another Secretary of State's office, ten miles east, right off the 290 Expressway." And all for crimes I didn't commit. I am still chafing at the thought that some stranger, pushing through post-Christmas rush at Union Station, would have the nerve to zip open my purse and steal my wallet. The inconvenience of it all is not made any easier today when I arrive here, only to find that I have to keep driving—first to a town thirty minutes away to obtain a Social Security clearance, and then another half hour to a second facility where, hopefully, the computers are functioning.

As though I have nothing better to do with my time, I mutter to myself as I take a number and join a third line, this one at the Social Security office. I sense that this is not a happy place to be. Toddlers whine. Adults complain. Being reduced to a number seems to have drained those of us who wait of any semblance of goodwill and peaceful understanding.

"Never have I seen such a rude place in all my life," an old man with a leathery face laments as he pounds his cane on the tile floor. "Have to take a number before they will even answer your question." He addresses his comments to no one in particular, but we all nod in silent accord. The cold efficiency, the impersonality of it all does not sit well with me either, especially when I know there is more to come after I leave this place.

And all because someone had the nerve to steal my wallet. I return to the source of my misery and feel my jaw tighten again. I have gone through the scenario before. An unguarded moment. Divided attention. Rushing crowd around me. And how often have I reminded my teenage daughter to carry her purse in front of her when she's in a crowd. I do not easily forgive myself or the thief.

I am still bothered and disturbed, not only by the theft, but by the hassles of the day, when my number is called and I step to the counter. I am aware that someone in a pink coat steps up beside me. I am also aware that it is not her turn. *I sat and waited. Let her do the same,* I think to myself.

"I'm sorry, miss. You'll have to take a number and wait your turn." The clerk speaks with irritation I feel.

"But all I needed was . . ." Two small children pull at her coat, and the baby in her arms cries a hacking cry. The clerk repeats her instructions with growing force and irritation.

"Please, ma'am," the young mother starts again. This time her words come out with a sob. "All I wanted to know . . . is this where I get my husband's death certificate?"

We are stopped short, the clerk and I. Neither of us knows what to say. I want to gather the mother into my arms, wipe away her tears, hold her crying baby, calm her restless toddlers. Instead, I step back from the counter and mumble something about being sorry and, "Go ahead." The clerk speaks to the grieving woman in hushed tones, then hands me the necessary forms, and I return to my seat to write. But I have been silenced and humbled. *A lost wallet, and she has lost a husband,* I reflect as I fill out the forms. My losses seemed tragic until now.

I drive to my next stop with a thankful heart. In my mind, I see the woman in the pink coat again and hear her sob. And even as I drive, I pray about her loss and begin the process of forgetting my own.

Ruth Senter

Never Give Up

What we do today, right now, will have an accumulated effect on all our tomorrows.

Alexandra Stoddard

At twenty-three, Chad's life was just beginning. Handsome and popular, he had been a long-distance runner and a top wrestler in school and was still pursued by young women of all descriptions. People who met Chad couldn't help but like him instantly. He had a wide, infectious smile, brimmed with good humor and was the sort of person who would drop everything at a moment's notice to help out a friend.

He had purchased the motorcycle to have transportation to the two jobs he held. Working two jobs would help him save for a better apartment and maybe a car and some furniture of his own. But one night on his way to job number two, a drunk driver, who carried no insurance, careened into him, spilling the bike and shattering Chad's leg. Now, at twenty-three, his life seemed to be ending.

For seven agonizing months, Chad lay in a hospital bed, staring at the metal framework of skewers that penetrated his leg at several points, holding it together. Pieces of his bone had been left in the street, and Chad went through operation after operation in a vain attempt to save the leg from amputation. His friends organized blood drives for Chad's operations, and his supervisors at work held his job open for him in hopes he would be able to return to work.

When the doctors announced the leg had to come off, Chad sank into a bitter despair. How would he function with only one leg? Would he become repulsive to women and never marry or have the family he had always dreamed of? And how would he ever find a way to pay the hospital bills that had now soared to the cost of a new three-bedroom house?

Nothing we did cheered Chad or eased his deep depression, as we waited for his bone infection to be cured before the leg was amputated. It would not be good to undergo such an operation with Chad not caring if he survived it.

One night, I brought the husband of a colleague of mine at work to Chad's hospital room. Gene began talking at once, joking with Chad, telling him he was "on his last leg" and he "only had one leg to stand on."

Chad was furious. "How can you come into my room and talk like that when they're going to cut off my leg?" he demanded to know.

Gene just shrugged. Then he bent over, unbuckled his own leg and threw the prosthesis on Chad's bed. I left them alone.

When I returned an hour later, Gene was gone and the light had come back into Chad's green eyes.

"You should hear his story!" Chad said. "He stopped late at night on the freeway to change a flat tire. He was opening the trunk to fetch the spare when a drunk driver going sixty-five miles an hour honed in on his taillights and rear-ended Gene's car. Gene jumped as high as he could at the last moment, but one of his legs was cut clean off at the knee and the other was so badly mangled he came very close to losing it, too. The drunk driver had no insurance, and Gene had a wife and three children to support. And I thought I had problems! Gene manages the San Diego sports arena and is going to get me front-row tickets to my favorite rock band as soon as I recover from surgery and have learned to walk on a prosthesis!" His eyes softened then. "Gene says that people who give to others always get back more than they give. He said not to worry about my future. It will work out. He said the main thing was never to give up."

Four months later, Chad was back at work. He was self-conscious about his limp, exhausted at the end of every day, and the new prosthesis rubbed endless blisters on his tender stump. But he remembered Gene's words. He learned to ride a bicycle with his "fake leg," rode a horse bareback for the very first time, took off the prosthesis and swam one-legged in the ocean and at night when no one could see, he practiced running slow, jagged laps at the high school track.

A month after returning to work, Chad plucked up his courage and asked a pretty new girl at work if she'd like to go out with him. He was surprised when she said yes. He didn't know it then, but he had just asked out his future wife and mother of his three children-to-be. Jane didn't care how many legs Chad had. She cared only that he had a big heart.

The hardest problem for Chad was wondering how he would ever get back on his "foot" financially. The hospital bills he owed would take thirty years to pay. He would never be able to afford a car or a home, but he refused to give up. He remembered Gene's words and paid whatever he could afford to the hospital twice a month.

Not long after he met Jane, one of his doctors called. Often they called to ask Chad to rush to the hospital and offer comfort and support to an injury victim facing amputation. No matter how tired or sore Chad was, no matter what hour of the day or night he was called, he never refused to drop everything and help out a fellow human being in need. But this call was different.

"Chad," the doctor began, "because you underwent experimental procedures during the months we tried to save your leg, many people became acquainted with your case. I am calling to tell you that an anonymous stranger has just paid all your medical bills."

Gene was right. People who give freely to others get back more than they give.

Anita Grimm

The Little Leaguer I'll Never Forget

He was a 100-percent, rollicking, sure-of-himself kid—and because of him I stopped going to the games.

All across America, thousands of kids swarm over Little League baseball fields, their faces alight with anticipation, flushed with victory or clouded with momentary disappointment. I used to be directly involved, and afterward a frequent visitor at the field in my town, rooting not for any particular team, but taking delight in what I'd always considered a marvelous concept.

Then one day, some years ago, I stopped going. I stopped because of Channing Allen Jr. He had a fancy, family middle name—I forget what it was—but everyone called him Chippy.

I managed the Tigers in the mid-1950s, when Chippy was the star pitcher. In the years I managed Little League teams, I never had a kid like Chippy. Once, a friend from an advertising agency phoned and said he was looking for an all-American kid for a big color ad. Freckles, towheaded, a mischievous smile. And in a baseball uniform. By chance was there a kid like that in our Little League? Was there ever! Right on my own team.

They rubbed a bit of dirt on Chippy's face, skewed his

cap around a bit and shot the picture. The ad was a huge success and Chippy got a hundred bucks.

Chippy was one heck of a twelve-year-old pitcher, who could "throw a baseball through the side of a barn," as big leaguers like to say. I still recall him standing calmly on the mound with bases loaded (usually because of infield errors). He'd glance over at me, kneeling tense and agitated on the dugout step—and grin. There wasn't a raw nerve ending in that kid's body. His grin was telling me to relax. Then he'd rear back and burn three straight fastballs right past the batter for a strikeout.

We discouraged our pitchers from throwing curveballs because their young wrists and forearms are not ready for the stress a curve puts on them. I had to watch Chippy like a hawk, or he'd nip one in. It wouldn't "roll off the table," as the saying goes, but it had a nice nickel bend to it. And Chippy would punch the air with his fist as it fooled the batter.

I'd yell at him, and he'd turn to me with a "Who me?" face of freckled innocence. Or he'd come into the dugout after the inning and say slyly, "Heck, I thought you weren't looking."

You couldn't get mad at him. He was just being a 100-percent, rollicking, sure-of-himself kid.

Chippy was our leading home-run hitter and enjoyed swinging for the fences. At least twice, I recall, he was at bat with bases loaded and the count three balls, no strikes. He knew my instructions. You take the next pitch, hoping for a fourth ball to walk in a run. And, of course, the opposing pitcher knew the game, too: Play it right in there for the called strike.

I can still see the grin on Chippy's face as the ball left the pitcher's hand. He would dig in and swing. Thwaak! He'd nail it for a homer. "You were supposed to take that pitch," I'd remind him sternly as he trotted into the dugout.

"I know, Mr. B.," he'd say. "But it came up there like a big balloon, and I couldn't resist."

Nor could I resist Channing Allen Jr. Irrepressible. Unpredictable. An emerging man-child one moment; a little kid the next.

When Chippy didn't pitch, he played third base. With his strong arm, he'd often drive me batty. On a grounder he'd field the ball cleanly, bring it up to chest level, and then turn it over in his glove, as if he were examining the seams before getting off his throw and nipping the runner by a half step. I'd once told him Ken Keltner of the Cleveland Indians did the same thing, and after that there was no chance of breaking Chippy of that mannerism. "Don't worry," he'd say. "I'll get him." I knew he enjoyed my anxiety, and knowing it was part of his fun.

Chippy made our town's all-star team but was bitterly disappointed that we didn't get far in the play-offs on the road to the Little League World Series in Williamsport, Pennsylvania. He took defeat seriously. Most kids shrugged it off twelve minutes later, but Chippy wore defeat like an open wound. He was a competitor. "I don't want to be a good loser. It can lead to bad habits," he once told me with that impish grin.

I knew he'd be a competitor in life, too. But I lost track of him after he graduated from Little League. Then I heard that he'd gone to college . . . or he hadn't gone . . . that he'd dropped out "to find himself," for a while. That was in the mid-1960s. The next thing I heard left me sick to my stomach. . . .

Recently I went to Washington, D.C., on business. But there was something more important I wanted to do there. I took a cab to the Mall and walked along the highly polished black-granite Vietnam Veterans Memorial. It was beautiful and hauntingly dramatic, a fitting tribute to the 57,939 names of the fallen engraved on it.

A park ranger turned the pages in a huge book. His finger sought it out. "Panel 15E," he said quietly, "line 38."

I walked down the pathway until I found panel 15E and counted down the lines etched into the gleaming, reflecting granite. There it was: Channing Allen Jr. I stared at it, trying to bring my feelings into focus. But all I could see through my misting eyes was a freckle-faced twelve-year-old on a Little League mound, grinning down at the batter.

It was years ago that I'd heard how he'd been wounded by a sniper's bullet, and then killed after helping evacuate others who had been hit. The news had stopped my going to Little League games.

I reached up and ran my fingers over Chippy's name. Then I strode quickly away. But I had noted other names as I sought his. Chippy was in a well-mixed lineup. John Hornyak . . . Ismael Soto . . . Carmine Genovese . . . Leonard Gurwitz . . . Tyrone Jackson . . . Peter Schmidt. A lineup as varied as our own Tiger team: Kelley . . . DiMassio . . . Rappoport . . . Stankowicz. Both sets of names were in perfect American counterpoint. And I knew I could no longer repudiate all that Chippy Allen had epitomized. Not to watch kids play ball again was a false estrangement from reality and unworthy of that name in black granite.

This year I was at the opening of the Little League season, enjoying it immensely. And praying those names like Hornyak, Genovese, Gurwitz, Soto—and Allen—would never again be etched in a stone war memorial.

Jerome Brondfield
Submitted by Barbara Chesser, Ph.D.

Hold On to Your Hair!

*A person has two legs and one sense of humor,
and if you're faced with the choice, it's better to
lose a leg.*

Charles Lindner

By far, the funniest day of my life was Sunday, January 26, 1997.

Jim had invited me to go to a Super Bowl party on this day. Although I felt a chemistry between us during our previous meeting, I was really unsure if this invitation was a date or a friendly get-together. We had lunch at the Hard Rock Café in Boston and were trying to figure out what to do next before the party that evening. Eventually, we decided to walk a couple of blocks to the Hancock Building and take in a view of the beautiful city from the observatory.

Well, it was very windy—or perhaps I should say it was gusty. I was thinking to myself, *Do I hold on to my hair? No, because then he will know that I am wearing a wig.* So I decided to just go with the "bearing down" technique. Well, this wasn't the best decision that I had ever made.

The next thing I knew, the wind had whipped my wig right off my head. I stopped dead in my tracks as I felt the cool wind on my lovely bald head. I tried to remember that someone had told me once that I had a "really nicely shaped head." It is so easy for people with hair to say that! I turned my head slowly to look over my shoulder, only to see my hair rolling down the sidewalk like a tumbleweed in the desert. Jim was still walking and talking ahead of me, ignorant of the chaos that was unfolding behind him. After what seemed like minutes, Jim turned around as he realized that I was not with him. As our eyes met, Jim was one with me in my secret.

I turned to run after my hair as it was really getting away from me now. Quickly I remembered that there was no running allowed after a hip replacement last year. I asked Jim, "Would you get my hair?" Jim took off after it, and I found myself thinking of how much that brown mass looked like a squirrel running through piles of dirt. *Please, God, don't let it go into the street. That thing cost me a hundred bucks, and I still have to go to a party tonight.* Jim did rescue my hair. In fact, he held it over his head like a trophy and yelled back to me, "I've got it!" *Terrific,* I thought sarcastically, and waved him back. If anyone had caught this on videotape, I surely would have won the ten-thousand-dollar prize.

Jim returned with my hair, and his eyes seemed to say, "Don't worry. Here's your hair. I didn't see anything." He looked like he was dying for me and wishing that I did not have to go through this. I apologized to him as I could only imagine what it was like to be in his shoes. I shook out the dirt and tried to reposition the wig back on my head without a mirror. I couldn't stop laughing, and tears began to cloud my eyes as I could not believe that all of this was happening. I asked Jim, "Did you know that I had had cancer?" "Yes," he said. Our mutual friend had told him my story. I said, "Did you know I was wearing a wig?" "No," he said. I said, "It's a pretty good one, huh?"

We continued on our walk up to the Hancock Building, which is made of reflective glass. I caught a look at myself in one of the mirrors and realized that my wig was on the wrong way. It also wasn't really sitting down the way that it should. I could not get into the ladies' room fast enough to repair the damage to my helmet. I sat down on the cold floor and just laughed and laughed. I couldn't wait to get home and tell some of the people who loved me. I don't think that I came out for a while. Jim told me later that he didn't think that I was going to come out at all!

It occurred to me that my late Aunt Ginny, who had an outrageous sense of humor and struggled through her own cancer battle, may have had something to do with this. I imagined her looking down from heaven and telling me to "Cut it out!" I was trying to be someone that I was not and attempting to hide the painful truths of these past years. I had put on a nice outfit and made up my face. The wig was a pretty nice-looking one as far as wigs go, and I just wanted to be normal. I wanted to be a twenty-eight-year-old woman going out on a date without worrying about how to tell someone that I had survived breast cancer and a recent bone marrow transplant and what his reaction would be. I had gathered all my courage to accept this invitation from Jim, and it turned out to be one of the best decisions that I had ever made. I have experienced true acceptance from this man and a compassion that is hard to find. Jim is beginning to laugh now when we talk about this story. I think he was traumatized for a while there. Who wasn't?!

Kathleen M. Kelly

Memories and Laughs

Two weeks before Des Moines Roosevelt's twentieth high-school reunion, I began frantically working out with arm and leg weights, shackled like an escapee from a prison chain gang. As I gyrated in the living room with my vintage Stevie Wonder album "Signed, Sealed, Delivered" going full blast, my children looked on in horror at my flying flesh. "Why are you doing that, Mommy?" they wondered.

"Because Mommy is silly and vain," I replied. Of course, two weeks didn't repair the ravages of the two decades since I last saw my classmates. I didn't go to the ten-year reunion—I was living out East then, and too hell-bent on my career to give a rip about auld lang syne.

But my regimen did give me the psychological boost I needed to face those people I worshipped and envied, despised and admired, and wept, dreamed and giggled with twenty years ago. I comforted myself that even if the reunion was miserable, it would make good copy. High school. How those two words dredge up a world of memories.

We were all carefully casual at first, our newly purchased stone-washed denim togs painstakingly ironed.

But it soon came out that I wasn't the only one to indulge in useless preparations.

Several people succumbed to perms and crash diets. One woman confessed that she threw caution to the winds and baked like a lizard in the sun, on the theory that tanned fat looks better than pale. Forget the extra wrinkles she was creating for the thirty-year reunion. She wanted to look good now.

We all felt in our secret hearts that we were the only ones who hadn't changed appreciably. Naturally, we all went through the charade of peering nearsightedly at name tags with graduation pictures on them, trying to reconcile the track star with the paunch and then exclaiming shamelessly, "You haven't changed a bit!" People were heard to mutter, "My, this is strange." And more than one asked aloud, "Who are all these old people?"

My claim to fame in those long-ago days was having the longest hair in school, so several female classmates greeted me with the accusatory shriek, "You cut your hair!" Yes, ten years ago when it dawned on me that strands of gray looked mighty peculiar in a waist-length ponytail.

As I circulated, I learned that my fellow graduates include a columnist for the *New York Times*, a neurologist on the faculty of Harvard University Medical School and an actor-director whose first film won an international award. Gee, why couldn't they have made something of themselves.

As much pride as I took in hearing those classmates' accomplishments, however, I must admit that a high point for me was visiting with a woman who was once engaged to my former fiancé. We acted out every man's worst nightmare as we compared notes, our victim mercifully absent. If he could have walked in and seen us—wine glasses aloft, heads thrown back, teeth bared as we screamed with laughter—he would surely have turned tail and run.

The reunion held some other wonderful surprises, too. One was seeing a skinny boy who had worn thick glasses transformed with contact lenses and confidence into a witty, gregarious CEO. The rest of him had caught up with his Adam's apple, and he had married his high-school sweetheart, a painfully shy girl who never communicated much except for what shone out of her lovely eyes. Still soft-spoken but now self-assured, she worked the room making everyone feel remembered and unique.

Then there was the willowy girl whom we all expected to take the New York modeling scene by storm. She did, briefly, and is now back in Des Moines with six children, living happily ever after.

One of the school's most irrepressible boys (not major-league bad, just frequent-detention naughty) is now a probation officer. He told me that earlier in his career, when he worked with troubled youth, he challenged his charges to come up with an excuse he hadn't used himself.

And then there was the fellow who was legendary in grade school for his command of dirty words, now become a warmly friendly family man. He touched me by remembering the day I was introduced in kindergarten as the new girl, thirty-three years ago.

Of course, some things haven't changed. The homecoming queen was as ridiculously beautiful and unassuming as ever. And the class cynic lounged by the wall, owlishly observing, "Same old cliques."

Spouses looked on, eyes glassy with boredom and jaws aching from the effort of grinning at strangers as we classmates endlessly reminisced. My own beloved gave himself up to the indifferent canapés early on, and finally found a classmate's pregnant spouse who wanted to sit in a corner as desperately as he did.

Meanwhile, we Rough Riders remembered the time Diana's skirt fell off in the hall, and the time Jeff, on a dare, munched on a cow's eyeball during dissection in biology lab.

Between us, my five hundred classmates and I have survived bizarre religious cult experiences, drug experimentation, children, mortgages and a couple hundred divorces. We came from all over the world to take stock of ourselves and each other, and to remember the joys and insecurities of those wonderful, excruciating days.

We lifted a toast to those classmates who remain eternally young in our memories, claimed too soon by cancer, suicides and accidents. We are old enough now to know that we know very little—only that life is short, and we must all try to be good to one another.

All in all, I'm awfully glad I went, and awfully glad my arms can go back to jelly now. My only regret is that not a single cheerleader had gotten fat!

Rebecca Christian

Make Mine Vanilla

Life's greatest joys are hidden in unsubstantial things.

May Riley Smith

It was a plain-old-vanilla kind of night. My husband, away on a business trip, had just phoned to say his good nights to us. Before hanging up, we played our usual game of "kissy face," making kinky promises that we never intended to keep. I hung up the phone and stared at it, trying to hold on to his presence a little longer. Carefully, I placed the name and phone number of where he would be staying on the refrigerator door with the same rainbow magnet I always used. *Plain-old-vanilla life,* I thought.

A glance at the clock jolted me back to reality and the fact that it was a school night. Jade, our six-year-old daughter, should be in bed by now. I proceeded to walk down the hall, knowing exactly which plank on the hardwood floor would creak when I walked on it. Jade knew, too, for I immediately heard the hurried sounds of a little girl trying to pretend she was already in bed.

Upon reaching the stairs, I took slow, deliberate steps

to give her more time to look believable. Fourteen—fifteen—sixteen, I've counted these steps a million times. Going up—going down, it was always the same—sixteen. At the top of the stairs, I paused for a moment to gaze at the moon, which always looked better from that cathedral window than any other place I can remember. Plain-old-vanilla life, but good vanilla, like Häagen-Dazs.

While entering Jade's room, I admired how perfectly we matched the pale green walls with pink heart border to her pale green covers with pink, heart-shaped pillows. Her priceless treasure chest of "dress-up" clothes, placed at the foot of her canopy bed, allowed her to easily transform herself into a royal princess by day and a fearless pirate by night. The collectible dolls stood in beautiful gowns, patiently waiting for the ball to begin, while the Barbie dolls, half-dressed in their townhouse, were still trying to decide what to wear. The perfect little girl's room filled with the jubilant magic of childhood.

I walked over to Jade's bed, where she sat hugging the white tiger that her dad had brought home from one of his trips. "Ready for your prayers?" I asked. With the innocence of a child, Jade asked God to bless everyone and everything she loved. "And God please bless Daddy, who has to sleep on the big airplane. Amen." With that I tucked in her covers and kissed her forehead. "Go to sleep," I whispered. "Tomorrow's a school day."

Walking out, I made sure to turn on the nightlight and leave the door half-open, just as she liked. Still within earshot, I heard her whisper to her tiger, "We have the best mommy in the whole world."

"Go to sleep, Jady Wady," I called, and the last sweet sounds I heard were giggles.

Vanilla with sprinkles, I thought, and smiled.

Adrienne C. Reynolds

8

ECLECTIC WISDOM

There is more to life than increasing its speed.

Mahatma Gandhi

Write Your Own Life

Whatever the mind can conceive and believe it can achieve.

Napoleon Hill

Suppose someone gave you a pen—a sealed, solid-colored pen.

You couldn't see how much ink it had. It might run dry after the first few tentative words or last just long enough to create a masterpiece (or several) that would last forever and make a difference in the scheme of things. You don't know before you begin.

Under the rules of the game, you really never know. You have to take a chance!

Actually, no rule of the game states you *must* do anything. Instead of picking up and using the pen, you could leave it on a shelf or in a drawer where it will dry up, unused.

But if you do decide to use it, what would you do with it? How would you play the game?

Would you plan and plan before you ever wrote a word? Would your plans be so extensive that you never even got to the writing?

Or would you take the pen in hand, plunge right in and just do it, struggling to keep up with the twists and turns of the torrents of words that take you where they take you?

Would you write cautiously and carefully, as if the pen might run dry the next moment, or would you pretend or believe (or pretend to believe) that the pen will write forever and proceed accordingly?

And of what would you write: Of love? Hate? Fun? Misery? Life? Death? Nothing? Everything?

Would you write to please just yourself? Or others? Or yourself by writing for others?

Would your strokes be tremblingly timid or brilliantly bold? Fancy with a flourish or plain?

Would you even *write*? Once you have the pen, no rule says you *have* to write. Would you sketch? Scribble? Doodle or draw?

Would you stay in or on the lines, or see no lines at all, even if they were there? Or are they?

There's a lot to think about here, isn't there?

Now, suppose someone gave you a life. . . .

David A. Berman

Nice Timing

*Life is the game of boomerangs. Our thoughts,
words and deeds return to us—sooner or later—
with astounding accuracy.*

Florence Shinn

I had spent over five grueling years on my dissertation
for my Ph.D. and was frantically preparing for my oral
boards. The boards were to be held in California, and I had
scheduled a flight through Minneapolis, where I was to
change planes and get to John Wayne Airport. My incom-
ing flight was very late, and I was soon in an all-out sprint
to catch my flight to California. Very few people were left
in the concourse. I had to stop to catch my breath on a
moving sidewalk when I noticed a woman in her fifties
struggling with a carry-on bag.

I don't know why, but I looked at her face and blurted
out, "Are you going on flight 567 to California?"

She responded, "Yes."

"So am I," I responded. "Give me your bag. I'll run
ahead and tell them to wait for you." I took her bag and
started sprinting again.

I raced onto the plane and told a flight attendant that one more passenger was behind me and to please hold the plane for her. I seated myself with her bag, and a few moments later she arrived and was the last person on the plane before they closed the doors and took off. After the plane leveled off, I presented the bag to her, and she smiled at me and thanked me.

I didn't sleep a wink in the hotel that I stayed at before my oral boards and arrived at the university at seven o'clock in the morning. The board kept me waiting for an hour in a room before the defense of my dissertation began. I walked into the boardroom and was initially intimidated by all the professors in their regal robes. As I slowly glanced at the faces of all the board members, I noticed the bright face of a woman directly in the center of the board. She looked at me, gave me a flirtatious smile like a young schoolgirl and winked at me. It was the same woman whose bag I had carried ahead the night before. Needless to say, whenever I stumbled on any questions, she did a great job of extricating me.

Thomas De Paoli

Take Some Time

Take some time to smell the flowers
As you walk the paths of life.
Take some time to ease the tensions
From the challenges and strife.

Take some time to hear the birds sing
As they usher in the dawn.
Though the day be just emerging,
Too soon it will be gone.

Take some time to watch a sunrise,
Now and then a sunset too.
Just be sure that seeking pleasure
Isn't all you ever do.

Take some time to count your blessings,
Though you feel they're not that great.
You will find they're more abundant
Than you thought, at any rate.

Take some time to banish hatred
When and where you can.
Just detest man's evil ways
And not your fellow man.

Take some time to love your children
Every moment you are free.
The benefits exceedeth
A university degree.

Take some time to love your neighbor
And even more important still,
Take some time to love yourself
Or not many others will.

And if you don't like that image
Of yourself that others see,
Take some time to make some changes,
Be the best that you can be.

Take some time to help another
Who you think might need a hand.
You will find the satisfaction
Leaves you feeling sort of grand.

Take some time to live by virtue
In the best way that is known,
And respect the rights of others
As equal to your own.

Take some time to just appreciate
The fact that you are here,
And to know that Higher Power
And to trust It without fear.

If you do these things with diligence
You will eventually be glad.
If you don't attempt to do them
You may one day wish you had.

Although this no doubt could impose
Upon your time for seeking wealth,
There should be little question
That it could improve your health.

And though you might not be as wealthy
Nor drive so fine a car,
You'll find you will be richer
In other ways by far.

Leon Hansen

"That's what I get for stopping to smell the roses."

The Movers and the Gentleman

The day began like any other moving job in the city. The moving crew was on the job at the agreed upon time, 8:30 A.M.

After introducing themselves to the customer and a brief tour of the residence to assess that plan for loading, the old gentleman asked them if they would like some coffee. The men, being charged by the hour, declined his offer. He smiled at their honesty and gestured to them to continue.

The old house had a redolent fragrance of musty rose petals. The bereaved seventy-nine-year old husband merely watched and quietly chatted and quipped with the young-strong men as they went about their work. It was obvious he was lonely and welcomed the rather captive audience into his home. Even under the albeit necessary circumstances of having to move to the nursing care facility, their presence heartened him.

The young men were kind to the old gentleman, tolerating his rather one-sided conversation. Occasionally, they had to ask him to 'move to one side' while they removed furniture and memories all at one time right before him.

In a way he was as glad to be leaving the house which really had no relevant significance for him anymore since his partner of sixty-two-years had died two years ago. He found peace each day in prayer. The responsibilities for his care would be a welcomed solace.

The hours sped by and the house became but a shell of past occupancy. Upon near completion of the job one of the movers went through the house to check each room to make sure nothing had been left behind. In the upstairs bedroom under a small alcove there was a chest almost imperceptible because it was the same wood hue as the paneling on the wall behind it. When he started to remove it, the entire contents fell through the bottom of the chest. Papers were strewn all over the floor, along with photos. He began to collect everything into some semblance of order when a yellowed newspaper clipping caught his eye: TWIN BOYS DIE IN BOATING ACCIDENT. After quickly scanning the article, he learned that they were indeed the old gentleman's sons, lost to him and his wife forever over three decades ago.

When the movers had completed the move, the man thanked them for their diligence and careful concern for his precious belongings. He told them that their kindness to him was more appreciated than they could ever realize.

Six months later, almost to the day of the move, the gentleman died. In his will, he left his entire fortune of one and a half million dollars to the "Two movers who were so kind and reminded me of my own sons."

Barbara Chase-Pace

Old Wives' Tales

The more sand that has escaped from the hour-glass of our life, the clearer we should see it.

Rabbi Harold Kushner

I always loved going to visit my grandmother. She lived in New York City, and we often took the train up from Washington, D.C., for a weekend. I got to sleep in her huge old four-poster bed on sheets that always smelled faintly of lavender. And I was awakened by the smell of Grandma's specialty—blintzes, a delicate golden crepe-like pancake filled with a cinnamon-laced creamy cheese mixture. I loved those blintzes, and my grandmother tried to teach me to make them myself. But no matter how closely I watched her and imitated her technique, I could never get those pancakes to turn out like hers. But she told me not to worry. It was all in the kind of pan you used, she told me, and one day, she said, she would give me hers, thus ensuring my success.

I suppose my grandmother tried to teach me other things when I was a child besides how to make blintzes. I don't remember now. What I do remember, and what has ultimately been most important to my happiness in life, are those lessons I learned from her when I became an adult.

My mother—my grandmother's daughter—died ten days after I was married. I was twenty-two years old. I felt lost and abandoned, and I did not want to see my mother at the end in the hospital. I did not want to discuss funeral arrangements and last wills. But my grandmother insisted. She wanted her daughter to die peacefully, knowing that the people she loved would be taken care of. And she wanted me to have the closure that comes from being able to say good-bye. She knew I'd need it.

She didn't dwell on her own grief. Instead, she set about the business of helping her daughter's child see that even if I was dissolved in chaos, losing a parent was the natural order of things. There was a small comfort in this. Even though grief washed over me in huge debilitating waves, I believed somehow, sometime, there would be symmetry again in my life. There was an order, and I could have faith that once again I would feel joy and calm. Grandma, who had already lived close to eighty years, had a perspective of a bigger life picture than I did.

She knew where to find joy.

When I met a man I loved, my grandmother was the one to tell me that marriage should be joyful and fulfilling both spiritually and physically. I could maintain my sense of self even while I cultivated my life as part of a couple. Equality, mutual respect and loving kindness were what a happy marriage was built on. Nothing much had changed in this regard in the sixty years since she had been a bride, she maintained.

At the time I married, in the mid-1970s, the feminist movement was well under way. Women of my generation felt tremendous pressure to build careers first and to defer, if not marriage entirely, then certainly children. But my grandmother had been an original feminist, building a career outside the home not by choice but by necessity. She had been in both arenas—home and work—and knew where her joys had been found. So she encouraged me to have children.

My grandmother felt that true feminism was about having choices, not pressure. And she let me know that creating a loving family was as worthwhile and valuable and just as fulfilling as any job could ever be. When the voices of feminism were at their most strident, telling us we must have it all, my grandmother counseled me to listen carefully to my own inner voice. She said that any woman who did not admit to the innate desire to love and nurture a child was either an aberration or kidding herself. And she foresaw the pain that childless women would experience when they let their biological clocks run down while they were busy pursuing other things.

And so I had my children—four daughters whom I struggled to give the kind of love and support that I'd had. If I doubted my mothering skills, my grandmother gave me confidence.

When I had trouble nursing my first daughter, well-meaning friends had plenty of advice. Only my grandmother waited to be asked. Then she told me to take my cues from my baby—to let her tell me how much she needed and when. She felt that being guided by the baby's instincts and my own would make us both happy.

That philosophy has continued to work as my daughters have gotten older, too. When I follow their leads, they still let me know just how much intervention they really need from me.

The result has been that I learned to trust my own instincts, and my daughters have learned that they are capable of making good decisions for themselves. All of us are women empowered by confidence in our own good judgment.

Toward the end of her life, my grandmother taught me about friendship. She lived in a home for the aged where the attendants were kind and the care was good. But what kept my grandmother's spirit refreshed and happy was her friendship with her roommate. The two of them lived together for eight years until my grandmother's death.

They knew each other's families, what medication each should take and when, what special foods the other liked and what each other's breathing should sound like when they were sleeping. Twice, when her roommate's pacemaker failed in her sleep, my grandmother sounded the alarm and attendants got there in time. My grandmother said the silence woke her.

The two of them were more than friends, closer even than spouses. They met at a time in their lives when they each needed something that only someone in the same place and time in her own life could give. They shared a dependence and trust that grew into love and sustained them in the truest sense of the word.

But, having been my grandmother's granddaughter, that friendship did not surprise me. It was typical of the way my grandmother conducted herself with those she loved—wholeheartedly giving the best of herself to bring out the best in them.

She set an example for me and taught me about love, marriage, children and friendship—the elements of life that make it worth living. And she taught me to draw on my own strength to get me through the sadness and pain that were inevitable in life. She caused me to have confidence in my own good judgment, and faith that life would hold good things for me and for those I loved.

I remember exactly where I was when I got the phone call that told me my grandmother had died at ninety-two, lucid till her last breath. I was standing in my kitchen. And I remember clearly what I did then. I dug her old crepe pan out of the closet where I had stored it away. And, smiling happily to myself, grateful for having known her, I proceeded to make a batch of blintzes. This time, they turned out perfectly.

Marsha Arons

The Runaways

One winter morning the year before I started school, my dad came in and asked if I would like to go with him to feed the cows. That sounded like fun, so I dressed in my warmest clothes, including the mittens connected by a string through the sleeves of my jacket, and went out with my dad to take my place in the world of work.

It was a pleasant morning. The sun shone brightly, but it was cold and the ground was covered with a blanket of new snow. We harnessed the team, Babe and Blue, and went over the hill with a wagon full of hay. After we found the cows and unloaded the hay for them, we started home. Then my dad came up with a good idea. "Would you like to drive?" he asked. And I responded in typical manly fashion. I like to drive anything: cars, trucks, golf carts or donkey carts. I think the attraction must be the power. There is such a sense of power to be in control of something larger than I am, and it's good for my male ego.

I took the lines from my dad and held them looped over my hands as he had shown me, and we plodded back home. I was thrilled. I was in control. I was driving. But the plodding bothered me. I decided that while I was in control, we should speed up. So I clucked the horses along, and they began to hurry. First they began to trot, and I decided that was a much better pace. We were moving along, and we would get home much faster. But Babe and Blue came up with a better idea. They decided if they would run, we would get home even sooner.

The horses went to work on their plan and began to run. As I remember it, they were running as fast as I have ever seen horses run, but that observation might have a slight exaggeration factor built in. But they did run. The wagon bounced from mound to mound. As the prairie dog holes whizzed by, I concluded that we were in a dangerous situation, and I started to try my best to slow down this runaway team. I pulled and tugged on the lines until my hands cramped. I cried and pleaded, but nothing worked. Old Babe and Blue just kept running.

I glanced over at my dad. He was just sitting there, looking out across the pasture and watching the world go by. By now, I was frantic. My hands were cut from the lines, the tears streaming down my face were almost frozen from the winter cold, stuff was running out of my nose and my dad was just sitting there watching the world go by.

Finally, in utter desperation, I turned to him and said as calmly as I could, "Here, Daddy. I don't want to drive anymore."

Now that I am older and people call me Grandpa, I reenact that scene at least once a day. Regardless of who we are, how old we are, how wise or how powerful we are, there is always that moment when our only response is to turn to our Father and say, "Here. I don't want to drive anymore."

Cliff Schimmels

The Journey of Success

When choosing the path to follow, I selected the road
heading west.
It began in the Forest of Childhood, and ceased at the City
of Success.

My bag was packed full of knowledge, but also some fears
and some weights.
My most precious cargo was a vision of entering the city's
bright gates.

I reached an impassable river, and feared that my dream
had been lost.
But I found a sharp rock, cut down a tree, and created a
bridge, which I crossed.

It started to rain, and I was so cold, I shivered and started
to doubt.
But I made an umbrella out of some leaves and kept all the
cold water out.

The journey took longer than I had planned; I had no food
left in my dish.
Rather than starve before reaching my dream, I taught
myself how to fish.

I grew awfully tired as I walked on and on, and I thought
of the weights in my pack.
I tossed them aside, and I sped up again. Fear was all that
was holding me back.

I could see the City of Success, just beyond a small grove
of trees.
At last, I thought, I have reached my goal! The whole
world will envy me!

I arrived at the city, but the gate was locked. The man at
the door frowned and hissed,
"You have wasted your time. I can't let you in. Your name
is not on my list."

I cried and I screamed and I kicked and I shook; I felt that
my life had just ceased.
For the first time ever, I turned my head, and for once in
my life faced the east.

I saw all the things I had done on my way, all the obstacles
I'd overcome.
I couldn't enter the city, but that didn't mean I hadn't won.

I had taught myself how to ford rivers, and how to stay
dry in the rain.
I had learned how to keep my heart open, even if sometimes it lets in some pain.

I learned, facing backwards, that life meant more than just
survival.
My success was in my journey, not in my arrival.

Nancy Hammel

Who Is Jack Canfield?

Jack Canfield is a bestselling author with over twenty-three books published, including nine *New York Times* bestsellers. In 1998 *USA Today* declared that Jack Canfield and his writing partner, Mark Victor Hansen, sold more books during the previous year than any other author in the United States. Jack and Mark also have a syndicated *Chicken Soup for the Soul* newspaper column through King Features and a weekly column in *Woman's World* magazine.

Jack is the author and narrator of several bestselling audiocassette and videocassette programs, including *Self-Esteem and Peak Performance, How to Build High Self-Esteem* and *The STAR Program.* He is a regularly consulted expert for radio and television broadcasts and has published a total of twenty-seven books—all bestsellers within their categories—including twenty-two *Chicken Soup for the Soul* books, *The Aladdin Factor, Heart at Work, 100 Ways to Build Self-Concept in the Classroom* and *Dare to Win.*

Jack conducts keynote speeches for about seventy-five groups each year. His clients have included schools and school districts in all fifty states, over one hundred education associations including the American School Counselors Association and Californians for a Drug Free Youth, plus corporate clients such as AT&T, Campbell Soup, Clairol, Domino's Pizza, GE, New England Telephone, Re/Max, Sunkist, Supercuts and Virgin Records.

Jack conducts an annual seven-day Training of Trainers program in the areas of building self-esteem and achieving peak performance in all areas of your life. The program attracts educators, counselors, parenting trainers, corporate trainers, professional speakers, ministers, youth workers and interested others.

To contact Jack for further information about his books, tapes and trainings, or to schedule him for a keynote speech, please contact:

The Canfield Training Group
P.O. Box 30880 • Santa Barbara, CA 93130
phone: 805-563-2935 • fax: 805-563-2945
To send e-mail or to visit his Web site: *www.chickensoup.com*

Who Is Mark Victor Hansen?

Mark Victor Hansen is a professional speaker who, in more than two decades, has made over four thousand presentations to more than 2 million people in thirty-two countries. His presentations cover sales excellence and strategies; personal empowerment and development; and how to triple your income and double your time off.

Mark has spent a lifetime dedicated to his mission of making a profound and positive difference in people's lives. Throughout his career, he has inspired hundreds of thousands of people to create a more powerful and purposeful future for themselves while stimulating the sale of billions of dollars worth of goods and services.

Mark is a prolific writer and has authored *Future Diary, How to Achieve Total Prosperity* and *The Miracle of Tithing*. He is coauthor of the *Chicken Soup for the Soul* series, *Dare to Win* and *The Aladdin Factor* (all with Jack Canfield) and *The Master Motivator* (with Joe Batten).

Mark has also produced a complete library of personal empowerment audio- and videocassette programs that have enabled his listeners to recognize and use their innate abilities in their business and personal lives. His message has made him a popular television and radio personality, with appearances on ABC, NBC, CBS, HBO, PBS, CNN, Prime Time Country, Crook & Chase and TNN News. He has also appeared on the cover of numerous magazines, including *Success, Entrepreneur* and *Changes*.

Mark is a big man with a heart and spirit to match—an inspiration to all who seek to better themselves.

For further information about Mark contact:

P.O. Box 7665 • Newport Beach, CA 92658
phone: 949-759-9304 or 800-433-2314
fax: 949-722-6912
To send e-mail or to visit his Web site: *www.chickensoup.com*

Contributors

Jack Alexander turned to memories of his childhood to write his short stories. He can be reached at 252 Colonial Heritage, Doylestown, PA 18901, by calling 215-230-0118 or by e-mail at *jaxletter@webtv.net*.

Andy Andrews is an author, comedian, motivational speaker and national television celebrity. Andy's purpose is to positively affect the attitudes of those who are touched by his wide scope of talent. He has authored a four–book series entitled, *Storms of Perfection*, and has written a book of short stories entitled, *Tales from Sawyerton Springs*. Andy can be reached through his Web page at *AndyAndrews.com* or by calling 800-726-ANDY.

Terry Andrews is a writer who lives on the coast of Oregon. She has just completed her first novel. This story is based on her memories of a family Christmas when she was growing up in Iowa. You may reach Terry by e-mail at *25terrya@mail.seasurf.com*.

Marsha Arons is a writer and lecturer in Skokie, Illinois. She is thrilled to be associated with the *Chicken Soup* series, and her stories appear in *Woman's Soul, Mother's Soul* and *A 5th Portion*. She also contributes to national magazines such as *Good Housekeeping, Reader's Digest* and *Redbook*. She has authored a book for young adults and is currently at work on a collection of short stories dealing with mother-daughter relationships. You can contact her via e-mail for speaking or other assignments at *RA8737@aol.com*.

Beverly Beckham is an award-winning columnist and editorial writer for *The Boston Herald*. She is the author of *A Gift of Time*, a collection of personal essays. An at-home mother who embarked upon a writing career at age thirty, she routinely ponders the universal experiences that connect family and friends. You can reach her at P.O. Box 216, Canton, MA 02021 or by e-mailing her at *BevBeckham@aol.com*.

David A. Berman is a high school English teacher, weekly columnist, freelance writer, event host and public speaker who lives in rural New Hampshire with his wife, Kim and daughter, Jessica who have helped him rediscover what life has to offer. He hopes to someday make writing and speaking his primary focus. He may be reached at P.O. Box 280, West Rumney, NH 03266.

Michael Biasini is currently teaching special education in Mesquite, Texas. He enjoys teaching, motivational speaking and cycling. He is happily married to Valerie, and has been blessed with two wonderful children, Andrew, age five and Matthew, age three. Michael can be reached at 972-681-7035. Remember: Never give up!

Shawn Blessing is an educational consultant with the Education Service Center in Richardson, Texas. She received her B.S. degree in home economics from Texas Tech University and her M.A. in educational administration from New Mexico State University. She currently resides with her thirteen-year-old son, Joshua, an all around great kid, in McKinney, Texas.

Captain Ross Bryant is an active duty armor officer and a sixteen-year veteran of the U.S. Army. He has served as a tank platoon leader, executive officer and a company commander. He has served in Germany, Egypt and the U.S. He is currently training ROTC in California. He can be reached at 909-829-1654 or e-mail: *coyotesix@worldnet.att.net*.

Krista Buckner graduated from the University of California, Irvine and earned her master's degree in clinical psychology from California State University,

Bakersfield. Krista founded her own company called Fitness for the Mind which provides keynote presentations and self-development seminars. She has spoken at universities, medical centers, government organizations, athletic clubs, private businesses and various non-profit organizations. She can be reached at P.O. Box 10839, Bakersfield, CA 93389 or call 877-348-6463.

Felice Buckvar's young adult thriller, *Dangerous Dream*, was recently published by Royal Fireworks Press, and her articles appear frequently in the *New York Times*, *Newsday*, *Family Circle* and other publications. She gives readings from her books, lectures, and teaches courses on creative writing and writing for publication. She can be reached at 212-406-7265.

Mike Buettell is a highly respected junior high school counselor in Irvine, California. Partially disabled, he is a living inspiration to his students that courage, perseverance and a sense of humor can overcome any obstacle. He can be reached at Rancho Middle School, 4861 Michelson, Irvine, CA 92715 or call 714-786-3005.

Heather Bull is still a stewardess and enjoys traveling with her husband. She originally shared this story with her brother who is the creator of the Web site *CyberStory.com*. *CyberStory.com* features inspirational, heartwarming and uplifting real-life examples of how one person can make a positive difference in someone's life.

Dave Carruthers is a well-known coach and a motivator of young people. He is also the author of *Athletes Achieving Peak Performance*. Dave is listed in *Who's Who Among American's Teachers* and his talks are inspirational and challenging. He can be reached at 4010 Bill Moxley Rd., Mt. Airy, MD 21771 or call 301-662-1965 or e-mail *carruthersd@Hotmail.com*.

Natalie M. Cadavid is a practicing attorney in Chicago who enjoys writing short stories and essays in her spare time. Natalie attended the University of Michigan Law School and currently is a law clerk for a federal judge in Chicago. As a college student at the University of Illinois, Natalie was a reporter for the campus newspaper, the *Daily Illini*.

Diana Chapman has been a journalist for fourteen years, having worked at the *San Diego Union*, Copley Los Angeles Newspapers and the *Los Angeles Times*. She specializes in human interest stories and is currently working on a book involving health issues, since she was diagnosed with multiple sclerosis in 1992. She has been married for nine years and has one son, Herbert "Ryan" Hart. She can be reached at P.O. Box 414, San Pedro, CA 90733 or call 310-548-1192.

Barbara Chase-Pace has owned and operated a family-owned moving company for over fifty years. She has gained a wealth of experience in "taking people home" as they call their services. Barbara has never forgotten a brief note on an article while in college that said "you have it in you to write." Thirty-five years later, after raising three sons, and working in a secretarial career, she took a class "Creative Writing 101." The pleasant discovery: She not only "had it in her to write," but she finds it difficult to stop. She considers it a gift from God.

Rebecca Christian is a writer who lives in Des Moines, Iowa.

Regina Clancy-Hiney is a teacher, mother and writer. She has written her child's name in over fifty articles of clothing—many of which have yet to return home. She specializes in giving homework on Fridays and pop quizzes on Mondays.

Jo Coudert is a freelance writer, a frequent contributor to *Woman's Day* and the *Reader's Digest*, and the author of seven books, among them the bestselling *Advice from a Failure*. Her most recent works are *Seven Cats and the Art of Living*, *The Ditchdigger's Daughters* and the forthcoming *The Good Shepherd*.

Valerie Cox's poem, "The Cookie Thief," was published in *A 3rd Serving of Chicken Soup for the Soul*. In between traveling and speaking, Valerie serves on two nursing home ministry teams and is currently working on a second volume of poetry and prose. She can be reached at 31849 Pacific Hwy. South, Suite 210, Federal Way, WA 98003 or by calling 253-941-3209.

Mark Crawford made the switch from exploration geology to writing four years ago because he was more excited seeing his first story in print than finding a gold mine. He is the author of five books on history and science and numerous articles for regional and national publications. You can reach Mark at 5101 Violet Lane, Madison, WI 53714; e-mail: mandm@itis.com.

Thomas De Paoli is a management professional with twenty-plus years of experience in many areas of business. He has extensive experience in reengineering and coping with mega-change. He has traveled to over forty countries and has been published in *Manufacturing Engineering Magazine, Purchasing World* and *Purchasing Today*. He conducts seminars on reengineering purchasing, negotiating, supply management, pay-for-skill compensation, dealing with mega-change and various human resources topics with a special emphasis on empowerment. Contact him at 920-457-1658 or *tdepaoli@Excel.net.*

Paul Dean is a staff writer and automotive critic for the *Los Angeles Times* and has been a journalist for thirty-five years. He was a feature writer and correspondent for British newspapers, worked with United Press International in Canada and came to the United States in 1963. He was nominated for a Pulitzer Prize and the Ernie Pyle Memorial Award for coverage of the Vietnam War. Dean has more than fifty writing awards and has a syndicated column, *Behind the Wheel*, that goes to over eight hundred clients. Dean's hobbies include tennis, vintage race cars, sailing, collecting antique clocks and flying WWII airplanes.

Jean Oliver Dyer is an exceptional woman who will receive her master's degree in May of 1988. She will begin work on her Ph.D. in June. She is currently a full-time background investigator working for the Richmond Police Department. She is a private tutor in reading, math and computer skills. Her hobbies include reading and cooking. She can be reached by writing to 1112 Hollister Avenue, Richmond, VA 23224.

Mary Gardner is president and CEO of the Coaching Certification Institute, an authorized training center under the wing of The Learning Studio (Langhorne, Pennsylvania). A dynamic motivational speaker, she has helped numerous business executives, entrepreneurs, celebrities, attorneys and other professionals achieve success in both their personal and professional lives. Mary resides in New York City.

Rabona Turner Gordon gets her inspiration for writing poetry from her five children. She is a single mother and she and her children have endured and enjoyed many of life's challenges. She quite often does customized poems for her church, friends and co-workers. Rabona resides with her children in Marietta, Georgia. She can be reached by e-mail at *rabona.gordon@respironics.com*.

Stacey A. Granger lives in Maryland with her husband and their six children, and is the author of *The Portable Mother, The Portable Father* and *The Workout Cop-Out*. She can be reached at 48 Anna Speakman Road, Elkton, MD 21921 or by calling 410-392-7612.

Anita Grimm is a former teacher and businesswoman who lives with her husband, horses and dogs on a small Oregon farm in the shadows of the Siskiyou Mountains. She adopted Chad on his thirty-eighth birthday and is the grandmother of three. She can be contacted at *akneetah@mind.net.*

Nancy Hammel makes her publishing debut in *Chicken Soup for the Soul.* At nineteen, she is a student at Daemen College in Amherst, New York, where she is studying to become a social studies teacher. She hopes to continue to write inspirational poems and stories in honor of her inspiration—her family and friends.

Leon Hansen was born on a farm in eastern Nebraska. He farmed along the Missouri River for many years, and served three years in the Air Force during WWII. In 1969 he and his family moved to Oregon. He has written poetry since he was twenty. Some of his publications include, *Memories in Rhyme, It Could Be Verse* and *Thoughts for Thinkers.*

Jerry Harpt has taught and counseled in the public schools for thirty-three years. He has a regular newspaper column entitled Challenging Our Limits, teaches creative writing to adults and has recently completed two children's books that he hopes to get published. He can be reached at N. 3231 River Drive, Wallace, MI or by calling 906-863-8862.

Kathie Harrington holds a master's degree in speech pathology. She specializes in autism, serving the autistic population of the Clark County School District in Las Vegas, NV as Mentor Teacher—Autism and provides consulting services to state agencies. Kathie is a national speaker on the topic of autism focusing on the informational as well as the inspirational aspects of the disorder. She has authored four books/programs in the field of speech therapy, numerous short stories and poems. Her most recent publication is *For Parents and Professionals: Autism* (LinguiSystems, East Moline, IL) which blends both personal and professional experiences. Contact Kathie at 3611 Maria St., Las Vegas, NV 89121; phone: 702-435-8748; fax: 702-436-9161; e-mail: *TappyH@aol.com.*

Michael Haverty was a student at Queens College, NY taking a course in writing. This story is about his father-in-law who was an influence in his life. He has been married for thirty-three years and has five children. This story was a labor of love for Michael.

Bill Holton is graciously allowed to share his home with three demanding yet adorable Siamese cats and his demanding yet adorable wife, Tara. Bill is a freelance writer from Richmond, Virginia. When not feverishly begging magazine editors for assignments, he actually dreams of retiring to the Florida Keys where he will concentrate his boundless energy on fishing. He can be reached at *BHOLTON@REPORTERS.NET.*

Darcie Hossack is a freelance writer living in Canada's beautiful Okanagean Valley. Her writing reflects the joy and humor she looks for in every new day. Besides short stories and articles, her latest ambition is *36" 24" 36" and Other Fairytales About Womanhood,* a lighthearted laugh at women's common woes. Darcie can be reached by email at *allegro@cnx.net.*

Kim Kane is retired from the Navy and mother of three. She now writes a family humor column for the *Amazing Instant Novelist* site on America Online. She lives on a small island off the coast of Seattle. Her hobbies include jigsaw puzzles, (now that her kids are big enough, she doesn't have to worry about them eating any of the pieces) and writing.

Kathleen M. Kelly is currently writing a book about her healing from metastatic breast cancer entitled *Hold On to Your Hair!* Kathleen is more than two years into her second remission and she feels it is the love that surrounded her from family and friends and colleagues at Glastonbury Youth and Family Services that enabled her to cope with the most challenging time of her life. And yes, Jim is still in the picture! Kathleen can be reached at 8114 Town Ridge, Middletown, CT 06457 or by calling 860-632-1243.

Misty L. Kerl teaches science to middle school and high school students in Angola, New York, just south of Buffalo. She is currently working on her master's degree, which will be completed in December, 1998. She is twenty-eight years old and has been married for three years, although she has been with her husband for the past eleven years. She can be reached at 716-549-3043.

Joe Kohl has been an internationally published magazine cartoonist and illustrator for over twenty-five years. His cartoons and designs also appear on numerous greeting cards, tee-shirts, mugs and books. Joe has several of his own cartoon books out. He can be reached via e-mail at *joekohl@aol.com* or visit his Web site at http://*www.newl.com/jkohl*.

June Cerza Kolf retired after twelve years of hospice work and is the author of five books relating to grief. She is a frequent contributor to inspirational magazines and has just completed a book for suicide survivors. Currently she and her husband enjoy traveling and their four grandchildren.

Tom Krause is a motivational speaker, teacher and coach. He is the founder of Positive People Presentations. He speaks to teenagers, teaching staffs and any organization dealing with teen issues. Also business organizations in the area of motivation and stress reduction. Tom is the author of the poem Just Me from *Chicken Soup for the Teenage Soul*.

Lawrence A. Kross practiced restorative dentistry in northern New Jersey for thirty years, publishing only professional articles. Upon retirement, he has been writing fiction with over twenty stories published. (This story is nonfiction). Nowadays you can find Larry skiing, playing tennis, hiking and biking. (Normal adult activities he attributes to Sandy.)

Delores Lacy was born and raised in Tampa, FL; served twenty-two years in the Navy; married and bore three children—Christian (deceased), Rebekah and Matthew—and later divorced. Now retired from the Navy, she works as a civilian at the Naval Air Station in Pensacola full time and as a Mary Kay consultant, part time.

Linda Lawrence (Hunt) teaches with Forest Baird at Whitworth College in Spokane, Washington. An English professor, she is also freelance writer with articles in many national magazines and newspapers and is presently writing a book drawn from a true story of two women who walked across America in 1896. She can be reached at *lhunt@whitworth.edu*.

Mike Lipstock's stories have previously appeared in the *Chicken Soup* books. They have also appeared in well over a hundred magazines and nine anthologies. He recently received his second nomination for a "Pushcart Prize" and a nomination for a story to be presented on National Public Radio. He lives in Jericho, New York and his telephone number is 516-681-0171.

Patricia Lorenz is an internationally-known inspirational, art-of-living writer, speaker, columnist and teacher. She is a frequent contributor to the *Chicken Soup for the Soul* books. She is the author of *Stuff That Matters for Single Parents* and *A Hug A Day for Single Parents* and the writer of over 400 articles published in many national magazines. She's a contributor to eleven *Daily Guideposts* books; a regular columnist for the Milwaukee archdiocesan newspaper; and the author and voice on *Hugs for Your Heart* audio books. Patricia is a speaker who entertains her audiences from the get-go and packs a wallop with her take-away messages. You may contact her at 7457 S. Pennsylvania Ave., Oak Creek, WI 53154. For speaking engagements contact Associated Speakers, Inc., at 800-437-7577.

Meg Lundstrom lives in New York, and coauthored *The Power of Flow: Practical Ways to Transform Your Life with Meaningful Coincidence* (Harmony, 1997).

Vincent Luong is an entrepreneur who lives in New Jersey.

Barbara Mackey is a veteran feature writer for international corporations, national magazines such as *Woman's World*, and local publications, including the *Dayton Daily News* and the *Palm Beach Post*. Her favorite topic is ordinary women who display extraordinary courage. She lives in Dayton, Ohio and Bellaire, Michigan.

Angela Martin is the mother of two, and is currently majoring in social work at the College of West Virginia. A volunteer at the AIDS Task Force in Beckley, she works with families who are HIV-positive. She can be reached at P.O. Box 582, Prosperity, WV 25909 or by calling 304-255-4584.

Jacqueline Moffett has always enjoyed writing. She recently joined the National League of American Pen Women, Boca Raton, Florida branch and attends the monthly writing workshops. Jacqueline enjoys writing poetry and also short stories with happy endings. She can be reached at 3009 S. Ocean Blvd., #801, Highland Beach, FL 33487.

Kolette Montague is a wife, mother and grandmother. An elementary school teacher and freelance writer, she is member of the League of Utah Writers and the Utah State Poetry Society. She has won numerous awards for poetry and has been published in several anthologies. She is a professional editor/coach. Kolette may be reached via e-mail at *lmeelurg@slkc.uswest.com*.

Michele Morris is the author of *The Cowboy Life: A Saddlebag Guide for Dudes, Tenderfeet and Cowpunchers Everywhere* (Fireside/Simon & Schuster, 1993) and the coauthor of *Chinese Cookery* (HP Books, 1981). She has written articles and essays for many national publications, including *Travel Holiday, Travel & Leisure, Ladies' Home Journal, More, Money, McCall's, Parenting, Working Woman, Outside, Self, The Chicago Tribune, New York Daily News* and the *Los Angeles Times* Syndicate. She lives in Tucson, Arizona with her husband and two sons.

Diane Nelson is a newspaper columnist and essayist. She lives with her family in a home beside the Stanislaus National Forest, amid the mountains and trees that feed her soul. You can reach her at P.O. Box 5256, Avery, CA 95224.

Rick Phillips is a veteran of three decades of sales and sales management. He formed Phillips Sales and Staff Development in 1984 and since that time has trained sales professionals throughout North America in skills necessary to be successful in the new millenium. Rick can be reached at P.O. Box 29615, New Orleans LA 70189 or call 800-525-7773. You may e-mail him at *pssd@web-net.com* or visit his Web site at *http://rickphillips.com*.

Kay L. Pliszka retired from teaching to pursue her role as child advocate and educator by facilitating teen workshops, writing and public speaking. She has received a Wisconsin Bell/Ameritech Teacher Award, MCADD Award, Walkers Point Community Service Award, State Recognition for Exemplary Educational Grants and is included in *Who's Who Among American Teachers*. Kay may be reached at 1846 W. Halsey Ave., Milwaukee, WI 53221 or you may e-mail her at *UBZR26A@prodigy.com*.

Penny Porter is a mother of six and a grandmother of seven. She is a former teacher and school administrator. Award-winning Penny Porter is a frequent contributor to *Reader's Digest*. She has also been published in a wide range of national magazines and is the author of three books. Her inspiration is rooted in the love of family and human values which children of today need so desperately.

Adrienne C. Reynolds is an educator and a writer. Her love of teaching has traveled with her from Louisiana, North Carolina and Florida. Life experiences have afforded her a huge collection of stories that she is now taking time to write down. Her biggest fans are her husband, Juacane, and her children, Jade and Kyan. She can be contacted at 4501 NW 85th Ave., Coral Springs, FL 33065 or by e-mail: *clasywritr@aol.com*.

Nancy Richard-Guilford is an author and inspiring speaker who ignites audiences with her passion for life and contagious high energy. She teaches practical skills in a setting filled with humor and heart. Nancy loves listening to Three Dog Night songs, ordering Happy Meals so she can play with the toys, and her husband, 3-D character animator James Guilford. Her client list ranges from the U.S. Navy to metaphysical churches. To join this growing list, call 888-236-2629.

Ed Robertson is the author of *The Fugitive Recaptured, Maverick: Legend of the West* and *This is Jim Rockford*. He is also a consultant with Columbia House Home Video and has written for such publications as *The New York Post, Television Chronicles, New Media Review* and *San Francisco Giants* magazine. Ed lives in San Francisco, California.

Heather Roth and her husband are newlyweds and recently moved to California. With them they have brought their strong family values from the Heartland. She hopes to soon contribute to her families with children of her own and pass on those values. Things are going well for her and her husband and she says they couldn't be happier!

Hope Saxton is a freelance writer who resides in Ontario, Canada with her husband and two sons. Her work has appeared in *Happy Times Monthly*, and *The Edge Tales of Suspense*, among numerous other publications. She is currently working on her third novel. Hope may be reached via e-mail at *hopewrites@yahoo.com*.

Cliff Schimmels roamed the plains, herded the cows, chopped the cotton, and learned to tell stories while listening to those expert story tellers who made up the community around him during his boyhood years in western Oklahoma. After fifteen years as a high school teacher and coach, seventeen years as a professor of education at Wheaton College, and seven years as a professor of education at Lee University where he is now, he is still telling stories, just as those boyhood heroes taught him. Although he has written twenty-four books, Cliff's greatest accomplishment is being the father of three and the grandfather of four.

Jim Schneegold is a legal printer in Cheektowaga, New York (a suburb of Buffalo) who writes personal experience stories spanning from childhood embarrassments to yesterday's wait in the grocery line. His Erma Bombeck/Andy Rooney writing style works to keep his feet on the ground, right where they belong. He can be reached at 630 Beach Road, Cheektowaga, NY 14225 or via e-mail at *goldensnow@aol.com*.

Ruth Senter is the author of eleven books including the Angel Award Winner, *Have We Really Come a Long Way* (Bethany House Publisher). Her most recent publication is a chilren's book: *Annie Ashcraft Looks into the Dark* (Bethany House Publisher). Ruth's other books include *A Tribute to Moms* (Multnomah), *Longing For Love: Conversations with a Compassionate Heavenly Father* (Bethany) and *Beyond Safe Places* (Harold Shaw Publishers). Ruth has served as editor, columnist and freelance writer for many Christian publications as well as co-host for the TV series "Adventures in Learning."

Jolie "Jes" Shafer-Kenney is a freelance writer with over two-hundred articles published on America Online. Jolie is best known for her popular advice column on AOL (keyword: Online Psych) as well as facilitating many online support groups. She is listed in Marquis's *Who's Who of American Women* (1999-2000 edition) and can be reached via e-mail at *JESMOSK@aol.com*.

Mildred Shreve is a retired health aide. Her life these days are filled with pets. She is an animal activist and an active member of a very exciting bluck club.

Donna Smith is a retired English teacher. She is married and has five children, ten grandchildren and one great granddaughter. She has taught Sunday school at First Baptist Church for the last forty eight years. Donna is a freelance writer, speaker for inspirational writers' groups and a newsletter editor. She has been published in *Oklahoma English Journal, Teaching Today, Teaching K-8, Guideposts, Christian Reader, Mature Living, The Lookout* and several others. Donna is also a teacher-consultant and speaker.

Lizanne Southgate is the author of *Mother Musing, An Unlikely Princess* and *The Boy Who Swallowed a Dream*. She is a ghostwriter and the mother of five. To contact her regarding her books or ghostwriting services, write to her at P.O. Box 878, Brownsville, OR 97327 or e-mail her at *lizannes@proaxis.com*.

Denise Syman lives with her husband Phillip in Farmington, Michigan. She writes mainly of her experience as a mother as well as about home and family. Her son Daniel is in the U.S. Coast Guard and her daughter Delana is a full-time student. You may write to her at 22566 Lilac, Farmington, MI 48336.

John E. Welshons is a highly respected grief counselor, lecturer and business consultant who has worked with Ram Dass, Pat Rodegast and Stephen Levine. One of his most popular audiotapes, "Healing the Grief (. . . of the loss of a loved one)" features a conversation between John and Mark Victor Hansen. John is available for lectures and seminars. His book and tape catalogue and personal appearance schedule can be obtained by calling OPEN HEART SEMINARS at 800-555-0844 or by writing: P.O. Box 110, Little Falls, NJ 07424.

Mary Jane West-Delgado is a physical therapist, author, designer of safety products for the home and a cartoon writer. She would love to hear from you! Her e-mail address is *delgado@silcom.com*.

Jeannie S. Williams is an inspirational writer, motivational speaker and a professional magician. She conducts dynamic staff development, parenting and student presentations using her "magic"as a teaching tool. Jeannie is president and founder of the "Unlock the Magic" creative writing workshops and has been entertaining audiences for years with her own special blend of creativity and humor. She shares the magic of working with children in her newest book, *What Time Is Recess?* Jeannie can be reached at P.O. Box 1476, Sikeston, MO 63801.

Marvin J. Wolf is a journalist and author and was the only United States soldier to arrive in Vietnam as a private and leave as an infantry lieutenant. He lives in Los Angeles and is now writing a history of the Jet Propulsion Lab, his tenth non-fiction book. For more of his work, visit Marvin's Web site at *http://come.to/marvwolf*.

www.chickensoup.com